PRAISE FOR
FULLY PRESENT:

"This book with exciting up-to-the-minute mindfulness research findings and filled with wonderful vignettes that make it a joy to read can change your school, your clinic, your workplace . . . your life."
— Sylvia Boorstein, author of *Happiness Is an Inside Job*

"*Fully Present* is a wonderful book. It does a great job of presenting the psychological and biological science relevant to understanding and benefiting from 'mindfulness.' Just reading it made me feel better, but I also now have compelling reasons for wanting to pursue mindfulness myself."
— Joseph LeDoux, PhD, Director of the Center for the Neuroscience of Fear and Anxiety, New York University; author of *The Emotional Brain* and *The Synaptic Self*

"Be aware, be very aware! *Fully Present* will bring you into the current moment and keep you there. A must for any student of life."
— Jeff Skoll, Founder and Chairman, Participant Media

"*Fully Present* is a fresh and innovative examination of the 'why' and 'how' of the state of consciousness known as mindfulness. It is science based with practical applications. I hope everyone who wants to learn more about both the science and the art of mindfulness will read it."
— Tipper Gore, author, photographer, and mental health advocate

"*Fully Present* offers a wonderfully practical introduction to the cultivation of mindfulness and how it can be applied in daily life from childhood on through adulthood. Such practice helps to counteract the disruptive influence of the rapid pace of life and the sensory and information overload that characterize modern life. I heartily recommend this work and hope it will receive the widespread attention it deserves."
— B. Alan Wallace, author of *The Attention Revolution: Unlocking the Power of the Focused Mind*

"How to live in these extraordinary times? Do we embrace the exhausting cacophony of a world that never sleeps; or in a desperate search for solitude shutter the windows of the self, risking the blackness of despair? In *Fully Present* Smalley and Winston offer a middle ground: one where through mindful practice we can each find our own contemplative place and from there the strength to build a clearer personal vision. Melding the science and the art of mindfulness with its daily practice this concise, well-referenced work will stand apart from others as an invaluable compendium."

    —Peter C. Whybrow, MD, Director of the Semel Institute for
        Neuroscience and Human Behavior at UCLA; author of
        American Mania: When More Is Not Enough

"*Fully Present* is a highly readable, practical guide to the science and art of mindfulness meditation. For those wishing for a succinct summary of both the scientific evidence and the experiential descriptions along with specific meditation instructions, this book is an ideal place to start."

    —Richard J. Davidson, William James and Vilas Professor of Psychology
        and Psychiatry Director, Center for Investigating Health Minds
        University of Wisconsin-Madison

Fully
Present

Fully Present

The Science, Art, and Practice of Mindfulness

Susan L. Smalley, PhD
and Diana Winston

Second Edition
WITH A NEW AFTERWORD

hachette
BOOKS

New York

Copyright © 2010 by Susan L. Smalley, PhD, and Diana Winston
Afterword Copyright © 2022 by Susan L. Smalley, PhD and Diana Winston
Images on page 31 and 212 by Jim Formanek
Image on page 125 C. R. Cloninger, *Feeling Good: The Science of Well-being*, figure 3.3; page 128; © 2004 by Oxford University Press, Inc.
Images on pages 80 and 101 used with permission of Elsevier. All rights reserved. Modified with permission.

Cover design by Sara Pinsonault
Cover photograph © CravenA / Shutterstock
Cover copyright © 2022 by Hachette Book Group, Inc.

Hachette Go, an imprint of Hachette Books
Hachette Book Group
1290 Avenue of the Americas
New York, NY 10104
HachetteGo.com
Facebook.com/HachetteGo
Instagram.com/HachetteGo

Previously published by Da Capo Press: 2010

First Hachette Go Edition: December 2022

Hachette Books is a division of Hachette Book Group, Inc.
The Hachette Go and Hachette Books name and logos are trademarks of Hachette Book Group, Inc.

The publisher is not responsible for websites (or their content) that are not owned by the publisher.

Library of Congress Control Number: 2022917097

ISBNs: 978-0-306-82940-6 (trade paperback); 978-0-306-8294-37 (ebook)

Printed in the United States of America

LSC-C

Printing 1, 2022

To everyone with the curiosity to explore their mind and heart using the tool of mindfulness

A human being is a part of the whole, called by us, "Universe," a part limited in time and space. He experiences himself, his thoughts and feelings as something separated from the rest—a kind of optical delusion of his consciousness. This delusion is a kind of prison for us, restricting us to our personal desires and to affection for a few persons nearest to us. Our task must be to free ourselves from this prison by widening our circle of compassion to embrace all living creatures and the whole of nature in its beauty.

—Albert Einstein

CONTENTS

ACKNOWLEDGMENTS

The authors would like to thank our editor at Da Capo, Renée Sedliar, for her insightful comments; Matthew Lore for bringing the project to Da Capo; our agent, Stephany Evans, who saw how this book might fill an important niche; and our wonderful copy editor, Cynthia Buck.

Thanks to Jim Formanek for creating two illustrations for the book.

We are grateful to the many readers of early versions of the manuscript who provided helpful suggestions: Marvin Belzer, Susan Kaiser Greenland, Lisa Henson, Ellen Meyer, Phillip Moffit, Paula Ravets, Roni Rogers, Olivia Rosewood, Donald Rothberg, and Amita Schmidt.

We would like to thank the scientists and doctors who provided expertise on specific topics in the book: Lori Altshuler, Joan Asarnow, Robert Cloninger, David Creswell, Amishi Jha, Joseph LeDoux, Emeran Mayer, Max Muenke, Judith Piggot, Russell Poldrack, Lobsang Rapgay, and Elizabeth Smalley. Their expertise and that of the other scientists and researchers described in this book were interpreted by us, so any errors in presentation or interpretation of research are ours alone.

Thanks to Lauren Asarnow for her endless hours tracking down references and tending to small details of the book; to Alisha Musicant for her transcription work; and to Jennifer Kitil and Judith Rivero for their administrative support.

We would also like to thank our MARC collaborators and the UCLA faculty and staff who help our center grow: our co-director, Dan Siegel, as well as Shea Cunningham, Lisa Flook, Sigi Hale, Michael Irwin, Emeran Mayer, Bruce Naliboff, Lobsang Rapgay, Jeffrey Schwartz, Cathy Thomas, and Lidia

Zylowska. Special thanks to the MSST Foundation for its generous support of MARC and to our institute, the Jane and Terry Semel Institute for Neuroscience and Human Behavior, and its director, Peter Whybrow, for supporting the work of MARC in so many ways from the very beginning.

We would also like to thank Jon Kabat-Zinn, whose programs have had such an influence on our work.

Sue would like to thank her husband, Kevin Wall, and their three children, Patrick, Timothy, and Kelly, from whom she figured out the meaning of life. Special thanks to the friends who help her live a more mindful life, including those in the Book Club and Friday Morning Meditation, among others.

Diana would like to thank her many dharma teachers and her Spirit Rock Teachers Council colleagues, who have deeply influenced her teaching and articulation of mindfulness over the years. She would especially like to bow down before the feet of her husband, Martin Matzinger, who supported her in endless ways through the year of writing. And most love of all to Mira Lucia, who was in utero throughout the book's gestation. Both were born around the same time.

INTRODUCTION

An unexamined life is not worth living.

—Socrates

While most of us would agree with Socrates' sentiment, how many of us actually know *how* to examine our life as it unfolds and how to examine it skillfully? Furthermore, how many of us think we have the *time* to do that? We are immersed in a society of speed, technology, and information overload. Despite extraordinary advances in science and technology, from mapping our genomes to information access via the Internet, we live in an age of increasing anxiety and increasing doubt in our capacity to make decisions and to effect change, whether in our bodies, our lives, or the world around us. Feelings of fear, frustration, stress, and confusion seem to be on the rise globally, and the elevated rates of psychiatric illness among adults and children worldwide probably reflect this rising distress.

In the midst of our techno-savvy yet anxiety-producing culture, scientific investigation has become increasingly interested in the ancient practice of mindfulness as an antidote of sorts to the ills of the modern world and as a tool for skillfully examining our lives. Extracted from the religious settings in which it was developed, mindfulness practice has become a secularized tool for investigation of the modern mind. This book is an introduction to the why and how of mindfulness, from a scientist (the why) and a mindfulness teacher (the how).

WHAT IS MINDFULNESS,
AND WHAT CAN IT DO?

Mindfulness may be thought of as a state of consciousness, one characterized by attention to present experience with a stance of open curiosity. It is a quality of attention that can be brought to any experience. Mindfulness can be cultivated through explicit practices, such as meditation or yoga or t'ai chi, or even through creative processes in the arts or walking in nature. Mindfulness can also be enhanced less explicitly by adopting a generally mindful approach to life. As you learn the principles and techniques of mindfulness, you can apply them to any moment in the day, whether you are eating, driving, showering, or sending an e-mail.

Meditation can be considered a general term covering a wide range of practices that affect your awareness or utilize contemplation in the service of self-discovery. There are hundreds of kinds of meditation practices, including relaxation, concentration, visualization, and forms of religious chanting and prayer; a large subset of these practices, such as mindfulness meditation, Zen Buddhist meditation, and Transcendental Meditation, specifically focus on enhancing awareness, as do movement-based meditations such as yoga, t'ai chi, and chi gong. While these forms of meditation may differ in how they affect your awareness, all of them are various means of enhancing or, as some would say, "expanding" your awareness. We coined the term "Mindful Awareness Practices," or MAPs, to refer to this general class of practices. We also call the mindfulness classes we teach at our UCLA Mindful Awareness Research Center (MARC) by the name MAPs.

MAPs, in general, have been around for at least 5,000 years. While mindfulness meditation as a MAP is generally seen as being rooted in the 2,500-year-old Buddhist tradition, variants are evident in the practices of the ancient Greeks, Taoists, Native Americans, various religious traditions, and writings of poets, philosophers, and scientists throughout history. Although ancient in roots, mindfulness meditation is completely suited for modern times. It is a practice that can be done by anyone, regardless of age, background, or religion. The research exploring mindfulness, although still relatively new, is demonstrating that repeated practice can lead to changes in our lives, including:

- Reducing stress
- Reducing chronic physical pain
- Boosting the body's immune system to fight disease
- Coping with painful life events, such as the death of a loved one or major illness
- Dealing with negative emotions like anger, fear, and greed
- Increasing self-awareness to detect harmful reactive patterns of thought, feeling, and action
- Improving attention or concentration
- Enhancing positive emotions, including happiness and compassion
- Increasing interpersonal skills and relationships
- Reducing addictive behaviors, such as eating disorders, alcoholism, and smoking
- Enhancing performance, whether in work, sports, or academics
- Stimulating and releasing creativity
- Changing positively the actual structure of our brains

The emerging research on mindfulness makes it sound like a cure-all for whatever ails us, and perhaps it could be considered a simple solution for complex problems. For many people mindfulness practice is an excellent adjunct to other approaches they may be using to promote health and wellness, such as therapy, exercise, nutrition, or medication. Moreover, although mindfulness does not remove the ups and downs of life, it changes how experiences like losing a job, getting a divorce, struggling at home or at school, births, marriages, illnesses, death and dying influence you and how you influence the experience. In other words, *mindfulness changes your relationship to life.* Learning to live mindfully does not mean living in a "perfect" world, but rather, living a full and contented life in a world in which both joys and challenges are a given.

This book explores how to be more mindful in day-to-day life and how to use a mindfulness practice to promote well-being. But this book is also about our individual differences—both in our genes and in the environments that shape us—and how these differences affect our capacity to live more mindfully. Mindfulness meditation is itself a tool for discovering more about ourselves and how we relate to the world around us. This inward investigation, using the tool of mindfulness meditation, may help us understand more about ourselves from a first-person viewpoint just as science has done using a third-person lens of investigation.

HOW DID WE GET HERE?

Fully Present grew out of the collaboration of a scientist, Sue Smalley, and a mindfulness teacher and practitioner, Diana Winston, at their center, the Mindful Awareness Research Center (MARC) at the Jane and Terry Semel Institute for Neuroscience and Human Behavior at the University of California at Los Angeles. MARC is dedicated to increasing mindful awareness through education and research to promote individual well-being and a kinder society. Through MARC, we teach doctors, professors, students, teachers, mental health professionals, parents, seniors, and youth the science, art, and practice of mindfulness in MAPs classes, workshops, and trainings and conduct research on its effectiveness in promoting well-being.

Both of us are deeply committed to mindfulness and have a strong curiosity about the interface of the science, art, and practice of mindfulness. Even though science is the dominant cultural paradigm in the United States, we believe that the ancient practices from the East can inform, affect, and complement life in the modern West. We hope to articulate mindfulness in a way that feels relevant for our times. How can a secular language, based in science, be used to describe what once was the realm of the mystics and philosophers? And practically, how can mindfulness have a positive impact on lives in the twenty-first century amid the technology of Blackberries, iPods, iPhones, and the Internet? This book attempts to answer these questions by examining mindfulness through the lens of a scientist (Sue), the lens of a mindfulness teacher (Diana), and the lens of a practitioner, you the reader, as you learn the experiential practices we offer.

Here's how the two of us came together to write this book.

SUE'S STORY

When I was forty-seven, I had what might be called a mystical experience. At the time, I was living the hectic life of a full-time professor at UCLA, a mother of three, and a wife of a successful entrepreneur in the entertainment industry of Hollywood. Although I appeared happy, I was actually a cynical scientist who felt competitive, undervalued, envious, and angry at the world. I saw material reductionism—the idea that everything is explicable through a material lens—as a given, and I had no tolerance for others who felt differently. Friends of mine participated in "new age" activities like yoga and meditation, but I thought they were naive and rolled my eyes at these practices.

My world was one of typical twenty-first-century chaos—too much to do and too little time as I juggled career, motherhood, and Hollywood with a big chip on my shoulder over the burden I needed to carry. At work I conducted research to discover genes for autism and attention deficit hyperactivity disorder (ADHD), and although I had gone into the field with a passion and love of discovery, I was finding myself routinely going through the motions of science with little interest except for self-recognition. Subjects in my research had become "data points" through which we might understand the biology of disorders, but also through which I might find professional fame or fortune in my field of study. To counter these feelings of apathy and anger, I had begun therapy several years before and was slowly breaking down the external (and internal) barriers I had created for myself. I believe that this intense work to let go of the past and build a strong sense of self had laid the foundation for my mystical experience.

It arose following a brush with death—a tiny early-stage melanoma—and the experience lasted for some thirty days. Just prior to it, I had radically changed my behavior, convinced that change was necessary to save my life. I reasoned that my Western lifestyle was making me sick and that, if I chose a different route entirely, I might get well. I quit wearing a watch. I began yoga, meditation, a macrobiotic diet, acupuncture, massage, and holistic health care to counter the melanoma. Through these radical changes I became aware of my routines, habits, and conditioned behavior. Then one day, rather suddenly, I entered a state of "self-transcendence" in which I let go of my "self" and became part of a large, interdependent network, a deep interconnectedness of all things past, present, and future in which I knew the illusive nature of self, space, and time. While still functioning as a professor, wife, and mother, I nevertheless felt as though I had moved to a different dimension. Interestingly, the negative emotions I knew so well—anger, fear, greed, and envy—disappeared, and I felt only love, compassion, and kindness. After all, this experience showed me, if we are all interconnected and part of a whole, to hurt others would be to intentionally hurt myself.

In this experience, I felt deeply connected with all living and nonliving things—from rocks to ants to strangers to my deceased grandparents to my living children. And my world really began to change. I made new friends, became vegetarian, noticed and observed the world as if it were all new, found an unlimited sense of time, enjoyed every moment of every day, and seemed to live "in the present moment," experiencing each routine activity as if it were brand-new.

In the aftermath, I tried to make sense of what had happened to me, to understand the experience using the lens of science—the language of the culture I trusted. I researched all I could about brain changes that might explain what had happened, and I began to explore philosophy, physics, neuroscience, psychology, art and poetry, and the writings of the great religions. What I came to see was that the experience I had could be explained by science, but at the same time it could only be known through first-person experience. I discovered that many scientists also understood and wrote about this, from Albert Einstein to Jonas Salk. As Einstein noted, "The intuitive mind is a sacred gift, the rational mind is a faithful servant; we have created a society that honors the servant and has forgotten the gift."

It was the inner investigative journey that allowed my mystical experience to arise, but it is the day-to-day "living in awareness" that has enabled me to make sense of it. In the experience, I realized that letting go of conditioned habits and views of the world released newfound creativity. In this creativity I have often seen new connections and in that connectedness arises more and more compassion. That mystical experience shifted my work, how I act, think, and feel, and my way of interacting with my family, friends, and the world, and it has been a guiding force for where I am today. My own practice of self-discovery intensified five years ago but continues today in many quiet and steady ways: I practice meditation and yoga, but I also hike, write, paint, and walk in nature, and perhaps most importantly, I remain open and curious about both the joyful and painful situations of life.

In 2005 I founded MARC, with my colleagues at UCLA, to begin to study and to highlight the value of inner discovery—to find the key to compassion or "heart" that often feels lacking in institutional settings. Our center attempts to bring it out in the open by encouraging scientists, doctors, and students to remember to hone their own internal discovery process as intensely as they hone their scientific acumen. In this effort, we hope to instill a greater sense of value within academic institutions for both systems of knowing—the external system of science (reason) and the internal process of discovery (what Einstein called intuition).

DIANA'S STORY

Out of college, somewhat confused and despairing about what to do with my life, on a whim I traveled to India. At first I traveled like any tourist, enjoying glimpses of the Taj Mahal and experiencing the burning ghats of Benares, living on street curries and sleeping in seedy hotels, utterly fascinated by the culture with its juxtaposition of beauty and sorrow. It was in Dharamsala, India, home to the Dalai Lama's Tibetan government-in-exile, that I began my own spiritual journey. There I encountered Buddhist teachings that offered an answer to questions I did not even realize I had: What causes suffering? What can we do to find true happiness and well-being? I soon traveled to the south of Thailand, where I sat my first ten-day mindfulness meditation retreat at a jungle monastery. Each morning we rose in the dark at 4:00 AM to practice silent meditation amid the howling monkeys and the roosters crowing in the day. Day after day I sat on a hard cement floor, persevering, trying my best to remain aware of my breathing, to rein in my wild mind that simply did not want to stay put.

By the eighth day, although it was subtle and not dramatic, I knew something very significant had happened inside me. I was starting to feel the tiniest sense of peace. I encountered something unfamiliar. Deep below the surface waves—the drama, my identity, frustrations, and self-hatred— lay a vast calming sense that I was okay, that a still, clear, peaceful mind was available to me, that I could find happiness. This happiness was not the typical pleasure that comes from material success or acquisition, but a deep happiness from way down inside me that was not dependent on outside conditions.

This first glimmer led to a twenty-year journey of insight meditation. Called *vipassana* in the early Buddhist language and often translated as "mindfulness," this practice would become a doorway to peace, compassion, ease, and well-being. It would be the way in which I learned to trust myself, to gain access to my own inner wisdom, and to get to know myself deeply; ultimately it became the ground from which I understand and operate in the world.

I spent much of my twenties and early thirties practicing mindfulness in retreat settings in the United States and Asia, often spending months at a time in intensive meditation practice. In 1998 I lived as a Buddhist nun in Burma (Myanmar) for a year. I inhabited a tiny, spare hut in a forest monastery and practiced continuous mindfulness "boot camp style"—in complete silence, eating only two meals a day, both before noon, shaving my head, and taking the vows of a nun, which included not stealing, killing, or lying and, of course, remaining celibate. The year taught me a kind of fortitude and courage; I faced a landslide of inner demons and learned to overcome and find peace amid them, while at the same time achieving deep states of transcendence and joy.

Upon returning to the United States, I began to teach insight meditation at the Spirit Rock Meditation Center. For years I had been teaching teenagers about mindfulness, but in 2002 I began a four-year teacher training program, apprenticing under some of the leading Buddhist teachers in America. I learned how to lead retreats, workshops, and classes and how to find my own voice as I shared Buddhist teachings and practices with people of all ages.

One of my interests was in the intersection of Buddhist practice and social change. I had devoted many years in the mid-1990s to creating a Buddhist domestic volunteer corps called the Buddhist Alliance for Social Engagement. Much of my teaching and organizing involved bringing mindfulness to activists and other social change agents and organizations. But after a certain point I began to wonder how much impact I was really having. I was teaching about mindfulness, compassion, and balance in a frustrating world of vast inequities, but was society really changing?

About this time Sue contacted me to ask about my interest in teaching as part of a UCLA study on mindfulness and ADHD. My experience teaching teenagers, she suggested, would help researchers assess whether that population can benefit from mindfulness. Through the experience I saw even more strongly how the meditation tools and practices I had learned over so many years in the Buddhist context, as well as my own diligent application of them day after day, had created a body of knowledge and experience that could benefit people in many contexts outside of Buddhism. I was impressed by the work of Jon Kabat-Zinn, who had already taken mindfulness into the medical community to help patients with chronic pain through his Mindfulness-Based Stress Reduction (MBSR) programs, which, twenty years later, are a household name in secularized mindfulness. I thought about my own desire to bring values of compassion, connection, kindness, and justice to all people, and I realized that teaching mindfulness in a secular context in a university setting—with all its resources, research capabilities, collaborators, and community recognition—could be an exciting way to have an impact on society from the ground up. If we could then bring these values into institutions, huge shifts might happen. Sue and I shared this vision, so when she offered me a job at UCLA's newly forming MARC, I decided to take the plunge. It has been one of the most exciting endeavors of my life.

ABOUT THIS BOOK

This book arose because we found ourselves at a loss when participants in our MAPs classes would ask, "What book do you recommend?" While many excellent books on mindfulness are available, their orientation reflects the author's concerns—some are tied to Buddhism, some are directed toward mental health professions or neuroscientists, and some address specific issues like stress. We sought to present mindfulness in a way that reflects our own view, one that is focused on a balance of science (or reason) and art (or intuition). That balance is different for each of us, so this book attempts to find the balance point between these two orientations by combining our two voices. We hope that we have created an easy-to-read and user-friendly handbook that not only will offer you the practical, how-to aspects of mindfulness but will guide you in using your own reason and intuition to discover how these practices might benefit yourself as well as society.

Each chapter of *Fully Present* offers a scientific and experiential look at how mindfulness can shape your life, along with practical exercises, alternating between what we call "The Science," "The Art," and "The Practice." The practices are guided meditations that can be read aloud, pre-recorded, or read by someone to you as you practice; alternatively, comparable meditations can be freely downloaded from our MARC website, www.marc.ucla.edu.

Beginning with some practical and basic information, the early chapters explore "What Is Mindfulness?" and "Getting Started." We then look at the various facets of our lives in which mindfulness can have an impact: experiencing physical pain in the body, feeling negative and positive emotions, paying attention, engaging in stressful thinking, and working with obstacles we encounter. In the last chapter, we leave the art/science/practice format to explore our thoughts—supported by science when available—about taking mindfulness out into the world.

As we continue to collaborate with scientists and practitioners at MARC, we frequently discuss the need to describe mindfulness as a state of mind that can be initiated, cultivated, or enhanced by a variety of means—including the mindfulness meditation practices described in this book. All practices that enhance mindfulness promote self-discovery and awareness, but each of us must find the route that suits us best; your experience is likely to be very different from ours or that of anyone else. As Henry David Thoreau wrote in *Walden*:

> *Direct your eye right inward, and you'll find*
> *A thousand regions in your mind*
> *Yet undiscovered. Travel them, and be*
> *Expert in home-cosmography.*

Home-cosmography—the inner universe of your mind—is your own experience, and that is what we hope to foster with this book.

Mindfulness meditation has been helpful to us, and a growing body of research supports its effectiveness for many people, but we would stress that there is more than one way to "direct your eye right inward." Believing that one method is superior to another is a trap that we would urge you to avoid. If you look within, without preconceived notions, and let yourself be guided by the discoveries to be made in your inner universe, you may be surprised. Lao-Tzu, a Taoist master, wrote: "A good traveler has no fixed plans and is not intent on arriving." May the journey lead you toward a more fully present life.

1

WHAT IS MINDFULNESS?

"Well," said Pooh, "what I like best," and then he had to stop
and think. Because although Eating Honey was a very good
thing to do, there was a moment just before you began to eat it
which was better than when you were, but he didn't know what
it was called.

—A. A. Milne, *The House on Pooh Corner*

A world-renowned psychiatrist once posed a question to a room full of
mental health experts. He asked, "What is the 'seat belt' of mental
health?" Seat belts save lives; buckling up is a simple thing to do to protect
ourselves from physical harm. What is the comparable tool to protect us
from the mental hazards of life? What is the seat belt to protect against un-
happiness, depression, anxiety, pain, and suffering?

Mindfulness may be the mental "seat belt" that protects us along the
bumpy, twisting, turning road of life, whether we encounter unexpected
drop-offs, terrible accidents, or smooth sailing.

Merriam-Webster's Dictionary defines "mindful" as "inclined to be aware,"
and "awareness" as "vigilance in observing what one experiences." Synonyms
for "awareness" include "awake," "watchful," "wary," "cognizant," and "conscious." So mindful awareness (a synonym for mindfulness) means to be
"aware of awareness," an idea that implies an awareness of self and a capacity
to reflect, a definition closely associated with self-consciousness.[1] An expert
mindfulness teacher, Henepola Gunaratana, describes mindfulness as follows:

"When you first become aware of something, there is a fleeting instant of pure awareness just before you identify it . . . before you start thinking about it . . . before your mind says, 'Oh, it's a dog.' . . . That flowing soft-focused moment of pure awareness is mindfulness."[2] A mindful mental state differs from being lost in thoughts of the past or future or acting on "autopilot." To "practice mindfulness" is to exercise or work on honing this state of mind. We all probably agree that that sounds like a good idea; after all, who wants to be unaware or unconscious of their own experiences? Yet, as we will see, consciousness is pretty elusive and difficult to define scientifically, and it changes all the time. We think we know something one day only to discover that what we thought we knew was not quite right. We constantly "wake up" to knowledge, shifting from ignorance to awareness. What we are conscious of changes constantly.

This chapter explores the science of mindfulness, including how it is defined and measured, how it can be both a state and a trait, and how it works as a tool for self-regulation. We then turn to the practicalities of mindfulness to understand how it functions in our lives so that we can begin to cultivate it.

THE SCIENCE

We are still at the beginning of understanding mindfulness from a scientific perspective. Over the last twenty years, there has been an exponential increase in research on mindfulness, from some eighty published papers in 1990 to over six hundred in 2000.[3] Yet compared to other behaviors that are known to improve physical or mental health, such as diet and exercise, there is relatively little research on mindfulness. For example, a search of PubMed, the electronic library of biomedical research, using the keywords "mindfulness meditation" or "mindfulness-based stress reduction" yields 492 articles, while a keyword search on "heart disease and exercise" offers 46,136 articles and "heart disease and diet" returns 15,042 articles. Research on mindfulness is in its infancy.

There are two general types of research studies: studies that ask what mindfulness is and how to measure it, and studies that ask what benefits arise from practicing it. While the questions that scientists ask are probably no different from yours, the difference lies in how they seek the answers. Science is a methodology that uses third-person observation, by which we mean that it is an *objective* process that yields comparable knowledge no matter who does it. In contrast, mindfulness is a first-person, or *subjective*, methodology, the observation of which is quite challenging. (Imagine how hard it would be to decide which of two people is more "aware.") Putting mindfulness under the lens of science removes it from what it actually is—a subjective experience— yet in doing so we can gain an understanding of the shared elements of mindfulness as reported by many people and the changes in brain and body states detectable by current technologies and specialties, such as functional magnetic resonance imaging (fMRI), immunology, and genetics. Yet, no matter how well science describes mindfulness, it cannot capture the experience of it. Scientists can describe the chemical composition of an apple, its color, texture, and taste, but no description matches the experience of biting into an apple. When we name mindfulness and measure it using the tools of science, we may want to remember that the *name* and the *experience* are not the same. This is why we look at mindfulness from the perspective of both science and art in this book—to truly understand mindfulness is to not only know about the science of it but also practice the art of it.

Mindfulness is like the Indian proverb about the six blind men trying to describe an elephant: As each one touches a different part, he describes the elephant differently. If we look across the scientific literature, there are aspects of mindfulness described in research on creativity, intuition, self-awareness, insight, and positive psychology, to name only a few areas of focus. Yet to research mindfulness we must have a working definition and then ways to measure it objectively. The working definitions of mindfulness all include "an awareness or attention to present experience." Added to this basic definition are certain qualifiers describing the kind of attention or awareness a person has (receptive, open) or his or her orientation during the experience (impartial, curious, nonjudgmental, accepting).[4] Beyond this definition, there are varied opinions as to what mindfulness represents. Some scientists consider mindfulness to be a cognitive ability, a capacity to *think* in a certain way; others consider it part of personality, a *disposition* to respond to the world in a certain way; and still others consider it a cognitive style, a *preferred way of thinking*.[5] All three of these concepts may describe some aspect of mindfulness; it does not appear to fall neatly into any one category. To know where it fits best requires investigation, and that requires a working definition and tools to measure it.

Measuring Mindfulness

Most measures of mindfulness use self-report questionnaires, which include items such as: "I pay attention to how my emotions affect my thoughts and behavior," "I don't pay attention to what I'm doing because I'm daydreaming, worried, or otherwise distracted," "I disapprove of myself when I have irrational ideas,"[6] and, "It seems I am 'running on automatic' without much awareness of what I am doing."[7] Perusing those items, you can see that some describe attention, some describe a quality of observation, and some describe a tendency to be highly critical. The items are scored in such a way that the more curious and attentive to present-moment experience (without criticism), the higher the mindfulness score. Perhaps the most consistent set of items across all the instruments to date have to do with attention itself: the ability to maintain attention to present-moment experience.

The questionnaires have good *reliability*, meaning that they are stable over time; a person's score on the instrument could change because the person has changed, not because of the scale items. A reliable measure of weight, for instance, would be a doctor's scale; a less reliable measure would be a friend's estimation (perhaps a friend will always underestimate it). A measure with good *validity* is one that actually reflects the thing you want to measure. This is our central question here: How do we know how well the self-reports of mindfulness measure the construct of "mindfulness"?

There are currently no objective ways to measure mindfulness that we can use to compare and validate the self-report scales, yet, as we will see in later chapters, this is an area of active research. However, if practicing meditation increases mindfulness, we would expect to see a positive association between time spent in meditation and mindfulness scores; there is evidence to support this positive relationship, but only moderately.[8] Self-report scales, currently the only instruments of measuring mindfulness, may be a serious limitation. Perhaps the more mindful you *think* you are, the less insight you really have into your own mindfulness! That's not too hard to believe. By analogy, consider a piano tuner and a piano that is slightly out of tune. A

minor departure from perfect tone noticed by the tuner might be unde-
tectable to you or me. Indeed, we would probably describe the piano very
differently: What the piano tuner says is *out* of tune you and I might find to
be very well *in* tune. Perhaps the more mindful you are, the greater is your
ability to detect subtle deviations from present-moment attention compared
to the abilities of a less well-trained, less mindful individual.

Thus, it may be that self-reports are useful only up to a point and that
they fail to reflect the most mindful among us. Alternative methods of measuring mindfulness are needed, such as the physiological markers that are associated with mindful states, including brain, body, or even gene expression
patterns. Although research is beginning to uncover biological correlates of
mindfulness, as you will see throughout this book, none are as yet used as
direct measures of mindfulness.

Mindfulness as a Trait

In the last ten years of research on mindfulness, there has been an increasing
understanding that mindfulness has the qualities of both a trait and a state.
A trait is a feature by which individuals differ owing to genes and environment, and it is relatively stable over time; a state is a temporary biological or
psychological feature that may be induced but does not persist over time.[9]
Your eye color is a *trait*, but using colored contact lenses changes the *state* of
your eye color.

Even with little or no formal meditation training, people differ greatly in
their self-reports of mindfulness. Are some of us genetically destined to be
monks, contemplatives, or other mindfulness "experts"? Studies of mindfulness as a trait are just beginning, but preliminary findings suggest that differences reflect biological variation and are probably influenced in part by our
inherited genetic blueprints. For example, David Creswell, a psychologist at
Carnegie Mellon, and his colleagues demonstrated that people who vary in
trait mindfulness also vary in the brain activity associated with how well we
regulate our emotions (the more mindful the greater the ability to regulate
emotion).[10] Others have found comparable associations with attention regulation (the more mindful, or the more hours of mindfulness practice, the
greater the attention regulation).[11] Taken together, these findings show that

mindfulness may reflect differences in self-regulation as a whole, a trait known to vary in the population and to have genetic causes.[12]

Self-Regulation and Mindfulness

Self-regulation refers to the monitoring and modification of behavior (or of thought, emotion, or body states) to achieve a goal or adapt to the environmental context.[13] Many factors influence self-regulation: In addition to your DNA blueprints, how you were raised, and the culture, your self-regulation is also influenced by factors such as medication (like valium), your environment (notice your ability to calm yourself while on vacation versus when you're at work), and alcohol, among others. You are constantly regulating your body state (your activity level), your cognitive state (your thoughts), your emotional state (your feelings), and your relationship state (how you relate to yourself and others). Mindfulness meditation can influence any of these areas of self-regulation (as we will see in later chapters), and with repeated practice, state changes may even become more permanent traits.

Mindfulness as a State

Despite the idea that mindfulness is an inherent trait influenced by genes, biology, and experience, mindfulness is clearly a state as well, one that can be changed through a wide range of experiences but may or may not last over time. A large and growing body of research demonstrates that mindfulness practice changes subjective and physiological states. The immune system gets stronger, as reflected by an increase in the number of cells fighting infection. Brain activity changes, moving toward patterns that coincide with calm yet focused states of attention. Brain structure itself seems to change: Among long-time meditators, gray matter (the tissue containing neurons) is thicker in certain brain regions compared with nonmeditators. Lastly, even gene expression patterns seem to differ with the induction of a mindful state of mind. On a more subjective level, feelings of anxiety and depression lessen, well-being improves, and relationships toward self, others, and the planet are healthier. Taken together, this evidence indicates that mindfulness can be learned like any other skill and that the practice of mindfulness may be a powerful way to affect *neuroplasticity*—the brain's ability to form new connections in response to the environment—as well as *epigenetics*, the regulation of genes (turning on and off their expression) in response to the environment.

Until the midtwentieth century, scientists thought that our brains were pretty fixed, with a limited number of brain cells and, with only a few exceptions (like memory centers), a limited capacity to change once developed. Yet research in the late twentieth century overturned this assumption.[14] Our brains have a great capacity to change in both structure and function with experience, whether that experience is mindfulness practice, learning to ride a bike, speaking a foreign language, learning math, painting, or learning to think or feel differently. *Practice changes the brain.*

Perhaps one of the clearest examples of this idea is to look at the brains of musicians. A series of research studies show that learning to play music rewires the regions of the brain involved in processing sound (auditory cortex) and the integration of input to output (somatosensory cortex), as happens when a trumpet player monitors the pressure of the lips in playing the instrument, or when the hands of a pianist are in motion. The extent of brain change correlates with the age at which musical training began, the type of instrument learned, and the duration and intensity of practice.[15] We can rewire our brains, just as an electrician rewires a house, and science is beginning to show the possible range of such rewiring, as well as its limits.[16]

However, we can rewire our brains in ways that aren't always helpful. For example, musicians can overpractice, creating focal hand dystonia (involuntary contraction and spasms of the muscles) by being too forceful in musical practice.[17] By better understanding how practice influences the brain, we can perfect aspects of training and correct errors when they arise. The same may be true for mindfulness: With a better understanding of both the positive and negative consequences of mindfulness practice, you can hone its helpful aspects and minimize the harmful ones. For instance, a helpful application of mindfulness practice might be to enhance your awareness of negative behavior like gossip or self-destructive criticism, and an unhealthy application might be practicing mindfulness to yield praise from others. It is important to remember that mindfulness is a means of attending to experiencing and honing your ability at discernment; how mindfulness is integrated into life involves reflection, understanding, and ultimately the choices you make in the world.

Our brains are dynamic and malleable, just like our genes—whose expression, as already mentioned, is turned on or off as a function of our environmental experiences. In fact, much of twenty-first-century science is focused on the malleability of our biology as a consequence of experience, *including the experiences we create through our thoughts, feelings, and actions.* The circular nature of this relationship is like the chicken and the egg: Experience shapes our biology, and our biology shapes our experiences. Neither our brains nor our genes are fixed, and mindfulness is a means of discovering their fluidity.

Other Qualities of Mindfulness

Many studies of mindfulness have focused on the *outcomes* of practice, including changes in health, learning, decision-making, self-knowledge, self-regulation, insight, compassion, and creativity.[18] How should such outcomes be included in the definition of mindfulness, if at all? For example, if mindfulness is a tool for heightened self-awareness, how does it relate to our definitions of "self"? We know that at about two years of age a sense of self emerges—that is, an understanding of "I" as compared to "you." Alongside this sense of self emerges an understanding of time, and soon enough the "presence" of childhood dwindles against the thoughts of past and future that occupy much of adult life. Often we do not separate the "I" part of ourselves from the experiences we have—as in "I am happy" or "I am running"—and we may define ourselves by the rise and fall of our history of experiences ("I am a success," "I am a failure," "I am a doctor," "I am a mom," and so on). By bringing us to the present moment, mindfulness shows us how we relate to our self. In this way, mindfulness is related to concepts of self and the transcendence of self, a topic we return to throughout this book.

Mindfulness also brings our attention to how we see the world—that is, our *conceptual framework* of the world. As discussed later, our world is shaped by our experiences and the knowledge we accumulate through science, literature, poetry, and so on. Each person has a somewhat unique view of the world. A conceptual framework is generated by language, culture, and individual experiences from birth to death, memory, and a host of physiological and psychological factors. This framework changes throughout your life—think of how you saw the world at five, at fifteen, at thirty-five—but it plays a powerful ongoing role in how you experience the world. Imagine if you lived in the year 1750 and were introduced to a cell phone or a plasma TV screen. The experience would be inconsistent with your conceptual framework of how the world worked at that point in time, and it might lead you to refuse to believe in the reality of these objects or to attribute their workings to some sort of witchcraft. Mindfulness is attention to experience *as it is happening*—that is, *in the present moment*. In Buddhist literature, this kind of attention is often referred to as "bare attention," or seeing things as they are with no shading from the experience of past events—or in other words, seeing things as they are without reference to your conceptual framework, the memory and mind-set you bring to your experiences. Is this really possible? Can you separate your conceptual framework from your experience? If you can, what would you see?

Mindfulness is a means of asking yourself this question, and studies are suggesting that mindfulness practice can and does shift conceptual frameworks. Scientists have studied other methods throughout history, researching everything from the distorted worldview in many psychiatric disorders (such as psychoses) to the changes in worldview that arise via hallucinogenic drugs, brain tumors, hypnosis, religious convergence, near-death experiences, and other phenomena. For example, in the 1950s Aldous Huxley, as part of a research project on the effects of the hallucinogen mescaline, took the drug, and while he was on it scientists asked him questions and recorded his experiences in real time. When asked about space, Huxley noted, "When I got up and walked about, I could do so quite normally, without misjudging the whereabouts of objects. Space was still there; but it had lost its predominance." When asked about time, he said, "There seem[ed] to be plenty of it . . . but exactly how much was entirely irrelevant. I could, of course, have looked at my watch; but my watch, I knew was in another universe. My actual experience had been, was still, of an indefinite duration or alternatively of a perpetual present made up of one continually changing apocalypse."[19] Huxley experienced a change in his conceptual framework of space and time. A similar shift happened to Jill Bolte Taylor, a neuroscientist, when she experienced a left-hemisphere brain hemorrhage. During her stroke, her conceptual framework of the world and her "self" in it shifted as radically as Huxley's under mescaline. What she saw in the aftermath of this shift was the very nature of the different roles our brain hemispheres play in creating our conceptual frameworks and shaping our realities.[20]

Mindfulness is a tool we can use to examine conceptual frameworks, to lessen the influence of preconceptions, and to experience "what is" *by choice* rather than through drugs or neurological damage. Perhaps ironically, this echoes the basic principle of all science: *to observe data without preconceived ideas as to what the data will show.* Mindfulness and science share this principle about the discovery of knowledge, yet the former approaches it through first-person observational techniques and the latter through third-person observational techniques. As scientists move mindfulness into the lab (both experimentally and naturalistically), we will learn how to view it through a scientific lens, but a true understanding of mindfulness requires this first-person experience as well.

THE ART

With some foundation in an understanding of the many scientific questions, paradigms, and methods by which scientists are approaching mindfulness, let's turn to an experiential look at mindfulness. This section explores mindfulness from a first-person perspective, offering ways to understand mindfulness practically, as well as examples from our students' lives. At this point we invite you to give mindfulness a try. This book can describe mindfulness, explain its benefits, and analyze its meaning, but until you try it you are approaching it only on the conceptual level. Mindfulness is fascinating to study, but its transformative power lies in the experience.

Experiencing Mindfulness in Life

What might be an experience of mindfulness? Remember a time in your life when you were in the present moment—for example, strolling in the park, where your visual field came alive, or listening to your favorite music. See how clearly you can recall the scenario and try to remember the details: How did you feel? What did you see, hear, smell, or taste? Perhaps you were outside in nature, the sun was shining, and the sky was an uncompromised blue. Perhaps you were walking through the woods, or in a field or on a beach, and with each step you took you felt something that may be hard to describe but that seemed like a sense of connection with yourself or the natural environment. With each muscle movement you felt invigorated, alive, really "in your body" rather than lost in thought as usual. Perhaps for a little while you felt a welcome relief from countless annoying, trivial, or even important issues that had been bothering you. Perhaps these worries even seemed to evaporate. Simply walking, you were present and connected to the experience.

Most of us have had such an experience at least once in our lives, some of us more frequently. Nature is not the only place where this might happen. Similar feelings of well-being, ease, connection, and peace can come to us at any time. Maybe you have this sense in the midst of creative endeavors, like painting, writing, or making music. Maybe it happens when you are running that second mile, when you are cycling, or during a pickup basketball game. Maybe this is the sense you had when you fell in love and it seemed as if only the two of you existed on the planet. Maybe it accompanied the birth of your child or came to you while taking a walk and holding a grandchild's hand.

All of these scenarios are common, and most of us experience them at some point in our lives. Most of them happen spontaneously, without trying to make them happen. None of these experiences are particularly mystical, unusual, or exalted. We do not have them while fasting in a cave in the Himalayas but in the middle of our daily life. We may not have known at the time to call them "mindfulness," yet they are authentic, common, and lived experiences demonstrating our natural capacity to be mindful.

Is Mindfulness for Me?

The idea that mindfulness can have meaning for someone with a demanding job, endless responsibilities, and any one of a variety of religious orientations—including Christian, Jewish, Hindu, Buddhist, or no religion at all—might seem absurd. After all, even if there were some benefit to the practice, who has the time? Right away we can dispel the notion that mindfulness is time-consuming. In fact, it is time-*enhancing* and can be practiced anywhere, in the blink of an eye. *Mindfulness is the art of observing your physical, emotional, and mental experiences with deliberate, open, and curious attention.* And although it is an "art" that can be cultivated through a daily formal meditation practice (which we talk about throughout the book), you can easily practice it instantaneously by remembering to be aware of your present-moment experience anytime in the course of a day.

To incorporate mindfulness into your life does not require that you change your life in any drastic way—you still attend to your normal array of family, work, social, and leisure time activities—but you can learn to perform all of these activities with a different state of awareness, one that is open, curious, and nonreactive. Mindfulness may at some point lead you to change some behaviors, particularly those that may be harmful to yourself or others, but it is not a self-help methodology per se. In practicing mindfulness, *you are not trying to change who you are, but to become more fully present with your experiences*—with your body, thoughts, and feelings and with their impact on your life. In the process, you are likely to get to know yourself better, learn to relax and detach from stress, and find a way to navigate the intense pressures you may face. Through such increased awareness, you may also become more discerning of your thoughts, feelings, and actions, and that awareness will give you greater opportunity to make a positive change if you wish to do so. Says Charlie, a thirty-eight-year-old dockworker:

> I'm convinced mindfulness makes me a better father. It's not only that I'm able to listen better to my children, but also it's the fact that I somehow appreciate every moment I have with them, more than I ever have in the past. I don't take the time with them for granted anymore. I mean, they're six and eight now, but before I know it they'll be in college and . . . well, I get to enjoy them now.

No More Automatic Pilot

Many of us complain that we sometimes miss out on parts of our lives. During my cousin's college graduation, my mother was so busy photographing him receiving the diploma that she did not actually see him accept it. Her only memory is of fiddling with the camera. So often we are not present in what we are doing. We have no idea of what we may or may not have just done, whether it was driving across town, making dinner, or engaging in some other routine behavior. We tend to remember crises or extra-special events, but much of ordinary life—the daily activities of showering, grocery shopping, getting dressed, and so on—seems to slip by us. We might call this "living life on automatic pilot": You are functioning, accomplishing life's tasks, but it is as if no one is at the controls. You are not appreciating or even experiencing much at all; you literally are missing your life. Have you ever gotten into your car, then gotten out of your car and realized you had no idea what happened in between?

Mindfulness is an antidote to the dullness and disconnection of life lived on automatic pilot. By applying mindfulness, you can counteract that spaced-out feeling you may sometimes have in the midst of your day. You can learn to take an ordinary experience, give it your present-moment attention, and experience it as extra-ordinary. (This may happen for you as you try the eating meditation practice at the end of this chapter!) With many moments of your life taking on extraordinary qualities, you are likely to feel more "alive." Sometimes sights and sounds seem stronger, more varied and textured. Spicing up life with mindfulness can change the way you approach ordinary activities and bring you new enthusiasm and joy.

One of our meditation students told us about how bored she was with walking her dog. When she began to really pay attention, however, it suddenly became an entirely different experience. She felt more connected to her body, her senses came alive, and she saw her neighborhood as if for the first time. She saw details of trees and flowers she had never noticed. The scents seemed stronger and more varied. She relaxed as she felt the sun on her skin. As she connected to her present-moment experience, she felt a greater sense of appreciation and enjoyment in activities that she had been performing with reluctance. She felt that even her dog could sense the change in her.

From the Past and the Future and into the Present

If you ask people on the street where their minds are most of the time, they will probably think you are really odd, but then they will answer, "My mind is right here." Is it? Most of us spend a great deal of time lost in thoughts about the past or the future. Many of our thoughts are about things we regret from the past or things we are worried about in the future. We obsess, worry, grieve, imagine the worst happening in the future, and replay situations from the past that caused us pain. Theoretically, it might be wise to replay only pleasant thoughts, but we mostly replay negative thoughts, as if we have broken records in our heads. Most of our thoughts hardly seem to vary. We have been thinking the same (often painful) thoughts day after day! So our minds are often not aware in the present but living in a different time period, either the past or the future.

Mindfulness can take you out of your habitual thinking by bringing you to what is actually happening at the present time. Stop right now, take a breath, and pay close attention to the present. Exactly in this moment, are things, for the most part, okay? The future has not happened, the past is over, and right now, well, it just is. This foundational technique of learning mindfulness—learning to return your mind to the present, no matter what is happening—is tremendously helpful for working with challenging thoughts, emotions, and experiences. You will learn how to do this in subsequent chapters.

Emma, a twenty-three-year-old aspiring actress, struggled constantly with negative thoughts about herself. After a few weeks of the MAPs class, she came into class elated: "I had an audition today, and for the first time ever I didn't judge myself. Well, I did notice judgment in my mind, but I just stopped and took a breath and decided to be mindful instead of judgmental. I felt my body, noticed my thoughts, and all the judgment just stopped."

Coming back into the present moment by letting go of thoughts does not require that you eliminate creative ruminations, reflections on the past, or abstract thinking. Mindfulness is more about giving yourself a choice with your thoughts. You can exert some control over them rather than being at their mercy. As you learn to regulate your attention, you also learn when it is useful to focus on the present moment (particularly when working with difficult or negative thinking) and when it is useful to use creative and other functions of mind.

Sunila, who is a forty-four-year-old internist, tells us:

As a physician, it's important for me to be able to be really present with patients. But I also have so much I'm juggling, thinking through their case, not to mention the other cases I'm working with that day. Often times I'm trying to come up with an out-of-the-box solution. So I've learned to train my mind. When I'm with a patient, I listen with full attention. I focus on them fully. Once I leave the room, I allow my attention to wander, to ponder, to think creatively. It's only since learning mindfulness that I've had some facility doing this, and my patients have noticed a difference.

Less Reactivity

For our purposes here, "reactivity" means responding to stimuli in the world in ways that induce unnecessary stress. For instance, when you are verbally attacked, you may respond automatically, both physically and mentally. When you come into your office and find extra work on your desk, you may get irritated and say or do something you later regret. When your partner has committed to washing the dishes but you come home and find the kitchen a mess, you may react by getting angry or by isolating yourself or by trying to make your partner feel guilty. It may feel as though you have no control over your actions. You are behaving automatically—reactively.

Mindfulness offers another way. By practicing present-time awareness, *even in the midst of a difficult situation,* you can become aware of your impulses (your reactive patterns), stop, perhaps take a breath, and respond skillfully in a way that does not lead to more harm. With such insight into yourself, wise actions are likely to follow, as one meditation student discovered.

Gino, a twenty-eight-year-old graduate student, was running late as he drove on an L.A. freeway, and when someone cut him off, he missed his exit. Immediately, a flash of rage swept through his body. In the past he might have made an angry hand gesture or shouted fruitlessly at the long-departed car. He would have stewed in his anger, with his blood pressure rising, and obsessed about getting back at the other driver. But because he was learning mindfulness, he decided to use this experience as an opportunity to become aware of his reactivity and make a different choice. He took a breath, noticed his body—heart racing, heat in his face, a clenching in his gut—and thought, *Wow, I'm really angry.* After thinking about what a small thing it had been that triggered such massive anger, he was actually able to laugh about it. As he noticed this, his body began to calm down. In that moment he knew he could respond differently in the situation. He realized that he was still angry, but somehow not so overwhelmed. He even thought, *I might let that guy in the pickup into my lane.* Awareness allowed him to make that choice.

Mindful Attitude

A classic definition of mindfulness often includes the words "nonjudgmental," "open," "accepting," and "curious" to describe the attitude you can cultivate when being mindful. Mindfulness is an accepting and kind attitude toward yourself and your present-moment experience. So if you are trying to be mindful but have a reaction to your experience—that is, you are aware, but you're disliking, fearing, or judging your experience—then your mindfulness is colored by these reactions.

For example, if you are mindful of your breath but thinking, *Wow, this is utterly boring,* or *I'm doing this wrong,* then you are aware, but the quality of accepting things as they are is not present for you. To make it slightly more complicated, if you then notice that you are either bored or doubting your effort, but feel curious and open about this experience, even somewhat kind toward yourself for feeling bored or doubting, then your attitude would be accepting!

When you are aware of the present moment in a kind and curious way, accepting it exactly as it is, then you have the direct experience of mindfulness. This is not to say that sometimes judging, aversion, fear, and so forth, will not color your mindfulness, but that this is the ideal you can aspire to through practice—to be as kind as possible to yourself and your experience. This is also not to say that if you are truly mindful you will never have judgmental thoughts. Judgments arise unbidden in our minds, so we don't need to judge our judgments! Instead, recognize them for what they are: thoughts passing through your mind.

How might this work? Here is what Joan, a fifty-three-year-old musician, has to say:

> When I began my meditation practice, I was convinced I was doing it wrong. I couldn't breathe one breath without a voice telling me that I was breathing wrong! How can you breathe wrong? Anyway, I really worked on practicing kindness with myself, letting myself be okay with each breath, even letting myself be okay with not knowing if I was doing it right. It was like I could bring mindfulness to being unsure. Over time I began to relax, and now I don't judge my meditation so strongly.

Having a kind and open attitude does not mean that you accept all behaviors as equally appropriate. If you say to yourself, *Oh, I yelled at my partner when he didn't deserve it, but I was very mindful and kind to myself in the process,* you are misunderstanding this attitude. When you have a truly mindful attitude, you see yourself kindly but *clearly*, with no shadings from your own reactive patterns or ways of deluding yourself. As you become more mindful, you begin to see more clearly the effect of your behaviors on other people. Through a lens of mindfulness, you recognize behaviors that harm, such as abuse, lying, and malicious gossip, as hurtful to yourself and others, and you may choose to diminish or abandon these behaviors.

Over the long term, you may notice a striking effect: Kindness begins to permeate the rest of your life. Unfortunately, many people these days suffer from self-criticism and self-hatred. Learning to develop an accepting attitude through moments of mindfulness helps you develop a kind and compassionate attitude toward yourself and others over the long term. This idea is based on the principle that what you practice you cultivate. So if you spend many moments of your day learning to be open to experiences with kindness, openness, and curiosity, you are likely, over time, to find these attitudes and behaviors becoming a natural and more incorporated part of who you are. As we saw in the science section, this is mindfulness moving from "state" to "trait."

Mindfulness Is Simple but Not Easy

One of our students, Jade, age thirty, sums up how difficult it is to be in the present:

> I was on vacation in Mexico, and the whole time I was there, despite beautiful sunny weather and an amazing beach, all I could think about was whether or not I should be in Hawaii, or maybe another Central American country. Finally, I said to myself, "If I'm not going to be *here*, why bother to go anywhere at all?"

As obvious and simple as mindfulness can be, and despite its beneficial effects, doing it is another story. It is very *simple* to be mindful. Take a moment right now, stop reading, and feel your nose and body take one breath. You are present with that one breath. You are mindful in this single moment in time. It is simple to be mindful, but *remembering* to be mindful can be very difficult.

Modern society tends to condition us to be anything but mindful. The dominant American culture validates virtually mindless productivity, busyness, speed, and efficiency. The last thing we want to do is just *be* present. We want to *do*, to succeed, to produce. Those of us who are good at the doing seem to fare well in many of our institutions and corporations. Those who are not, well, they tend to fall behind. But this is life in America in the twenty-first century and, to an increasing degree, around the world. We are so focused on doing that we have forgotten all about being, and the toll this takes on our physical, mental, and emotional health is palpable. As the saying goes, we have become "human doings" instead of "human beings." In the science sections of this book, you will learn that many chronic illnesses (pain, depression, heart disease) may arise when we get the doing and being parts of ourselves out of balance. Mindfulness is a means to rebalance doing and being.

It has become so normal to be incessantly busy that many of us cannot even tolerate the feeling of stopping and slowing down. I know a man who needs to talk on his cell phone or read a book when walking down the street; he cannot face what he perceives as the sheer boredom of no stimulation. Josh, a beginning meditation student, reports that in all his waking hours he never chooses to be in silence. Even when he is relaxing, he turns on the TV or searches the Internet while ambient music pumps away in the background. His first attempts at mindfulness were quite discouraging to him, because the feeling of being alone with himself was so foreign and uncomfortable. He could not see the point of spending five minutes in silence with himself when he had so much to do to run a successful business. He assumed that a time of silence and self-inquiry was a waste of time when he had all those "important" things to do.

Learning mindfulness starts wherever you are. Whether you are busy, distracted, anxious, depressed, jealous, peaceful, or tired, all you need to do is to take a moment to pay attention to yourself. If you can stop, breathe, and notice what is happening in just this moment, then you have tapped into the power of mindfulness. This simple act, unassuming as it is, can lead to significant changes in your well-being and become a real "seat belt" for your mental health.

THE PRACTICE: EATING MEDITATION

This introductory exercise provides an excellent experiential understanding of mindfulness. We recommend that you try this practice with a grape or any simple fruit.

Settle back in your meditation posture, close your eyes, and take a breath or two to relax. The grape you have in front of you didn't magically appear at the supermarket. It actually has a long history. As I describe this, let your mind imagine the history of the grape. Feel free to make other associations on your own.

Some time ago, someone planted a grape seed. That grape seed began to sprout, and it grew into a vine. There was soil, sun, rain and water, and perhaps fertilizer; there were humans who tended to the grape. The vine grew and grew, and ultimately it began to sprout fruit. The fruit ripened until it was ready to be harvested. Then someone came along and cut the vines, whose grapes may have been packaged at that point, wrapped in plastic, loaded on trucks, and driven to supermarkets, where you purchased them.

There are also many secondary connections to reflect on . . . all of the humans involved in this process. There were people who tended, people who harvested, people who drove trucks. And we don't know the circumstances under which the farm workers lived and worked; perhaps their lives were quite difficult. We do know that each person had a set of parents. And their parents had parents, and *their* parents had parents. And so on. And each person was clothed and fed and ate countless amounts of food. And where did that food come from? Let your mind roam and imagine the answer to this question. The truck, for instance—where did *that* come from? Oil and metal and plastic and glass. How about the roads the truck drove on to cart this grape to market? Who tarred, cemented, and paved those roads? Let your mind consider this. Make one more connection you haven't yet thought of or I haven't descrribed.

Now notice what is going on inside yourself. How do you feel? There is no right or wrong answer to this question, which is a really important point with mindfulness. All we do is find out what is true in this moment for us. You might be feeling some sense of appreciation. Or you might be feeling some sadness, or sleepiness, or anything at all. Just check in with yourself and notice what is happening in this present moment.

Now open your eyes and pick up the grape. Look at it as though you have never seen a grape before—as if you were a little child who has been handed her first grape. You can roll it around in your fingers; you can notice the shape and the color and the way the light on it changes; you can find out whether it has a smell or a sound. See if you can look at the grape with the curiosity and wonder a child brings to a first experience—that is mindfulness.

Now bring the grape up close to your mouth and notice as you do so whether something inside you says, *I want to eat it!* Simply be aware of that impulse. Then close your eyes, open your mouth, and put the grape in. Begin to chew, but slow down the process. Use your awareness to feel and sense and taste; there's so much to explore—flavors, textures, sounds. And there's saliva—your teeth and your tongue know exactly what to do.

You also might notice what is going on in your mind. Maybe you are comparing this grape to one you had last week and thinking, *Oh, it's not as good*, or, *Oh, this one's better than the one I had last week.* Maybe you want another grape immediately. Maybe you are thinking, *Hmmm, this is kind of silly*, or, *This is so interesting!* Truly *anything* could be happening. With mindfulness, we simply notice. We become aware.

When you finish the first grape, eat the second grape with the same quality of attention. When you finish the second grape, notice your whole body present here, and when you are ready, open your eyes.

2

GETTING STARTED

If you want a quality, act as if you already had it.
Try the "as if" technique.

—WILLIAM JAMES

Changing behavior is hard. We are creatures of habit, and science merely corroborates this fact. If it were easy to change our behavior—to stop doing things that are bad for us and start doing things that are good for us—we would not be a nation in which obesity is a national health crisis, alcohol and cigarette abuse afflict millions, self-help books top the best-seller lists, and magazines spotlight "how to" lists for everything.

Mindfulness meditation is a method of becoming more aware of the obstacles that keep you from changing your behavior. Many obstacles may be encoded unconsciously as habitual patterns of thinking, feeling, and then action. Mindfulness can help bring these patterns into conscious awareness so that you can select alternatives and create change. But the practice of learning to live more mindfully itself requires attention and effort; like almost any skill, it requires repetition until skillfulness is achieved.

THE SCIENCE

What does it take to change our behavior? Clearly it takes effort to change behavior or learn a new skill because routines or behavioral patterns that are automatic are tough to change. When we can do something on automatic

21

pilot, our brains reduce the attentional effort directed toward the activity.[1] Automatic routines, like well-learned skills, require little directed brain energy to succeed, so it is no wonder that we don't stay present while we brush our teeth, take a shower, get dressed, and go through the numerous routines we have built into our days. By the same token, we certainly don't need to attend to our breathing for our bodies to breathe. In other words, our brains don't need an investment of energy from us to get routine tasks done, so why should we exert that energy?

This question points to a linchpin practice of mindfulness: investigating habitual patterns or habits of mind. Most of us are not aware of how many habits we really have, so noticing them is a first step in practicing mindfulness. You can begin to notice how much you function on automatic pilot by challenging it—for instance, don't wear a watch, use a different burner on your stove when you cook, or take a different route to work. Even though discovering your habits takes effort, you will immediately live a little more mindfully. If you then wish to add a formal mindfulness practice to your day, the science of behavioral change can help you succeed.

The Four Ingredients of Behavior Change

Although a large body of science on how to change behavior is available, applying it seems to be another matter: People still find it hard to change their behavior permanently.[2] How hard is it? In their book *Freakonomics*, Steven Levitt and Stephen Dubner describe a classic case to illustrate the point: medical staff personnel and the simple act of hand-washing.[3]

You might think that hand-washing would be a no-brainer, especially with 44,000 to 98,000 people dying each year because of hospital mistakes, bacterial infections being one of the top errors. In one study reported by Levitt and Dubner, doctors—our experts in medical care—reported washing their hands 73 percent of the time. However, when observed on hidden camera, they were found to do so merely 9 percent of the time. In efforts to get medical staff to turn on the faucet and use a little soap, administrators at Cedars-Sinai Hospital in Los Angeles made it a top priority to change the hand-cleaning behavior of staff from an average of 65 percent to close to 100 percent, and they succeeded. What worked? Following all four of these steps:

1. *Simple steps:* Placing hand sanitizers all over the hospital made hand-washing easier and more accessible.
2. *A supportive environment:* A reward system for being caught in the act of hand-cleaning was created with gifts such as $10 Starbuck's gift cards.
3. *Motivation:* Doctors were asked to put their hands on petri dishes to culture the bacterial colonies (invisible to the naked eye) thriving there, and then visual images were displayed on screen savers throughout the hospital. The living-color bacterial colonies proved to be a powerful motivator. These three steps boosted hand-washing to close to 100 percent.
4. Then *repetition* made it a habit.

These four steps seem to be crucial to behavioral change, whether your focus is dieting, exercising, stopping smoking, or adding mindfulness to your life.[4]

Simple Steps

All of the relevant science shows that baby steps are of critical importance in making behavioral change.[5] You wouldn't try to play a Mozart sonata without first learning how to play scales. Adding something new to your daily routine can seem overwhelming if you feel already feel pressed for time. This is perhaps the greatest reason to start small, with five to ten minutes a day, and build over time. Keep your mindfulness practice manageable and help yourself along the way. Research shows that success lies in setting simple achievable goals; for instance, weight loss is easier to achieve when you slow down your eating by putting your fork down between bites, take breaks during a meal, or eat fruit for dessert. Setting such small achievable goals makes mini-successes possible, and that puts you on course to achieve long-range goals, such as a specified weight loss or incorporating mindfulness into a daily practice.[6]

A Supportive Environment

A new environment can be conducive to behavioral change. David Heber is an expert on getting people to lose weight. One secret to his patients' success in achieving their weight loss goals is their attention to the environments that shape their eating patterns. Just knowing what to eat (how to diet) is doomed to fail if the world in which you operate is not supportive of your eating habits. The first thing his patients do is identify the "ABCs" of their uncontrolled eating: Antecedents, Behavior, and Consequences. Antecedents are the events that occur immediately before a behavior like uncontrolled eating and that are linked to it, such as stress and raiding the refrigerator, or a mid-morning sugar binge after drinking a morning latte without breakfast. In his book *The L.A. Shape Diet*, Heber gives an example of the ABCs: Feeling upset is an antecedent, eating chocolate ice cream is the behavior, and feeling better is the consequence. Changing eating behaviors requires understanding the ABCs and then taking preventive steps to create new patterns that support weight loss versus uncontrolled eating. In a similar way, creating the right environment to support a mindfulness practice is as key to its success as shaping the environment around food is to losing weight.

In his weight loss program, Heber provides an example of changing the environment to achieve new patterns of behavior. "Stay away from people who criticize you for being overweight," he notes, "and seek out those who will say positive things as you lose weight."[7] The same kind of social support can help you develop a mindfulness practice. Notice what happens, for instance, when you feel tired (the antecedent). After you start watching television (the behavior), you feel distracted from yourself (the consequence). Finding the ABCs about practicing mindfulness may help you maintain it by increasing your awareness and helping you create new patterns, such as meditating first thing in the morning before you turn on the television or computer and noticing a positive feeling in the aftermath. And as Heber suggests when it comes to weight loss, finding others who support your efforts while staying clear of those who are cynical or verbally critical of mindfulness or meditation may help you keep going.

Motivation

Behavioral change requires motivation.[8] When embarking on a new regime—whether it be fitness, studying for the bar exam, or exploring mindfulness—you may be highly motivated in the beginning; it is common to have initial experiences that are so novel and out of your ordinary routine that they are highly reinforcing. Over time, however, meditation—like all other skills—waxes and wanes in its immediate feedback. The need to practice drills in sports training or play scales to learn music often deters people from continuing. Similarly, many people start to meditate and quickly stop because their motivation lessens as the novelty wears off. To counter this natural tendency to lose motivation, you can do certain things to keep your motivation high until it shifts from extrinsically to intrinsically rewarding. Again, we can take examples from Heber's successful weight loss programs, which suggest using "self-talk" as a way to follow through with an intention. Self-talk is an inner voice that directs you toward your intention and away from disruption. Examples of self-talk to avoid eating an ice cream sundae, for instance, might be to tell yourself how many hours on a treadmill it will take to counter it or practicing how to say "No, no, no," when offered a sundae.[9]

A friend once told me that it takes her forty-five minutes of deliberation to achieve three minutes of meditation. Most of us have "self-talking" inner voices that deliberate incessantly, particularly when we are trying to add something new to our lives or make a behavioral change. When your inner voice tries to convince you not to begin your practice of mindfulness, counter that kind of message with self-talk about the science of its health benefits, the "yes, yes, yes" of its impact on your feeling of happiness, and its relatively short duration.

Repetition

Creating a new habit requires repetition.[10] Some skills are harder to learn than others, and we vary in our capacity to learn different things. Think about learning to play a musical instrument. How long do you think it would take you to learn to play the harmonica? One hundred hours? Science suggests that you could be pretty good at playing the harmonica in just fifty hours of practice; if you stay home from work for a week and dedicate your days to harmonica playing, perhaps you could approach a Dylan song by the end of the week. It is a little harder, however, to learn other instruments: It takes about 450 hours to be pretty good at the piano, and 1,200 hours for violin.[11] How many hours do you think it takes to become a proficient meditator? One hundred? One thousand? Five thousand? One study shows that changes in attention may arise *in as little as twenty minutes of meditation a day for just five days.*[12] But studies also show that the health benefits and effects on well-being increase with more hours of practice. Indeed, some of the most striking brain changes are found in lifelong meditation practitioners who have logged more than nineteen thousand hours of practice.[13] Yet radical changes in consciousness can arise in a millisecond, as reflected, for example, in reports of creative bursts or of near-death experiences. The fact is that no one knows how long it takes for mindfulness practice to yield beneficial effects. As with any skill, change increases with continued practice. So start small, make it manageable, keep it simple, and *practice*.

Getting Started in Inward Discovery

The basic tenet of both mindfulness and science is to observe things as they are. Getting started in mindfulness is a matter of honing your subjective skill of investigation, which is a skill complementary to science as a means of obtaining knowledge. These two investigative paths have a lot in common.

Both science and mindfulness rely on observation, the former using a third-person perspective, the latter a first-person perspective. Both expect the practitioner to observe with an unbiased point of view, one not shaded by personal beliefs or attitudes. Both science and mindfulness start by taking observations and forming hypotheses or statements about the world at large (both external or internal) that can be tested. In science a hypothesis looks like this statement: "Stress causes heart disease." In mindfulness practice you learn to examine first-person experiences by forming "hypotheses" like: "When I am stressed, my stomach tightens." Both science and mindfulness meditation utilize data collection to test the hypothesis in question. A scientist might design an experiment that places people under stressful conditions, and then he or she examines the changes in their heart rates or other physiological measures associated with heart disease. In mindfulness applied to day-to-day life, you might pay attention to the situation whenever your stomach tightens and observe whether that happens whenever you are feeling stressed. Based on data collection, science and mindfulness can lead to conclusions about their hypotheses and open the door to more questions.

Applying mindfulness as a tool of inward exploration, like scientific investigation as a tool of outward exploration, is a never-ending process. With each new discovery comes increased understanding and then another question. Alan Watts once described this process of discovery as a perpetual game of hide-and-seek in which we keep finding ourselves again and again.[14]

Mindfulness Is Like a Nice Bath

One way to explore the receptive nature of mindfulness is to see its similarity to taking a bath—another receptive experience, yet one that cannot be enjoyed without some effort. When setting out to take a relaxing bath, you fill a tub with water, add bath oils or salts, set the mood by putting on some soothing music, and set your cell phone on vibrate or take other steps to avoid being disrupted. You prepare to take a bath like you prepare to meditate. When you get in the tub, you relax into the water; feeling its warmth, sensing the calmness of the water, you are receptive yet attentive in the experience. In meditation, you set up the environment (as you do to prepare a bath), and then you sit (or lie down or however you might practice) and become receptively aware of your experience. In meditation, you direct your attention to your breath in the same way you direct your attention to relaxing while bathing. Both experiences require preparation, and both experiences are receptive in nature. Although meditation requires initial effort, over time its receptive nature is likely to take effect. To encourage this effect, remember the analogy of the bath and let the meditation process guide you more than you guide it.

THE ART

Anna curled up on her overstuffed couch, closed her eyes and tried to make her mind go blank. *I'm going to meditate for an hour*, she declared to herself. She waited a moment . . . *Everyone told me meditation would be good for me. It doesn't seem good, but I guess the books say it is. Hmmm, what's wrong with me?* Then her thoughts really started zooming. *Maybe I should be doing yoga instead. Or guided visualization. Or should I be sitting cross-legged on the floor? Maybe that would make me really a good meditator.* Her cat slinked over and promptly sat on her lap, demanding attention. After five minutes Anna gave up. *Meditation shouldn't be this hard*, she thought.

Actually, meditation is not this hard. Anna had set some unrealistic expectations for herself, and so, not surprisingly, she was disappointed when she could not meet them. Subsequently, she had a very difficult time, as she had not properly prepared herself for meditation. This section will help prepare you to meditate, beginning with an explanation of meditation techniques and attitudes, before moving into the practical advice. Once you have a basic understanding of postures, locations, timing, and other things a beginner should know, you will then be ready to learn the techniques and principles of mindfulness meditation throughout the book.

Scientific Attitude

In the spirit of self-discovery, we invite you to attempt meditation with a very specific attitude—one of scientific exploration. In the science section, you saw some ways in which mindfulness and scientific inquiry have similar trajectories. Now we invite you to actually be a scientist as you try meditation— a scientist of your own mind, that is. As you begin your practice, don't assume that mindfulness is a doctrine to be unquestioningly accepted. A good scientist would look for evidence that it is useful or not. So if you are skeptical at first or have a lot of questions, that is a very appropriate attitude to have. Investigate meditation as any scientist would.

Pay attention to how you feel as you begin your meditation practice. Notice how you feel before and after. You may not necessarily see an impact right away, so take this attitude of curiosity and rigorous examination with you as you practice over the coming months. Over time you may see changes in your stress level and in your physical or mental health. If those changes are helpful in your life, they may serve as sufficient evidence that mindfulness meditation is effective, a useful tool, and worthwhile enough for you to continue with it. If you find over time, however, that it is not for you, you can find many other practices to explore.

In this way, our minds become laboratories for inner exploration. Always trust your own best wisdom when trying a new method, whether it is mindfulness or some other kind of meditation. (This is a pretty good rule of thumb for anything else for that matter!) Follow the example of Juanita, a fifty-two-year-old medical technician:

> I was encouraged in the meditation class to take a rigorous scientific attitude towards starting my practice. And good thing too, because I was really skeptical. My doctor recommended I take the class to lower blood pressure and be less stressed out. I thought mindfulness was some new age thing, not something we do in my culture. So I asked a lot of ques-

tions, a whole lot of questions. And I kept paying attention to the impact of meditation on my life. Did it make sense with what I already knew to be true? A lot of times it did. Some things didn't jibe with me. I let go of those. And over a few months, as I kept examining things, I did start to see differences—actually my coworkers mentioned it first: "You seem so much calmer. What are you on?" "Meditation," I'd tell them. It was true: I was getting calmer, less jumpy, less prone to outbursts of anger.

The following sections explore some of the basics needed to set yourself up to meditate.

Postures

You can meditate sitting, walking (which we talk about in Chapter 4), standing, or lying down, as well as in the midst of activities; generally, however, people practice meditation in a sitting posture. In sitting meditation, you have the choice of sitting on a chair or on a cushion on the floor. Have you seen those stereotyped images, in advertisements or other places, of hard-bodied meditators in pretzel-like contortions on the floor? You do not need to look like that or to sit like that to practice meditation. There are a wide variety of postures, and you can find the one that works for you.

Then why do most meditators sit on the floor? Many of the cultures from which the practice of mindfulness is derived sit on the floor as a matter of course. In these cultures, many everyday activities, such as eating or relaxing, take place on the floor. And for some people, sitting cross-legged on the floor is a comfortable position in which to hold a posture for an extended time. In some schools of meditation, the cross-legged position is seen as important to maintaining energy and alertness. When meditation came west and the first students sat on the floor, some of them found it to be supportive and a helpful meditation posture, but others did not; the latter could have avoided a lot of unnecessary agony by simply sitting in a chair instead. Most Western cultures are "chair" cultures, although some of us might benefit from floor sitting—witness the epidemic of back pain in America.

Your choice of position is completely up to you: If sitting on the floor feels natural, enjoyable, and supportive and your body is fairly pain-free in this posture, please meditate on the floor. Otherwise, feel free to sit in a chair.

Some people even prefer to lie down. Any and all positions are okay for meditation, although some may help you stay more alert than others. (Lying flat often makes people sleepy, so I don't recommend it unless you have an injury.) And of course you can change your posture over time or even use different postures on different days.

If you wish to sit on the floor, it is helpful to get yourself a small round cushion (called a *zafu*); they are available at many yoga studios or specialty stores that sell products used specifically for meditation.[15] It can provide just the right amount of lift and may help with the flow of circulation. You can always use a sofa or bed cushion if you do not have a meditation cushion.

Try not to sit directly on top of your cushion but move toward the front so that your rear is higher than your knees and your knees come as close as possible to the floor. You can spread your knees wider so that they rest on the floor. Some people prefer to sit with their feet on top of each other, but I don't recommend it because your feet may fall asleep that way. You can also experiment with putting the floor cushion in between your knees. Some common ways in which people like to sit are shown in Figure 1 on page 31.

Sitting in a Chair

Pick a chair that is fairly firm yet comfortable. Not *too* comfortable because you don't want to set yourself up to fall asleep. Don't go for the big overstuffed living room chair. A desk or kitchen chair that gives you adequate support but is not your cushy La-Z-Boy is preferable. Put your feet on the floor so that you feel firmly supported. If you cannot reach the floor with your feet, put a blanket or cushion under your feet so that you have stability. It is best to keep a fairly upright posture, but one that is not too tight or rigid, as shown in Figure 1. Sometimes it is helpful to put a cushion behind your back; this supports you by keeping your back straight. If a cushion is uncomfortable, sitting naturally against the chair is fine, but try not to slouch.

In all postures, keep your back as upright as you can to promote alertness, but try not to make it too rigid, too tight, too loose, or too relaxed. You want to be at ease *and* alert. Your hands can be resting on your lap or your legs or on the arms of the chair. Your tongue can be wherever it is comfortable; many people like to rest it on the roof of their mouth.

The important point is to be at ease. If you are in pain or trying to hold an awkward position, your meditation becomes much more challenging.

FIGURE 1 Various positions used in meditation practice.

You may notice that it takes a while for the muscles of your back to become accustomed to this posture. You may find that your legs fall asleep if you sit cross-legged. If so, don't be alarmed—this happens to many people. Over time, as your body gets used to the posture, your legs will fall asleep less frequently. Some yoga poses that open the hips are helpful to increase flexibility and strength for sitting cross-legged.

A Modified Lying Down Posture

If you have had an injury that makes it difficult to meditate sitting up, I recommend a modified lying down posture with your back on the floor, your legs at a ninety-degree angle, and your feet up on a chair. The one drawback to the lying down posture is that you can easily fall asleep while meditating, so try to do it at a time of day when you know you will be most alert.

Eyes

Most people find it easiest to meditate without a lot of external distractions, so I recommend closing your eyes when practicing. However, open-eyed meditation—softly gazing down at the ground—is fine if that is your preference. Some people are uncomfortable meditating with their eyes closed.

Location

Choose an area in your home to be your meditation spot, such as the corner of a room where you can close the door. Try to pick a place where you will not be disturbed. (There's nothing like the phone or doorbell ringing to provide a great excuse to stop!) Sitting at the same spot every day helps you become conditioned to your meditation setting. As we saw in the science section, our environments have a huge effect when we are trying to change our behavior. Once you have created a new environment for yourself, repetition is key—keep going back!

Sometimes it helps to decorate or personalize your spot. Some people create a special meditation area with flowers, candles, a meaningful picture (of family members or an inspiring person, or a nature or art image), and perhaps a meaningful passage written out. Decorating your meditation spot is absolutely not necessary; do what feels right to you. You really do not need any props in order to meditate. It is a low-tech sport, and all you need to do is create a space that you think will help you start doing it.

Distractions

Like so many of us who have active and busy family lives, you may find that trying to fit silent meditation into your home life is a challenge, to say the least. You may feel that you have an endless list of things to do other than meditation—cooking, shopping, housework, repairs, and so forth. The only way to develop the habit of meditation is to make it a top priority. Self-care and reflective time are just as important as the many other things you need to do each day. Over time you will come to see this more clearly. And of course, your children or partner may call for attention. (Have you noticed that children often want attention just as their parents have planned some quiet time?) If you can keep your attention to these distractions open and curious, even that can be a source of mindfulness practice, and over time, with some direction and repetition, the kids will probably learn to leave you alone. In fact, some children learn to join in (and meditation cushions are available in children's sizes!). Occasionally our students complain that their pets won't let them meditate. You might think of that as an excuse of the "dog ate my homework" variety. Most people can close the door, but I know students whose cats and dogs learned to sit on their lap and join them in meditation. Yes, you can teach your dog to sit!

When to Meditate

Choose a time of day when you will be most alert and least distracted. Many people meditate when they first wake up. Some have a routine of meditating when they come home from work or school. Others meditate before bed or at some point in the evening. A favorite meditation time for some of our students is during work. There is nothing like closing your door (if you have one) and practicing mindfulness for five or ten minutes in the middle of the day to become more relaxed and reduce your stress. Some parents report having their best sessions when they are waiting to pick up a child from an after-school activity. They insert a meditation CD into the car stereo and meditate away.

The important thing is to find out what is going to work for you—as opposed to following your ideas about when you think you *should* be meditating. Over time you will experiment with different times of day to figure out what is most helpful to you. Ultimately what is important is that you settle on a regular daily time that you follow consistently.

Length of Time

Since so many people feel overwhelmed by the busyness of life, as if there is never enough time to do everything that needs to be done, we recommend starting small—say, with five minutes of meditation each day. Although it is hard for many people to incorporate a new habit into their day, five minutes seems within the reach of most of us. Over time you can work your way up to twenty to forty minutes or even more. Don't set high expectations of meditating for an hour; you will be disappointed if you find it too hard to do. You may get discouraged and give up too soon if you set the bar too high. If you meditate for a few weeks at five minutes per day and you find that it does not feel long enough, then you can increase your time in small increments until you find a length of time that feels beneficial yet works within your lifestyle.

You can keep track of the time by putting an alarm clock or kitchen timer in front of you. You can also buy a meditation timer with a bell that chimes in an array of sounds (see resources section). You can even use a clock or watch and just open your eyes from time to time to check it. Another option is to meditate with a guided CD that will give you a clear ending point and guide you in the basic instructions. (You can download free meditations from our MARC website, www.marc.ucla.edu.) Over time you may find that you prefer to meditate without the recording, although some people have used the same recordings for years. It is up to you. Experiment to find out what feels supportive and makes the process easy.

❧

Clearly, there are a variety of ways in which to meditate, lots of postures, lots of eye and hand positions, and many places and times to do it. There is no formulaic way to meditate, although you may be given many suggestions of what has worked for people over time.

Mindfulness has to do with figuring out who you are and what fits your life. So give yourself a lot of leeway to experiment and explore, don't set the bar too high with high expectations that are likely to lead to frustration, and approach meditation with a scientific attitude—test it out and see what works for you. It may take several weeks or even months before you begin to establish a routine with which you feel comfortable. You will soon see that your daily practice is both an end in itself—one that enhances well-being, provides joy, and promotes self-reflection—as well as your foundation for cultivating mindfulness throughout the day in all aspects of your life. So to get started, right now, try the following practice to help you relax into your posture.

THE PRACTICE:
RELAXING INTO YOUR POSTURE

Get into a comfortable position on a chair or the floor. Bring your attention to your seated body. Take a few deep breaths to let yourself relax more deeply. Then, after a few deep breaths, let your breathing return to normal.

Bring your attention to your feet. Feel the contact that your feet make with the floor. Notice their weight, pressure, heaviness, touch. Then notice the posture that your legs are in. Notice the place where your legs make contact with the chair or the floor. Again, feel the heaviness, pressure, touch. You can also notice how your back rests up against the chair or how you hold your body in space. What sensations do you notice?

Turn your focus to your abdomen. We often hold a lot of tension in that part of our body. Do you notice any tension or tightness? If so, try to relax or soften your belly. If it is helpful, direct your breathing into your belly by breathing into that area more fully.

Now turn your attention to your hands. Are they tense or tight, or are they relaxed? Soften or relax your hands. Also notice your arms and focus on how they are resting, how they feel. Next, bring your attention up to your shoulders. Are your shoulders tight or relaxed? Let them release. Try to drop and soften them—even wiggle a tiny bit if it helps relieve tension. Make sure you continue to breathe regularly.

Now notice your throat and jaw—another place where many people hold tension. Relax your jaw and then soften your face, letting it relax. Relax and breathe. You can then notice that your whole body is seated. Take another minute or two to silently scan your body. Notice whether there are still areas of tension, and if so, invite them to relax. Observe the parts of your body that do feel relaxed. When you feel very relaxed, enjoy this state for as long as you wish, and when you are ready, open your eyes.

3

BREATH AND AWARENESS
Essential Components

Breathe, and you know you are alive. Breathe, and the
whole world breathes as one.

—ANNABEL LAITY

Our relationship to the world is at the core of every breath we take.
Our breath connects our individual lives with those of others and
with the planet through the exchange of oxygen and carbon dioxide. Yet
most of the time we barely notice that we are breathing, unless our breathing is disrupted.

Breath can reveal a lot about you: It can signal what you ate for lunch or
how you might be feeling—calm, stressed, happy, sad. A leading neuroscientist who studies emotion, Antonio Damasio, suggests that breath (along
with heart rate and a few other physical measures) can predict one of four
emotions—fear, anger, happiness, or sadness—with 65 percent accuracy.[1]
Your breath (and cardiorespiratory activity) can pretty much reflect your
mood before you even know it. When you smell something unpleasant, you
experience a shortening of breath, and pleasant odors induce deep breathing
(which may be one reason why most people feel relaxed in a garden).[2] Both
of these reactions happen well before you recognize the smells as good or
bad. The breath can tell us a lot about ourselves and each other.

THE SCIENCE

Breathing is a central focus of mindfulness, meditation, and most mind-body practices. Even the word "spiritual," which is often associated with mind-body practices, stems from the Latin *spiritualis*, which means *of breathing*. Breath is an index of health and well-being. The Greeks thought that the heart and lungs represented the core of *vitality*—the most important faculty of life.[3] In Chinese medicine *qi* (or *chi*) is a measure of the life force of the body, assessed through examination of pulse and breath.[4] In Indian philosophy, *prana* is equivalent to this life force. In Western medicine, breath is a basic vital sign of health as reflected by the routine use of stethoscopes in almost any health examination.

No Two Breaths Alike

DNA contributes to how we breathe. For most of us, breathing is automatic, but for a very few it never is. In a rare genetic condition called central congenital hypoventilation syndrome, the automatic system of breathing never develops. Although rare, scientists have learned a lot about how genes influence our breathing by studying disorders like this one. It appears that this rare mutation can lead to a failure of the brain to control breathing; in mice the mutation causes death in the first few hours of life, and in humans a child can survive with artificial life support. Moreover, it isn't just one gene that is involved; it seems that different mutations lead to different degrees of severity *and* that these genes are also influenced by the environment (at least for the mouse—human studies are not available on this point). For example, mice raised in hot temperatures with exactly the same gene mutation as those raised in cold temperatures are less severely affected by this disorder.[5] This highlights the fact that the genetic blueprint we inherit is not fixed in stone; the environments in which we are raised can greatly alter the influence that our genes have upon us. Our genetic and environmental experiences shape and reshape our bodies, including our breathing, throughout our lives.

Lance Armstrong is known to have exceptionally efficient lungs—he can consume 83 milliliters per kilogram of weight per minute of oxygen in a single breath during exercise; the average non-athlete might consume only half as much oxygen.[6] The Framingham Heart Study, with over ten thousand participants, showed that our DNA blueprints shape some 30 to 50 percent of our lung efficiency, with the environment accounting for the rest.[7] But the same study showed that how individuals *change* with age—whether lung capacity declines or strengthens—is largely (82 to 95 percent) influenced by environment.[8] This means that the choices we make and how we live—whether we work out every day, smoke cigarettes, live in areas with high air pollution—are key to our respiratory health as we age.

Can mindfulness actually influence our gene expression in some way? The answer to that question is one of the most exciting new discoveries emerging from the science of mindfulness: *We have the capacity to regulate our own genes—to turn them on or off in expression—by changing our mental states*, and attention to breath is a key means to do that.

Many factors are known to change gene expression, but only recently have data supported the idea that a consciously directed mental state is one of them. A 2008 study by researchers in Boston shows how powerful such an effect can be.[9] In the study, nineteen longtime practitioners of meditation (or mind-body practices that elicit the relaxation response) were compared with nineteen nonmeditators in terms of the patterns of their gene expression.* Many differences were detected between the two groups, with some twelve hundred genes showing more activity in the longtime practitioners than in the novices and some nine hundred genes showing less activity. When the gene expression patterns of the nonmeditators were compared before and after they were taught a specific relaxation response technique (developed by Herbert Benson at Harvard), some fifteen hundred genes showed differences. Combining all the information, a small set of fifteen genes was considered most likely to be influenced by the relaxation response, and many of these were genes known to be involved in the body's response to stress, cellular metabolism, and oxidative stress.

---

*Gene expression is analogous to a lightbulb and a dimmer switch used to turn a light up or down (on and off). When gene expression is turned up, it is "up-regulated," meaning that the molecules encoded by that gene increase in number compared to when the gene is "down-regulated" and the number of molecules decreases. Because our cells carry the same genetic complement, it is the gene expression patterns (the dimmer switch settings) that account for how cells differ—for example, the ways in which a liver cell differs from a heart cell in the molecules it produces.

Breath and the Health of the Lungs and the Heart

Breathing is both automatic and under voluntary control. Most of us breathe twelve to fifteen times per minute, gulping in a pint of air each time. The involuntary or automatic system of breathing arises in the respiratory center of your brain (the medulla of the brain stem) and stimulates your chest muscles to change in pressure and force air in and out of your lungs. Your voluntary control over your breathing arises in higher brain centers that modify the automatic pathway when you hold your breath or sing or speak.[10] The automatic nature of breathing makes paying attention to it difficult, and as you will see throughout this book, *effort* is needed to attend to your breathing or other habitual or automatic responses. Learning to be mindful of breath is a great way to discover and exercise more effortful control over breathing itself.

Researchers have begun to investigate how mindfulness can affect breath and heart health. For example, altering the breathing rate changes what is known as respiratory sinus arrhythmia, which is our hearts beating more times when we breathe *in* than when we breathe *out*. This difference is a sign of good health, and it decreases with health decline caused by aging and certain illnesses (diabetes, cardiovascular disease). A study of mindfulness using a body-scan meditation (similar to the one at the end of this chapter) at McGill University in Canada found that mindfulness, like exercise, leads to increased respiratory sinus arrhythmia.[11]

Mindfulness also seems to improve heart health. In a study conducted at Duke University, two groups of people at risk for heart disease were studied over a ten-month period. One group was given a program that included a health coach and guidance in mindfulness and stress reduction, while the other group received a written report of their health evaluations but returned, as usual, to their primary care physicians for follow-up health care. After ten months, the people who had been given the mindfulness program had much lower measures of heart disease risk and were found to be exercising more and showing greater weight loss.[12]

Another line of research has been to look at the effects of breathing practices on problems associated with breathing, like asthma. In a small but well-controlled study of breath training on asthma sufferers, twenty-two asthma patients were taught pranayama breathing, a common breathing practice found in certain forms of yoga and meditation that works with *prana*, or life force.[13] In one form of pranayama breathing the exhale is extended to twice the length of the inhale. (Right now you could stop and notice how long your exhales and inhales are relative to one another and attempt to increase the exhale to twice that of the inhale.) The researchers used a breathing device to create this two-to-one ratio of exhale to inhale in half the patients, while a placebo device was used in the other half. Over a four-week period, study participants used their "breathing devices" for fifteen minutes, two times a day. Results of the study showed that lung function in the group doing pranayama breathing had improved, their asthma symptom scores were reduced, and they used less medication to treat their asthma. The changes observed were similar to those found for the use of medication (low-dose inhaled corticosteroids) in patients with mild asthma.

Mindfulness and Blood Pressure

A review of 311 scientific studies of the effect of mind-body practices (including mindfulness) on physiology reveals clear evidence that these practices can reduce blood pressure.[14] These practices are also often similar in their effects to other interventions, such as doing daily blood pressure checks. For example, mindfulness meditation and daily blood pressure checks were equally effective in reducing blood pressure, while Transcendental Meditation and health education were equally effective in reducing blood pressure, weight, heart rate, and cholesterol levels. What this implies is that blood pressure, heart rate, and cholesterol levels improve *if we increase our daily awareness or attention to them*, regardless of the means by which we do so. Mindfulness is a valuable way to heighten awareness of your body physiology, but in some cases it may be no more effective than other sorts of behavioral change, like checking your blood pressure daily or learning more about health management.

The earlier we start practicing mindfulness—or other practices that increase attention to health—the better. We know that the seeds of problems with blood pressure and heart disease start early in childhood.[15] In a recent study of ninety-two middle school students, a simple breathing practice was introduced to half the students while the other half received lessons on how to keep their blood pressure healthy (through diet, exercise, and so on). None of the students had high blood pressure, and the study was designed to test how well youth can regulate their blood pressure in the normal range. In a relatively short period of time—ten minutes a day at school and ten minutes at home, for three months—the program had a positive effect. The youth given the simple breath meditation practice had lower blood pressure and heart rate compared to the students given the educational program.[16]

Breath as a Window on the Mind

When I was a child, we used to see who could hold their breath the longest while swimming underwater or driving through the tunnels sprinkled across the Pennsylvania landscape. Sometimes I would win, and other times I would lose to my two sisters, as my own breath capacity varied from day to day. In 2008 David Blaine, the magician and illusionist, made it into the *Guinness Book of World Records* by holding his breath the longest officially recorded, 17 minutes and 4.4 seconds.[17] We breathe differently when jogging, spinning, or swimming, or when we are exposed to environmental elements, such as smoky air or low oxygen at high elevations. Although external pollutants can directly affect our oxygen access, internal pollutants, like stress, can also harm us.

When exposed to stressful stimuli, such as an accident or a predator, breathing changes. In fact, the respiratory system is closely linked to emotions.[18] When we are anxious, our breathing rate increases under the influence of the heightened activity of emotional parts of the brain.[19] We are all familiar with the accelerating physiological signs of anxiety—including increased heart rate, increased blood pressure, tightening of the stomach, and perspiration—that signal the sympathetic nervous system's release of stress hormones (chemicals like noradrenaline and adrenaline) preparing the body for "fight or flight."* Many mind-body practices use slow deep breathing to counter the body's fight-or-flight response. Slow breathing (often deep abdominal breathing) may signal to the body that the parasympathetic nervous system, the one associated with calm, rest, and repair, is active. A. D. "Bud" Craig, a neuroscientist at the University of Arizona, suggests that many chronic illnesses arise when these two systems are out of balance and the fight-or-flight response is abnormally active.[20] Mindfulness may be a method

---

*The autonomic nervous system comprises the sympathetic branch, which is active during a flight-or-fight response, and the parasympathetic branch, which is active during a recuperate-and-rest phase.

of enhancing the capacity of the parasympathetic nervous system to bring the body back into a homeostatic state.

The mind-body relationship is bidirectional—the mind can influence the body, and the body can influence the mind. As we will examine in more detail later, when you experience an emotion, your body often acts before you feel the emotion. A recent science study showed that people who had been asked to hold a cup of hot liquid for less than a minute were much more apt to describe people as kinder, warmer, and happier than if they held a cup of cold liquid.[21] If you feel warm, you act more warmly toward others. The body's capacity to pair a physiological state with a conscious mental state is probably the reason why the body can take the lead in changing our mental and emotional states. Science has shown that even before a willful act, such as moving your finger, there are signals in the brain suggesting that the brain has registered and committed to this act seconds *before* we even know it.[22]

Mindfulness is a method of investigating the relationships between environmental events (whether internal or external) and their effects on your body, mood, and mental states. Breath becomes a key door of inquiry to help you identify the cause-and-effect relationships (habits) you may have established. Notice that mindfulness does not specify a particular *type* of breathing (as we saw with the pranayama breath study), but rather, it encourages the exploration of breathing itself—how it shifts and changes and what causes such change.

A mindfulness teacher once told me the story of how he learned to overcome his social anxiety by repeatedly noting the clenching of his stomach and the shortening of his breath throughout the day. He made a point of noting the physiological state of his stomach and breath every two to three minutes every day for two years! When his stomach was tight and his breath short, he would breathe slowly and deeply for a second or two to release it. Over a long period of time of this vigilant practice, his social anxiety gradually disappeared.

Why Breath May Be Such a Crucial Part of Mindfulness

There are five reasons why breath may play a central role in mindfulness meditation. First, breath is always present, free, and available to everyone, so it's a handy object for meditation. Second, breath is intimately linked to self-consciousness, since knowing that we breathe reflects our self-awareness. Third, breath reflects an outward sign of well-being, measurable by science. Fourth, our ability to change our breathing, up to a limit, reminds us that even though we are change agents we are also part of a process beyond our control. Lastly, breath is so automatic that it's like a built-in "trainer" of attention: It provides a constantly repeating practice in focusing attention, losing attention, and returning again.

THE ART

Fred pulled up to a stoplight. The light was green, but the car ahead of him was dawdling, trying to make a left turn. *Turn, go now!* he thought. *C'mon, you're going to miss it!* The light turned yellow and then red. Fred started to breathe heavily, and his face grew red from anxiety—he was already running late. *What bad timing!* And then he remembered his breathing. He took a mindful breath, and then another. At last he noticed that his breath had calmed a bit and he felt more refreshed; just as he was thinking, with a shrug, *Well, you can't control the lights, that's for sure,* the light turned green.

As Fred learned, breath is the very foundation of mindfulness practice. This section details the specifics of the mindfulness of breathing.

Meditating with a Focus

When you set out to establish a daily mindfulness practice, it is helpful to begin with a narrow focus. Meditating without a focus can be daunting, especially for beginners. If you tried to be aware of whatever came into your mind, you would probably be a little overwhelmed and start to wonder what you should be aware of.

Try it right now. Be aware. Stop, put down the book, and just notice—be in the moment and pay attention to what is happening right now.

What happened? Probably a lot. You may have noticed sounds or sights in the room or from outside. Internally you may have felt bodily sensations and noticed thoughts or feelings. Most of the time our minds are wandering all over the place, awash in a variety of stimuli. Some Hindu and Buddhist meditation texts compare our minds to chattering monkeys jumping from tree branch to tree branch—they call this "monkey mind." Being generally aware, without a center focus point, is possible, but not easy. And in the long run it can be tiring or perhaps a little overwhelming.

Some meditation traditions teach awareness in this manner, suggesting that we just sit, open our attention, and be aware. For some people this technique is very powerful. For most of the students we encounter, however, especially those who are just starting out, it is helpful to have a specific method to focus on, at least initially. For this, the mindfulness tradition has developed what we call "the anchor."

The Breath: The Meditation Anchor

The meditation anchor functions much in the same way as a ship anchor. A ship can be at sea, perpetually tossed and turned about by the waves, but when a sailor throws down an anchor, the boat stays steady in one place, not pitching about or running aground.

In meditation we use an anchor to keep our minds from being tossed and turned by the ocean of thoughts, stimuli, sensations, sounds, and emotions. In the mindfulness practice taught in this book, we use the breath as our anchor, although it is possible to use other anchors, such as sounds or bodily sensations. Other meditation practices use an image, a candle flame, another body part, or a mantra (a repeating word).

There are some obvious reasons to use our breath as an anchor. First, it is always with us. While we are alive, the one thing we can count on is that we will be breathing. Second, for most people it is pretty accessible and easy to feel. The majority of beginning meditators can quite quickly bring mindfulness to the breath in their body. Third, the breath is usually neutral—most of us do not have a lot of strong feelings about our breath. In general, the fact that breath is neither pleasant nor unpleasant makes it a perfect meditation object, because if we were to choose an anchor that conjures strong negative or positive feelings, we would be spending most of our time managing our feelings rather than being present with the breath.

Natural Breath

Many meditative and yogic practices (such as pranayama, described earlier) feature breathing and the regulation of breathing. In one practice, you inhale through one nostril, hold your breath, and exhale through the other nostril (holding your finger over the first nostril to direct the flow of breath). In yet another practice, you shorten your breathing and rapidly breathe in and out. There are many differences among mindfulness practices. In one mindfulness practice, you lengthen your breath deliberately and stay aware that you are breathing a long breath. Some mindfulness practices, such as one popularized by the Zen master Thich Nhat Hanh, even involve repeating a phrase as you are breathing, such as "Breathing in I calm the breath, breathing out I smile." Each mindfulness practice functions in slightly different ways. Some deliberately calm the breath in the process of bringing mindfulness to it.

The mindfulness practice in this book focuses on the unregulated, entirely natural breath. This practice does not require you to lengthen your breath, shorten it, hold it, deepen it, or anything else. There are two main reasons for this suggestion.

First, letting the breath be natural is a bit easier than trying to regulate it. If you are meditating for a period of time—ten to twenty minutes or longer—and spend the whole time trying to control your breathing, your mind and body can get tired. Letting your breath be natural is simple and easily sustained.

Second, and more importantly, the ordinary breath teaches us to be mindful of things as they are. One of the main tenets of mindfulness practice is to be aware of things exactly as they occur. We learn not to try to control our experience in life, but to let it unfold, exactly as it is. This cultivates a quality of calm acceptance of life—although we do not necessarily become passive! But if your breath is shallow, let it be shallow. Take the opportunity to observe what shallow breath is like. If your breath is long, let it be long. And so on. We gain skill in observation and acceptance rather than control.

Mindful Breath Regulation

Observing the natural breath is key to your daily meditation practice for the reasons described; however, it is also important that you understand and know when to employ mindful breath regulation. As discussed in the science section, your breath and your physiological states of well-being are intimately connected. Shallow, choppy breath may indicate that you are nervous—or that you have been running five miles! If your breath is fast, you may be angry. If it is very soft and subtle, you may be quite relaxed. Breath is a good barometer for your state of mind.

At times during meditation practice or daily life, you may wish to regulate your breathing in order to calm yourself down, feel connected to yourself, or relax a bit more deeply. In any of these cases, it is useful to elongate your breath. You can stop for a moment and breathe more deeply, yet you can maintain an awareness of your breath during this process.

So when you meditate, stick with the natural breath most of the time, but remember that it can be helpful from time to time to mindfully soften, deepen, or elongate your breath. You can also do this practice throughout your day, especially when you are challenged. Jenny, a forty-five-year-old software engineer, related this story:

> I left my boss's office really upset. She told me that several people were to be let go and I may be one of them. No guarantee, as they would have to see through to the next cycle. When I walked down the hall, I sensed my breath was tight and shallow. My heart was beating rapidly. So I stopped walking, right there in the hall, and took a few deep breaths, breathing into the tightness in my chest. Within a few seconds, I was able to feel slightly more relaxed. I reminded myself that I really did not know what was going to happen.

Direct Experience: Finding the Breath in Your Body

Sometimes when people try to be aware of their breath, they visualize or imagine their breath. Or they think about their breath. Sometimes they even talk to themselves: *Hey, I'm breathing, look, I'm breathing in, that was a long breath, now I'm breathing out. . . .* None of these tactics are what you are aiming for (although mental labeling can help you stay focused on the breath; see "Common Difficulties" at the end of this chapter).

The key to mindfulness in breathing practice is *feeling* the breath. It is important not to let your breathing practice become conceptual or cerebral. Mindfulness teaches you to connect to an experience directly, without getting lost in the concept of the experience. Breath is actually not a concept, but a physical sensation that can be directly felt. You can think lots of things about breath—such as when you take the trouble to understand the science of breathing and breath regulation—but to benefit from mindfulness you need to let go of the concepts and focus on the "felt sense"—how you directly experience your breath. This allows your cognitive functioning to relax and lets you learn on a less conceptual level.

To understand the felt sense, after reading this, close your eyes and simply feel your breath in your body. You may find yourself homing in on one area, or maybe you feel your breath throughout your whole body, moving parts of your body, or in specific areas of your body, like your belly or nostrils. You might notice wavelike sensations or little ripples of movement in various spots of your body. This is *feeling* your breath as opposed to thinking about it conceptually.

As it is possible to notice your breathing in a variety of places in your body, you can explore some of those specific areas. Try this:

- Focus your attention on your abdomen. Try putting your hand on your abdomen to feel it more clearly. Are you breathing without having to do anything in particular? Your belly is moving up and down. Take a moment to feel any sensations present in your abdomen.
- Now come back. What did you notice? We would guess that you felt a rising and falling sensation, a sense of expanding, a feeling of inflation and deflation, maybe a contraction at the end. Perhaps a little stillness before the next breath started. This is what you are aiming to become aware of: not what you're imagining or what you're thinking about the breath, but what you're feeling—the felt sense.

Another area to notice your breath is in your chest and throat area. Try this:

- Take a few breaths in your chest. What do you feel? Probably something very similar to your abdominal breathing, although maybe a bit more diffuse. Do you notice your shoulders getting into the action, heaving slightly? Don't forget, everyone is going to have his or her own experience with mindfulness, so you cannot feel the breath incorrectly.

Now pay attention at your nostrils:

- Take a moment to close your eyes and feel a few breaths at your nostrils. What do you notice? Here you might feel some coolness as the air rushes in and some warmth as it rushes out. Perhaps you feel a tickle at the top of your lip. Maybe you feel a slight movement of your nostrils.

Ultimately, as you develop your mindfulness meditation practice, you will want to find one spot to focus on that becomes your own anchor spot. The breath may be your anchor, but it is helpful to rest your attention on a specific part of your body where you experience your breath. After you have explored these three different anchor spots, choose your abdomen, chest, or nostrils to be your anchor for feeling the breath. Choose the spot based on what is most obvious, what is easiest, or what is most interesting to you. If you can't decide, just pick one—they all work equally well. What is important is that you feel comfortable with your spot. Alternatively, some people feel the breath most clearly when it is moving through their whole body, and that can work as a general anchor as well. It may take some time to arrive at your spot, so in the beginning of your meditation practice you can experiment with different spots until you settle on one.

The Wandering Mind

The basic meditation instruction (guided more fully in the practice section) is to choose an anchor spot (abdomen, chest, or nostrils) from which to be aware of your breathing. Try to keep your attention on this spot, one breath at a time. When one breath ends, the next begins. Keep your attention focused there to the best of your abilities over whatever period of time you choose—three, five, or ten minutes, or longer.

As you focus on your breath, you may find that, even with the best of intentions, your mind automatically starts to wander away from your breathing. Nothing is wrong with you if you can't be mindful of more than one breath before you are suddenly fantasizing about a chocolate ice cream sundae or adding to your to-do list. This is how our minds work. Contemporary culture is the master of distraction. Taught to look outward and bombarded daily with more and more information, we are constantly juggling a variety of responsibilities, under huge amounts of stress. It is no surprise that when you kindly invite your mind to focus, it goes wild.

In the beginning it may feel like you are aware of one breath but soon are lost in thought; after a while you return to your breath, but before you know it you are thinking all sorts of thoughts; you go back to your breath . . . and so on. This is a completely normal meditation session! Following your breath is a *practice*. No one does it perfectly from the start. You simply need to keep coming back again and again. This is where the learning occurs, and ultimately you can train your mind to return more frequently and for longer periods of time. Try to be kind to yourself. Don't yell at yourself in your mind (*Get back to the breath!*). You are learning a new skill that may take time; getting angry or frustrated at yourself will not make you more skilled; in fact, it will probably make you feel worse.

Think of it this way: If you want to build muscle, you need some resistance. That is why you work out with weights. Imagine how ridiculous it would be to try to build muscles by lifting a pencil. In meditation, our minds are working out too, trying to build a new brain pattern, something like a mindfulness "muscle." Resistance helps develop strength. The wandering, restless, fantasizing, thinking mind is the resistance, and a very high-quality resistance at that. The more you train yourself to return your attention to the present moment, to your breath, the "stronger" and more skilled you will become at doing so. As Gregory, a twenty-year-old college student, discovered:

> A few weeks into meditating, I was convinced I had gotten worse. In the first few weeks I had some focus, but in the third week my mind went crazy. I had about fifty commercials running through my head, replays of my last dating disaster, novels I wanted to write, and I couldn't stop thinking of sushi. I thought I was a meditation failure. But then my teacher explained, now I was just seeing things more clearly—I was aware enough to actually see how wild my mind was!

Common Difficulties

Most people struggle when they first start breathing meditation. Here are some of the most common difficulties that arise and ways of working with them.

What if the breath is difficult for me to find or it's not neutral?   Most people discover that breathing is a good, reliable, neutral anchor for them. A few people find that paying attention to their breathing can make them uncomfortable, even anxious. Others worry that they start to control their breathing when they focus on it (more on this later).

If you cannot use your breath as an anchor, there are other anchors you can use in meditation. Some people use sounds or their bodily sensations. In the beginning, please try breathing meditation, using your breath as an anchor, for a few weeks, and if it doesn't work for you, feel free to experiment with other anchors. Most people who cannot follow their breathing use sounds as an anchor. We will offer a hearing meditation practice in Chapter 8, but for now, when meditating, simply pay attention to the sounds around you. Let the sounds come and go, in and out of your awareness. Don't try to figure out the source of the sounds or make up a story about them. Just keep listening to the sounds, and when your mind wanders, continually return to the hearing of the sounds, as recommended with the breath.

Sometimes when I pay attention to the breath, I start to control the breath. This is a fairly common experience for people. Usually this difficulty shifts over time. Try paying attention to the breath at different parts of your body (abdomen, chest, nostrils) to see whether the same thing happens. You might also try to meditate lying down, since it is harder to control your breathing when you are prone. Try to relax, soften, and "sneak up" on your breath. If it gets too frustrating, you can switch your anchor to hearing, as just described, or you can notice changing sensations in your body. You might also ask yourself to notice what a "controlled" breath feels like. What is the direct experience—the felt sense?

Is it okay if I mentally label the breath "in/out"? Applying a mental label to help keep your attention on your experience is actually a very helpful tool that some people use when meditating. You may find yourself naturally repeating a word or phrase, such as "in/out" or "rising/falling." Try this technique and see if it works for you. If it is not helpful, just ignore it. Do remember to keep any mental label a very soft whisper in your mind. Keep most of your attention focused on feeling the breathing sensations so that you use the label only as a tool to keep your attention focused and it does not become a distraction or a new focus.

Being with the breath is kind of dull.   Some people do find that paying attention to the breath is dull—certainly not nearly as interesting as surfing the Web or watching television. Part of what you are learning through meditation is to take interest in things that are not so dramatic. In this utterly sped-up, high-tech world, it can be helpful to retrain yourself to take interest in the "boring" and "dull." Learning to take an interest in the not-so-exciting experiences of life helps you to appreciate and be present for the simple things of life, rather than constantly seeking new entertainment and experiences to excite you.

If you are a little bored while paying attention to your breathing, try to pay closer attention and to take an interest in the minutiae of your breath. Notice how the in breath differs from the out breath. Are two breaths alike? Can you sense a pause between the out breath and the in breath? Is it always the same part of your abdomen that moves, or does it change with each breath? You will be surprised how quickly the boredom can change and how you can transfer this newfound ability to other areas of your life. You may begin to see the world in more detail, as Ethel, a retired nurse and grandmother, reported: "I can't explain it, but ever since I started meditating, it's like the world has gotten more vibrant. I see colors more brightly, I hear sounds more strongly. I walk through life with a little more sense of awe and wonder, which is pretty good at eighty-one!"

I think I fell asleep while noticing my breath.   Sleepiness in meditation is extremely common. Considering how busy most Americans are and how little sleep they get—six and a half hours per night, one hour less than in the 1950s—when people meditate they often get really drowsy. Don't get too angry with yourself or discouraged by it. The best remedy is to try to practice at a time of day when you think you will be less tired. You can open your eyes, stand up, or try some walking meditation (see Chapter 4).

Paying attention to my breathing is difficult.   Many meditation students report how challenging it is to do something that seems deceptively simple. Students across the board report that it is hard to stay focused on their breath. Remember that paying attention to your breathing is not an easy task. Most of us have had twenty, thirty, forty, fifty, or more years practicing being distracted; being able to focus on your breath for an extended period of time is not going to happen overnight. As mentioned earlier, however, you can develop mental fitness by repetitively and kindly coming back to the present moment, just as you would do to develop physical fitness. Over time your mindfulness "muscle" will build. Jackson, a sixty-three-year-old investor, described it this way:

> I was hopeless at meditating. I think I was probably the worst meditator in the class. I don't think I could stay with even one breath before my mind wandered. I wanted to give up so many times, I have lots of other things to do, yet I knew this would be good for me, and it also felt relaxing. I also found that I stopped yelling at people so much, so I knew something was working (not sure what). So I kept at it, over weeks, months, and believe it or not, over time it started to get easier! I was able to be with a few breaths before wandering, and then longer periods of time. I could sense a very real difference in my mind by the end of the year.

THE PRACTICE: MINDFULNESS OF BREATHING

Begin this meditation by finding a comfortable place to sit, either in a chair or on a cushion on the floor. As you sit down, notice your posture: Feel your back remaining upright, but not too tense; try to stay relaxed. Keep your eyes closed and your tongue resting on the roof of your mouth or wherever it's comfortable, and rest your hands on your knees or lap. You can then notice your body sitting: the weight, the posture, and the shape of your body. Bring your mindfulness into your body and become aware of the present moment.

See if you can notice that one of the sensations in your body is the sensation of your breath. Find your breath in your body, feeling your body moving with the breath. Keep your breath completely natural, not elongating it or shortening it in any deliberate way. You might notice your breath in your abdomen as you feel a rising sensation, an expansion, a stretching . . . then falling, a contraction, a deflation sensation. Or you might notice the breath in your chest, where you feel movement, stretching, and expansion similar to what you feel in the abdomen. Try not to imagine the breath, or to think about the breath, but to *feel* the breath in your body. You also might notice a subtler presence of your breath in your nostrils—a coolness, a tingling movement. Choose one of these three spots where you feel your breath inside your body—your abdomen, chest, or nostrils—and try to keep your attention on these sensations of breath, one breath at a time . . . rising, falling . . . or in, out. . . .

As you're doing this, you might notice that your mind wanders and starts to think about all sorts of things. This is completely normal and happens for most people. So when you notice that your mind is wandering or thinking, just relax. You can say a soft word in your mind like *thinking* or *wandering* to acknowledge that you have wandered. And then, very gently but firmly, bring your attention back to the sensations of breathing. . . .

Do this practice in silence for five minutes, feeling one breath at a time, perhaps getting lost in thought, and returning to the sensations of your breath. Increase the amount of time you spend in this practice when you feel drawn to do that.

4

MINDFUL MOVEMENT
The Body and Awareness

The body says what words cannot.
—Martha Graham

The body never lies. That is the title of a book by Alice Miller, a psychologist whose work has been devoted to reading the body and understanding the other kind of language it uses—the language of gesture, facial expression, body movement, and even words that hold hidden meanings.[1] She tells story after story of patients burdened with traumatic pasts who reveal the secrets of trauma through this language of the body. But body language is not just a matter of gestures, facial expressions, and what we think of as nonverbal language; our bodies may also express themselves through physical aches, pains, and illnesses. Few of us are attuned to this other sort of language, but the practice of mindfulness* unfolds a new level of insight.

Our bodies are like vast landscapes, revealing hidden stories and emotions through their physical changes, both external and internal. It is possible to be quite aware of the cause of bodily sensations—heart palpitations in

---

*Mindfulness practice is one means of becoming more attuned to the body, but it is not a replacement for psychotherapeutic approaches, particularly in the face of abuse or trauma.

the face of danger, perspiration in the course of a rigorous workout—but to not be *attuned* to the body. So many of our body responses arise without consciousness that we are often "in the dark" as to what is causing them. Scientists have only recently discovered that there is what can be called a "second brain" in our bodies, located in the gut, and that when it is out of attunement with the brain in our heads, it can wreak havoc on our health, causing everything from butterflies in the stomach to severe abdominal conditions like irritable bowel syndrome. These two systems communicate all the time, sending chemical messages back and forth about experiences that affect our physiology.[2] Data show that becoming more attuned to the body can improve physical health, boost the body's immune system, and improve physical performance and sensory acuity.

THE SCIENCE

What kind of relationship do you have with your body? That may seem like an odd question. I mean, you and your body are one and the same, right? Well, yes and no. Which body is *more* you—the one you had at eighteen years of age or the one you have at thirty? The one that is twenty pounds overweight or the one you had at your ideal weight (even if that was ten years ago)? In Lewis Carroll's story *Alice in Wonderland*, we get a glimpse of this illusive relationship between "I" and the body it inhabits. Alice undergoes dramatic body distortions in the aftermath of drinking an unknown liquid and eating a small cake. And she notices, with curiosity, "Now I'm opening out like the largest telescope that ever was! Good-bye, feet." And later, "Let me think: Was I the same when I got up this morning? I almost think I can remember feeling a little different. But if I'm not the same, the next question is '*Who in the world am I?*'"[3] The question "who am I?" reveals a common illusion we share that the "I" and the body are one and the same.

Mindfulness is a tool for exploring the relationship you have with your body. Perhaps, like many people, you have a love-hate relationship with your body. At times you love it for letting you do certain things, but then you dislike it when it won't do what you want or does things without your consent, such as making noises, growing too large, or refusing to act as you intend it to. Most of us are pretty critical of our bodies, or at least some of their parts. We are not very happy when our bodies lose the tone of youth or develop the wrinkles of age. Often we forget the distinction between "I" and the body and dislike ourselves when our bodies are not what we want them to be. Or vice versa, we dislike, and even harm, our bodies when we are not too happy with ourselves.

Eating Disorders, Obesity, and Other Body Issues

Bulimia, anorexia nervosa, and binge-eating affect some 6 percent of women in the United States and other Western cultures. (Men and non-Western cultures are also affected, but to a lesser extent.) These eating disorders are conditions in which harsh treatment of the body (including starvation, gorging, and purging) emerge from a variety of factors, including a poorly developed sense of self.[4] Body dysmorphic disorder is another example of an unhealthy relationship with the body. In this condition, which affects 1 to 2 percent of the population, people become preoccupied to the point of obsession with an imagined or minor defect in the body that makes them feel defective and ugly. The rate of suicide among people with body dysmorphic disorder is forty-five times that of the general population.[5]

The incidence of these eating and body perception disorders pales in comparison to the prevalence of obesity. On the January 2009 cover of *O* (Oprah's magazine), a picture of thin Oprah next to a picture of overweight Oprah carried the caption, "How did I let this happen *again*?" Oprah suffers from a common struggle with weight and the all-too-common cycle of weight gain, weight loss, and gain again.[6] The obesity epidemic in the United States—affecting some 30 percent of the population[7]—is a sign that we *as a nation* are relating in unhealthy ways to our bodies and the foods we put in them. Evidence suggests that mindfulness practices directed toward eating and the body can help.

A recent study by scientists in the United Kingdom found that acceptance and commitment therapy (ACT), a mindfulness-based intervention program developed by Steven Hayes, Kirk Strosahl, and Kelly Wilson,[8] led to differences in exercise and weight loss between those participating in the program and controls. The group on the modified ACT program (tailored to eating and weight issues) exercised more than controls did, but no immediate differences in weight loss were evident. At the six-month follow-up period, however, the participants on the ACT program *who continued with the practice* had lost significantly more weight (an average of five pounds) than controls.[9] Most of the weight loss difference was accounted for by reductions in binge eating and an increase in exercise.

Other studies of mindfulness and eating disorders have been done within psychotherapeutic programs, including dialectical behavior therapy as well as acceptance and commitment therapy.[10] Controlled studies show that mindfulness within such programs reduces binge eating, whether or not it occurs with bulimia.[11] Researchers Jean Kristeller and C. Brendan Hallett at Indiana State University developed a "stand-alone" mindfulness program called MB-EAT and piloted it with eighteen obese women who suffered from binge-eating to see whether it would reduce the rate of their binge-eating.[12] Binging episodes dropped from an average of four times a week to less than two, and their severity decreased as well. Furthermore, the more time spent in mindfulness practice around eating, the greater the reduction in binge-eating and the severity of episodes. The program is now under investigation in a large-scale controlled study.

Mindfulness may also help reduce the excessive intake of harmful substances like alcohol, cigarettes, and drugs. Although research in this area is quite limited and methodological challenges like small sample sizes make conclusions tenuous,[13] there is growing support for the effectiveness of mindfulness-based approaches. Some of the best research in this area comes from the laboratory of Alan Marlatt, a psychologist at the University of Washington, and his colleague Sarah Bowen. Their group created a program called Mindfulness-Based Relapse Prevention (MBRP) and tested its efficacy in a group of 168 patients in recovery following intensive treatment for substance abuse.[14] Subjects were randomized either into an MBRP group that met weekly for eight weeks or into a "treatment as usual" (TAU) condition, which included a twelve-step program and weekly support group sessions. Two months after completion of the program, the MBRP group reported substance use at levels that were half those of the TAU group; they also reported significantly less craving. Four months after completion of the program, the differences were no longer evident, suggesting that the effectiveness of MBRP requires continuation of the practices. In a separate study by this same group of researchers, college student smokers showed greater reductions in smoking behavior following a short mindfulness practice to cope with the urge to smoke compared to students not given the practice.[15] Lastly, in a study of substance use in prison populations, a mindfulness intervention proved to be more effective than standard treatment for reducing substance use (marijuana, cocaine, and alcohol use) in that population.[16]

How exactly might mindfulness influence what we do to our bodies, whether what we do is harmful or helpful? A healthier relationship emerges when our growing awareness of physical sensations and the physical movement of our bodies *is accompanied by acceptance rather than criticism.* From a healthier relationship may emerge kinder actions toward the body. Second, mindfulness practice seems to help us make behavioral changes—such as exercising more, not eating as much, quitting smoking, and curbing drug use—because of how it helps us work with bodily sensations and thoughts. Mindfulness makes us more aware of the internal and external cues or triggers associated with overeating, smoking, or substance abuse. In addition, mindfulness practices increase our acceptance of both positive and negative emotions and thoughts, such as craving, so that we feel less need to alleviate them with such behaviors.[17] Often when people set out to stop doing things like smoking cigarettes or overeating, they try to *suppress* their thoughts (*I'm not going to think about smoking*, or, *I'm going to forget about those cookies in the kitchen*), and that effort ironically has the opposite effect: You actually engage in the behavior more.[18] With mindfulness, instead of suppressing a thought, you learn to let it arise, note it, and release or let it go. This process seems to account for some of the practice's success.[19] Mindfulness changes *how you relate to your thoughts and body.* Learning to be aware and to relate to your body with acceptance and kindness, rather than suppression, seems to improve how you treat your body.

Boosting the Body's Defense System

Perhaps one of the most profound and important ways in which mindfulness benefits the body is in boosting immunity. The immune system is like a vast spiderweb attuned to catching insects—in our case, it traps invading viruses, bacteria, and other pathogens. But just as a spiderweb can be damaged, so too can the immune system be weakened or damaged—by cancer, by other diseases, or by the cumulative burden of environmental stressors. Mindfulness appears to be a powerful tool to help strengthen the immune system.

The immune response can be measured indirectly, by signs of illness or rates of healing, and directly, by molecular measures of immune response.* Both types of measures have been studied with respect to mindfulness, and these studies indicate that the practice of mindfulness boosts immunity measured either way. Using the mindfulness scales in Chapter 1, people who say they are more mindful report less physical illness and fewer doctor visits. It is unclear whether this response is a sign of a healthier immune response in these individuals or a healthier lifestyle. But faster rates of healing were evident in a study conducted by the biologist Jon Kabat-Zinn, a leading expert in the field of mindfulness, when patients with psoriasis (a skin condition) were given a mindfulness program in addition to traditional treatment and compared to a group of patients who received traditional treatment only.[20] Using direct measures of immunity, the psychologist Richard Davidson's group at the University of Wisconsin found that flu resistance (as measured directly by antibody titer) was greater in a group of people given a flu shot following an eight-week mindfulness practice compared to those given the flu shot without the practice.[21]

Evidence that immune systems are stronger with mindfulness practice is evident in studies of immunocompromised populations (people whose immune systems are weakened). In a study of patients with HIV, T-cells—important cells that fight viral infections but decline in number over the stages of HIV infection—remained at the same level for a group of patients given an eight-week mindfulness class compared to patients given a one-day program (both groups received equivalent medical treatments for HIV).[22] Participants' T-cell counts were stronger the more they attended the mindfulness classes. A similar finding was observed among breast cancer patients given a mindfulness program (in addition to cancer treatment); their immune responses were stronger than those of a group not offered the program.[23] The direct impact of mindfulness on the immune response is not yet understood, but researchers like the psychiatrist Michael Irwin at UCLA are working hard

---

*Immune response is commonly assessed by measuring immunoglobulin levels (IgA, IgG, and IgM, the molecules that are important in antibody attacks on foreign cells) and the antibody titer (strength) of antibodies against specific antigens like influenza strains or tetanus toxoid. In addition, T-cell number, Natural Killer (NK) cell number, and interleukin levels (the proteins or molecules important in the immune response) are often measured.

to figure it out. Irwin is the director of the Center for Psychoneuroimmunology, a field of study seeking to elucidate the connection between the brain and the immune response and discover how our thoughts and feelings influence our immune system. His research has shown that other mind-body practices, like t'ai chi, have beneficial effects on healing and the immune response.[24] Irwin is also investigating the connection between the stress response and immune system changes at the genetic and molecular levels.

Maximizing Performance—Physical and Sensory

Philippe Petit is perhaps the world's most famous tightrope walker, having crossed the twenty-six feet between the twin towers of the World Trade Center on a narrow cable twenty-six years before their demise. Imagine walking across a cable no thicker than a jump rope, with no net to catch you if you fall. Any unplanned variation in movement, even just a centimeter right or left, would probably lead to your death. Like yogis, athletes, dancers, and t'ai chi experts, Petit has perfected awareness of his body movement through space. Even though the roots of athletic excellence probably lie in our DNA, environment and training are key to their expression. Petit practiced and planned for six and a half years before he walked between the twin towers. Olympic athletes spend five to eight hours a day in practice to reach their gold or silver medals. Genetics may predispose us to reach pinnacles of physical performance, but training is the only way to climb the hill.

Many athletes have described an experience of getting into the "zone" when practicing or competing, and most of us have had such an experience when jogging, cycling, skiing, surfing, playing golf or tennis, or bowling. Getting into the zone—or what is also called "flow"—is associated with optimal performance.[25] When someone is in the zone, or flow, there is a sense of losing oneself in the experience, forgetting about the "I" doing the exercise and becoming fully immersed in the experience. This state of full immersion is a form of self-regulation in which *performance flows without cognitive effort.*[26] It is an alternative state of consciousness, not our typical state in which the "I" calls the shots. Repetitive practice heightens the chance of flow experiences because the parts of the brain needed to carry out the action—whether it is playing a piano or running a track—no longer require effort for success. At this point, the action arises while the "I" rests.

Scientists don't quite understand flow, but it appears that we have the capacity to regulate our bodies via this process of completely losing ourselves (the "I") in an activity. Mark Leary, a psychologist at Duke University, calls this process "hypoegoic"—meaning an absence of the ego or "I" controlling things during the process, in contrast to hyperegoic regulation in which the "I" has a top-down control of things.[27] Perhaps with mindfulness practice we become more fully present in life by increasing the ease with which we can shift between such states. Research has shown that flow experiences are associated with higher mindfulness[28] and that flow states can be induced through mental training.[29] Such training may pay off in terms of excellence in performance as well. The psychologists Frank Gardner and Zella Moore created a mindfulness-based program designed specifically for athletes and tested its effects on female college hockey and volleyball players.[30] They found that mindfulness improved the athletes' game performance (based on coaches' ratings) compared to those not given the program, while also improving concentration and reducing negative thinking around performance.

The "I" in Mindfulness

The effect of mindfulness on "immersion," or flow, may seem contradictory to the experience of mindfulness as the "I," like a curious spectator, observing experiences and "separating" from the body, as we discussed previously. In the former there is a loss of self in the experience, and in the latter self and experience become more clearly distinguished. How can both of these seemingly different relationships be aspects of mindfulness? We defined mindfulness as attention to the present experience with a curious and neutral stance; where do these concepts of "self" and "loss of self" fit in?

As you will see throughout the book, mindfulness practice can lead to increasing levels of awareness of the relationship of your "I" to objects, your thoughts, your feelings, your body, and so on. It will become clear through mindfulness practice that your "I" relates to experiences in a variety of ways—sometimes separated, sometimes fully immersed—and that there is no constancy to it. Through mindfulness you can become more attuned to these varying degrees of relationship, and in this way mindfulness brings about a clearer understanding of the meaning of "I" itself. Although this insight is not part of the scientific definition of mindfulness, it may be a primary outcome; it may also turn out to be so integral to mindfulness that the scientific definition will need to be modified in the future.

Moving meditations, such as walking, yoga, and t'ai chi, increase awareness of the relationship of the self (the "I") to the body. Each practice uses different movement exercises to heighten attention to body and bodily sensations and thus foster discovery of this relationship. In these meditations we become more experienced observers of that relationship—astute detectors of bodily changes and the events (thoughts, feelings, experiences) from which they arise.

Physical yoga, mindfulness, and other mind-body practices can uncover many unconsciously held attitudes about body shape, size, and capacity to perform. Through practice, you may identify ways in which you subtly criticize your body, shedding light on how you relate to your physical form. I remember one time doing a sitting and twisting pose in yoga and hearing an inner voice say, *If you could just move your fat leg out of the way.* When our unconscious criticisms come to the surface during mindfulness practices, we can recognize them and then learn to let them go.

Sensory Acuity

Sensory acuity requires a different kind of physical attunement. Some of us perfect a sense (or senses) and harness that skill in our careers, as a musician does with sound, a chef with taste, a masseuse with touch, an artist with vision, or a perfumer with smell. Training can improve our perception of the five senses, as well as our balance and interoception—that is, our awareness of bodily sensations arising from internal organs, tissues, and bodily fluids. For example, blind Braille readers perform at higher levels than sighted people on tasks that require touch discrimination.[31] Pianists show greater touch discrimination than nonpianists, and this heightened sense correlates with hours of piano practice.[32]

By attending to sensory experiences, we can become more aware of them and of how we relate to them (attached, repulsed, avoidant, clinging, grasping, and so on). Have you ever had the experience of a smell bringing your attention to the present moment—such as the smell of bread baking, freshly mown grass, or coffee brewing—only to quickly see its link to something from the past? We often link sensory experiences to thoughts (for example, *I remember that smell from when I was a child*) or feelings (*I like that smell*). Mindfulness is about learning to notice those links and to experience the senses without connections (if and when you choose to do so).

Mindfulness can enhance your sensory acuity. In one scientific study, visual acuity (measured by the ability to detect light flashes of varying intensities) improved among people attending an intensive three-month mindfulness meditation retreat compared with controls who did not attend (and showed no changes in visual acuity).[33] In another study, the sense of touch—tactile acuity—was significantly heightened among t'ai chi practitioners compared with controls.[34] While tactile acuity is known to increase with tactile practice, the increase in tactile acuity among t'ai chi practitioners was not from direct tactile practice. In the study, practitioners used only mental training (directing *attention* toward fingertips and hands); it seems that just the *mental thought* of heightened sensory reception in the fingertips improved it. The researchers suggest that such exercises may slow the normal decline in tactile acuity with age.[35]

A body scan (see the practice section at the end of this chapter) is a common mindfulness practice that may attune sensory skills by enhancing *interoception*—the awareness of internally generated body states, including muscle activity, the movement of air through the body, and physiological changes. As we will see in the next chapter, one brain region important for interoception is the insula cortex, which looks different between longtime meditators and nonmeditators.[36] Some very longtime meditators show interoceptive abilities that are well beyond those of the general population. One example, a monk named Oser, was discussed in a meeting of scientists and the Dalai Lama as part of the "Science of Mind" meetings.[37] Oser showed brain and body changes never seen before by the scientists studying him. In a measure of the "startle response"—the body's basic response to any startling stimuli like a loud noise—Oser showed literally no response when in deep meditation. Although this seemed impossible to the scientists, they saw that Oser had mastered the capacity to move his body and brain states (as measured scientifically through MRIs, EEGs, and so on) into specific internal states by varying his meditation practice. Yet how finely tuned interoception can become is largely unknown. In one study of longtime meditators, researchers found that they could not detect their own heartbeats any better than nonmeditators, although the meditators reported being more highly attuned to their internal body states.[38]

THE ART

Christina was watering her garden. She waters daily, and because of her diligence she has had fresh green beans, tomatoes, and corn all summer. The problem is that she finds it a little boring to stand there watering every evening. So last week she decided to bring mindfulness to her experience. She stood out in the dusk and connected with her body and breath. She noticed herself standing there; she noticed the feel of the wind on her arms, the smells in the air, and the sights in her budding garden. She suddenly began to feel restful, at ease. No longer bored by the chore, she came alive in her body and connected to the experience of being present. To her eye, her garden took on a new vibrancy—it was filled with color and detail that left her awestruck.

It is unfortunate that many people today are disconnected from their bodies and just go through the motions of routine chores, with little interest, like Christina with her garden. We tend either to use the body as though it were a machine or to ignore it altogether. Sadly, many of us suffer from self-hatred that manifests as criticism of how we look, and we wage a lifelong war with our bodies for control and perfection.

An example of the mechanical approach to the body is Denise, who goes to the gym religiously, trying for the ever more perfect physique. Denise is not disconnected from her body, but she wants to control, manipulate, and regulate it as though it were a machine that she could simply tune up or whose parts she could replace when necessary. Her body will ultimately disappoint her when it slows down or gets ill and can no longer produce or "put out" to her specifications.

At the other end of the spectrum are those of us who are more like "heads with bodies dangling from them." Or as James Joyce wrote about one of his characters: "Mr. Duffy lived at a little distance from his body." These are people who tend to be cerebral, who do not feel at home in their bodies, and who certainly do not pay much attention to their bodies. Perhaps as we live more virtual lives through technology we will have fewer experiences of direct connection with our bodies. Maybe one day it will become more and more natural to elevate the virtual over the physical, as happened with the humans portrayed in the movie *Wall-E*: Their destiny was to become mere feeding tubes floated around by electronic devices.

I know several people who ignore symptoms of illness in their body, either because they are so out of touch with their body's messages or because they feel that acknowledging symptoms would be a sign of weakness. Julia, a mother who attended a MAPs class, said that she simply did not have time to deal with her persistent backache and shortness of breath. With three children and a part-time job, she told me, she could not "waste" time by stopping and taking care of herself, not even for a moment.

If you, like Julia and so many others, are alienated from your body, you will find that mindfulness is a way to get back into contact with your body. In fact, I believe that body awareness is the simplest of all the mindfulness practices. Through this practice, you can begin to approach your body with kindness, stop using it as a machine or ignoring it, and by learning to reconnect with it, feel more alive.

The Doorway to Mindfulness

Your body is the doorway to mindfulness. As you may have noticed by now, your mind can be anywhere at any time—brooding over the past or thinking about the future. And perhaps, like so many people, you know what it is to live on automatic pilot—sleepwalking through life and not truly living it—and are familiar with the state of being distracted, lost in thinking, imagining, planning, and worrying. Your body, by contrast, is *always* in the present moment, so bringing attention to it brings you automatically into the present. The task is to turn your attention to this reality, to put your attention on your body and become aware of whatever sensations you may encounter.

What do you notice when you bring mindfulness to the body? You can notice sensations like weight, pressure, heaviness, and temperature. You might notice vibrations, tingling, itching, pulsing, and throbbing. Sensations might be pleasant (a nice tingling in the stomach) or unpleasant (anything from an itch to strong physical pain). A lot of sensations are neutral, neither pleasant nor unpleasant. Sometimes you might not notice much at all, just a general sense of "hereness." Other times you might notice that you feel numb, or disconnected, or alienated from your body. And at still other times, like in the midst of making love, you might be lost in the intricacy and beauty of bodily sensations, although at other times you might have unpleasant, neutral, or numb feelings during sex.

Of course, each time you return to your breathing, as discussed in the previous chapter, you are returning to your body—becoming aware of the rising/falling sensations in your abdomen or chest or the in/out sensations in your nostrils. Perhaps you access your body through your breathing, feeling connected and present in the breath. Or maybe noticing the varied bodily sensations has a similar effect.

Nonconceptuality: What Being Mindful of Your Body Is and Is Not

To be mindful of your body means being aware nonconceptually of the present-moment experience. Being mindful does not mean having a particular *idea* or *concept* about the physical experience and labeling it as such. For example, when you notice an unpleasant sensation and call it a stomachache, then worry about what you ate last night or feel guilty about that extra-large hot fudge sundae, you're tuning into bodily sensations in a way, but you're not being mindful.

Here is another example of attending to the body in a nonmindful manner. Take a look at your hand. Look at its shape, the hue of your skin color, your palm lines, and the shape of your fingernails. You might think of all the ways this hand has served you—you write with it, you feed yourself with it, you can get dressed because of this hand, and so forth. This is what we might call conceptual thinking about hands. Now try this. Close your eyes (after reading this) and feel your hand from the inside. Notice the weight and pressure and any tingling, vibrating, or other physical sensations. You can move your fingers and feel the different sensations of muscular movement. How do you know it is a hand? Mostly you know it is a hand from experience and memory, but for now, just notice the sensations. This is a mindful, nonconceptual approach: You are aware of the actual direct physical experience as opposed to the concepts or stories of what you think your hands are. We referred to this as the "felt sense" in Chapter 3. The sensation in your hand is just one of many bodily sensations to which you can bring your attention. When you notice these sensations exactly as they are, you are present to your body—what we describe as being mindful of the body.

By the way, it is fine to think, *That's my hand*, or to have a stray thought like, *Hmmm, I've got to cut my fingernails*. Labeling experience is a natural

activity of the human mind, but rather than spending a lot of time continuing
to think about your broken nail, can you practice letting go of the thoughts
and returning to the direct experience by connecting with the sensations in
your body? If you practice doing this, you may find it becomes easier to notice
when you stray to thoughts and to gently bring your attention back to the felt
experience. That is the practice of mindfulness of the body.

Kindness Toward Your Body

As discussed in the science section, one of the benefits of shifting to a more
mindful relationship with your body is learning to bring more kindness to
yourself and then treating your body more kindly. For many people, the
body is the target of self-hatred or self-loathing. Perhaps self-judgment arises
as a hypercritical voice judging your performance at the gym or your weight
or how you appear in the mirror. You can learn to notice this voice as the
silent thinking it is rather than get swept away and hindered by it. When
you hear a negative or self-critical voice, try to view it as a story or "tape"
that is being played in your mind, one that you have heard before, and then
return your attention to the direct experience of the moment.

For example, in the midst of your daily run a voice might arise in your
head saying, *I'm the worst jogger ever.* Just notice that this thought is occurring and gently bring your attention back to the physical sensations that are
present in the moment. Perhaps you feel tired or sense an aching in your
legs or a cramping in your side. These sensations are all the *direct experience*
of the present moment. The story about being a terrible jogger is simply
that—a story you have added to your present-moment experience. As you
see more clearly the difference between the stories that critical voices tell you
and your own direct experience, you will begin to have more and more moments of relaxation and ease. And as you repeat the practice you will probably find that you are being kinder to yourself. If you catch these voices and
return to your physical body in the present moment, you will build up a capacity to be loving and compassionate toward your body.

Since your body carries you through life, don't you owe it to yourself to
treat it well? Walt Whitman wrote: "If there is one thing I know to be sacred,
the human body is sacred." You can relate to your body with judgment, com-

petition, fear, and ignorance or you can bring mindfulness to your body and learn to treat it with the love and respect it deserves.

Conscious Embodiment

I use the term "conscious embodiment" to refer to living connected to your body, to have that feeling of being comfortable in your own skin rather than lost in thought, overly identified with mental activity, and disconnected from physical experience. To be consciously embodied is to listen to information from the body (symptoms, desires, aversions) and then use that information to act wisely rather than ignoring it or responding haphazardly.

Through mindfulness you can become more embodied by training your mind to attend to the sensations of your body. You can learn to check in with your body more regularly, as a matter of course, rather than only when it demands attention because of injury or pain. This is not too difficult to do; mindfulness of the body is a matter of learning the skill and then practicing it. Over time, it becomes second nature and you become more attuned to the information conveyed by your body. Everyone has an example of not being attuned to the body—like forgetting to eat while working on a deadline or neglecting to stop eating when full. When you are mindful of the body, instead of ignoring or distrusting it, you take the information it gives you and use it as guidance that is just as valuable as your cognitive knowing. This might be called intuition, which meditators report becomes heightened over years of practice.

To become more adept at conscious embodiment, mindfulness of the body can be practiced using a variety of skills, including sensory awareness exercises or movement practices such as walking mindfully, t'ai chi, yoga, and chi gong. But bear in mind that not all movement teachers practice mindfulness and that not all movement exercises are done with mindfulness; you can easily take a yoga class or a walk without mindfulness. A mindful yoga teacher helps students be more aware of their breathing, physical sensations, thoughts, and emotions by teaching them to bring a kind and curious attention to the body. Some people find that it is easier to be mindful when their body is in motion; all forms of movement and exercise can be a practice for mindfulness.

Owen, a twenty-eight-year-old graduate student, practices "treadmill meditation":

> When I'm at the gym, it's pretty easy to get bored or just watch TV, but I decided instead to practice being aware. So when I'm on the treadmill, I turn my attention to the sensations in my legs. I walk with awareness. I sometimes pay attention to breathing. I can't tell you what a difference it has made. I'm no longer bored, and I get my daily meditation in, even if I miss it otherwise.

Throughout our MAPs classes I constantly refer students back to the body: What is going on in your body in this present moment? What sensations do you notice in your body? Are you having a strong emotion? If so, where do you feel it in your body? Are you having a difficult or repetitive thought? If so, direct your attention into your body.

This is a useful strategy because it tends to be our thoughts that get us into trouble. Our bodies simply function as they always do: pumping blood, taking in information from the senses, and experiencing sensory and emotional responses to stimuli. Our minds interpret these direct physical experiences—and often create stories around them—in ways that may increase discomfort or suffering and create more reactivity in our minds. We can short-circuit this reactivity by returning our attention to the felt experience of our bodies.

Daily Body Awareness

When we are distracted, anxious, worried, or lost in thought, the reminder to come back to our bodies can be very powerful. Through repeated practice, remembering to be mindful throughout the day becomes more and more of a habit. Even short seconds of mindfulness help relieve stress and promote relaxation. Body awareness is a tool you can use to become more connected to yourself, to regulate your emotions, and to increase your sense of ease and well-being. The more you do it throughout the day, the greater the benefit. (A helpful tool for practice is to use the acronym STOP and the steps it represents—see the STOP practice outlined in the sidebar).

I practice body awareness as frequently as I can—which means, whenever I remember to do so. I might be driving and let my attention move to the sensation of holding the steering wheel or feeling my back against the seat. I might take a breath or two to increase relaxation. I might notice my body when brushing my teeth, doing dishes, taking a shower, or opening a door. When I am in the midst of a difficult experience, such as a fight with my husband or the receipt of an unexpected e-mail, I notice my body in the midst of it. I stop and take a breath. The clearer I am about bodily sensations and the thoughts and feelings I assign to them (the stories), the easier it is to act with intelligence rather than react from habitual patterns.

Although being mindful is simple, remembering to be mindful is not as easy. To help myself remember, I have a program on my computer that rings a bell every half-hour (see the resources section for information on where to get one). This bell of mindfulness reminds me to check in with my body. I may be in the midst of writing or doing other computer-based work when suddenly I hear a low pleasant chime. Sometimes I'm a little resentful of the bell: *Hey, I'm in the middle of writing. I'm in the flow!* But most of the time I hear the chime, stop what I am doing, and bring my attention to my body. I notice the posture I am in (often contorted and ergonomically disastrous). I notice everything that I can in my body, from a tightening in my belly to a shortness of breath. Once I become aware of what is happening in my body, I then have the opportunity to shift it. For instance, I might readjust my posture or take a deep breath or remind myself to relax. I do this all with mindfulness, and it prepares me to continue working with renewed ease.

A PRACTICE: STOP

The acronym STOP, often used in Mindfulness-Based Stress Reduction, is a helpful aid in becoming more mindful of the body on a daily basis. This is how STOP works:

S: Remind yourself to STOP. Whatever you are doing in this moment, pause.

T: TAKE a breath. This reconnects you with your body.

O: OBSERVE what is happening for you in this moment. What do you notice in your body? You can be aware of anything: posture, sensations, tension in your body, or, once again, your breath. You might notice the sound around you. You might even notice your thoughts or emotions.

P: PROCEED: Continue on with whatever you were doing before you came to a STOP. ∎

Informal Meditation Practice

In the previous chapter, we talked about the importance of a daily formal meditation practice when you sit for five to twenty minutes to practice mindfulness. However, you can practice mindfulness informally throughout your day, in two ways.

First, you only need to *remember* to be mindful. No matter what you are doing, you can enhance your experience with mindfulness if you deliberately apply mindful attention to it. You might notice how mindless you are in a given moment and then stop and take a breath (using the STOP acronym) or take a generally mindful stance to your activity. Or you might pick one activity and have it be your mindful activity for the day or week or month. This is what thirty-two-year-old Alan, a father of three, tried:

> I made a commitment to practice mindfulness every time I took a piece of paper towel off the paper towel rack. At first it seemed like a silly exercise, but I mopped up my children's spills several times a day, so it seemed like a good activity to promote mindfulness. It became a mindfulness touchstone in my life. Whenever I touched the rack, I would feel my hands moving, notice the touch of the towel, and I would drop all the busyness in my mind and just BE HERE. The unintended consequence is that mindfulness started "growing" around it. I became more mindful while wiping up the spills, noticing inside my body when my son agitated me, and it was like my whole day grew more mindful.

Sometimes mindfulness arises spontaneously; after learning the basics of mindfulness, students recognize it and report the spontaneous arising of mindfulness in the midst of their lives. It is usually accompanied by a feeling of delight, as though the mind is taking on the new skill without a lot of prompting, as Ping, a fifty-three-year-old architect in our beginning meditation class, reported:

I was prepping for a meeting that I was quite nervous about. I really didn't want to go in there. Suddenly I noticed that I was, without even trying, feeling my breath moving in my belly and noticing my feet connected to the ground. It felt very soothing. Honestly, I was quite surprised. I went into the meeting in much better shape than I expected.

Walking mindfully is one way to bring mindfulness of body into your daily life (see the practice section). As Raja, a forty-six-year-old project manager, described it, walking mindfully can be a spontaneous meditation at any time of the day:

One day I was walking from my car to my office when I noticed how agitated I was. I had a million things to do that day, or that was what it felt like at least, and my mind was running all over the place about the call I had coming in at 10:00 AM and the form I had to submit by 11:00. Suddenly I remembered mindfulness, and it was like the channel changed in my mind. I shifted my attention from all the planning and just felt my footsteps as I walked. I then began to relax a little and started to feel my body moving through space, the wind on my face, and I saw this shiny little bird land right in my path. By the time I got to work, I was whistling a little tune. And everything I had to do that day got done, exactly as they would have whether or not I was worrying about them!

THE PRACTICES

Exercise 1: Walking Meditation

Read through the directions for the walking meditation a few times until you have a good feel for this mindfulness practice, then give it a try.

Find a place indoors or out where you can walk about ten to fifteen steps. This will be your walking path. Start by closing your eyes for a few minutes and feeling your body standing there. Notice the weight of your body as your feet touch the ground. Then begin to shift your weight back and forth. What do you feel? There are probably many changing sensations at your feet— muscular movements, pressure, weight, heaviness, lightness. When you take a step, you will notice similar sensations.

Now take a step and keep your attention as closely connected as you can to the sensations in your feet and legs. Begin walking back and forth on your walking path. You can walk at a normal pace, or you can try slower paces. You can even walk in slow motion. The important thing is to discover the pace you connect with, the pace that allows you to be the most mindful. When you get to the end of the path, stop for a moment and sense yourself standing. What do you notice? Then turn around, feeling the shifting sensations. Walk again, staying as aware of the sensations as you can. When your mind wanders off and drifts into other things, simply notice, as you do with breath meditation, that you are wandering and return your attention to the sensations of walking. You can do this practice for five to ten minutes, or longer if you choose. Doing it outside in nature is nice if you have the opportunity.

Exercise 2: Guided Body Scan Meditation

In this meditation, you will explore mindfulness of the body by "sweeping" your body—scanning it with your attention. There are many bodily sensations you might feel, such as pressure, tension, tightness, lightness, warmth, cold, pleasantness, unpleasantness, vibrating, pulsating, tingling, or itching. You might notice one very strong sensation, or multiple sensations, or nothing at all. Try not to make up a story about the experience (Wow, I must be getting old). *Just become aware of all that is happening in your body. Take as much time with each body part as you need to feel whatever sensations are present. This exercise can also promote relaxation.*

Find your comfortable, relaxed sitting meditation posture. (You may also try this practice lying down or standing up.) Bring your attention to the top of your head, where you might notice tingling . . . or movement . . . or itching. . . . Notice what's there. And now gently bring your attention down your skull. It's not always so easy to feel sensations in your skull, but notice what's present. Come back to your forehead, then down your face, your eyes, nose, cheeks, lips, and chin. Feel your whole face. You might notice pleasant sensation or unpleasant sensation. Can you simply be aware, in a kind, open, and curious way? In this process relaxation will come, bringing ease and balance.

Notice your neck and throat. . . . Bring your attention to your shoulders. We often carry lots of tension in our shoulders; if yours are feeling tight, let them relax. Help areas that are tense to relax by bringing your breath into that area. Have a sense of breathing into your shoulders, and let the relaxation happen.

Bring your attention to your left arm, noticing the upper arm, the elbow, the lower arm. Notice your hand and fingers. You're feeling your body from the inside; you're not visualizing it or imagining it, but actually feeling any and all sensations, subtle or not subtle, that are present.

Now go to the right shoulder, the right upper arm, elbow, lower arm, hand, and fingers. Take a breath. Do this scan slowly and gently, so that it feels helpful to you.

Come back to the top of your back. Notice your upper back. You can scan your attention back and forth, zigzagging. Or you can go up and down. Or you can do a global scan. Do whatever you feel drawn to. Notice your middle back. It's not always easy to feel the back. If you're experiencing an absence of sensation, that actually is a sensation. Notice the absence.

After scanning your lower back for sensations, come up to your chest. Feel any sensations that are present in your chest area, go down to your rib cage, and then bring your attention to your belly. Soften your belly. Take a breath and let your belly relax. Many of us carry a lot of tension in the stomach area. So just breathe, relax, notice what's present, notice what's true in this moment.

Notice your pelvis. Come to your hip joint, then the top of your left leg. Notice any sensations. Now scan your attention down your left thigh. Do you sense vibration, tingling, pressure, pleasant or unpleasant sensation? Can you sit with ease and balance in the midst of everything that's happening in your body? If you can, you can learn to transfer this practice to the rest of your life. Balanced and at ease, no matter what you encounter.

Now scan down from the knee to the left calf. Notice your ankle, your feet, even your toes. Go to your right hip joint, then down your right thigh, right knee, and right calf. Feel your right ankle, feet, and toes.

Now have a global sense of your whole body sitting. Just take it all in. You may have lots of little sensations, or just a general feeling of the body sitting or standing. You can either end the meditation or begin again, starting at your feet and going up toward your head. Then back down again. You can go at the pace described here, or you can go slower or faster. As you practice meditation, you will learn to check in with your own body and mind and trust your intuition. What feels appropriate right now? What does your body need? What does your mind need? What does your heart need? Learn to trust the answers.

5

WORKING WITH
PHYSICAL PAIN

The pain of the mind is worse than the pain of the body.

—Publilius Syrus
(Roman author, first century bce)

A mericans as a nation hurt a lot. In the United States alone, over half of adults say that they suffer from chronic or recurrent pain.[1] About two in five adults say that pain interferes with their responsibilities at work or home, their mood, their sleep, or their enjoyment of life. Our biggest physical complaints are back pain, joint pain, and headaches. We don't like pain, and we avoid it at all costs. The worldwide pain management market is expected to exceed $43 billion in the year 2010.[2]

"Pain" is a four-letter word that has its roots in the Greek word *poine*, which means "payment" or "penalty," as in punishment or revenge. Its origin may reflect what seems at times like a punishment—the pain of a hangover after a night of celebration, the pain of separation after a mad love affair, the pain of the climate crisis after decades of excess consumerism. Joys are sometimes followed by pain and suffering. Pain is part and parcel of human existence, be it physical, emotional, or cognitive. It is part of our shared human condition, and the knowledge that we *all* experience pain may weaken the self-centered belief that our suffering is somehow greater than another's. Mindfulness is a means to explore this aspect of human nature and its influence on us. We saw how mindfulness can heighten our physical awareness in the last two chapters; this chapter examines how mindfulness can change our relationship to those physical experiences that hurt.

THE SCIENCE

The biology of physical pain includes a vast array of chemicals and neural pathways. We have a complex system of cells located in our skin, nose, ears, eyes, tongue (and to a lesser extent our internal organs) dedicated to detecting noxious (painful) stimuli. Pain tells us when we are in danger, whether the risk is chemical (lack of oxygen, poison), thermal (fire, extreme cold), or mechanical (sharp teeth, insect bite), and *pain triggers a withdrawal from the harmful stimuli.* Acute pain is an evolutionary solution to avoiding things that can hurt or kill us. It is important for our survival.

It is probably not surprising that the skin, which presents the body's entire surface area to the external world, has the most sophisticated array of cells dedicated to the detection of pain. Pain is the body's early warning system to take action, and skin is the great detector of what may be harmful in the environment. There is much less cell specialization for pain detection in our internal organs, like the liver, heart, or kidneys, probably because damage to those organs comes more from the wear and tear of aging, especially after the reproductive years. Biologists suggest that natural selection probably perfected the pain response of the skin because our ancestors with poor "warning" systems for pain died more rapidly than those with better pain response. Conversely, internal organ "warnings" were under less selective pressure since conditions like arthritis and heart disease happen much later in life (after we pass our genes to the next generation).[3]

The Feeling of Pain

Humans are not alone in feeling pain, but it is difficult to determine what other species feel pain, because "feeling" implies consciousness and we haven't yet figured out exactly what that is or how to measure it objectively. Although most scientists would agree that a plant does not feel pain when it is plucked from a garden, that consensus disappears as we span across species. Who feels pain? Does an ant, a worm, a frog, a fish, a bird, a dog, a monkey, a dolphin, a whale? Almost all organisms show physiological responses to noxious stimuli, but many of these responses are purely reflexive, unaccompanied by conscious experience or sensation, without a *feeling* of pain.

Whether a physiological response is purely reflexive or has feeling attached to it is a question that philosophers, theologians, and neuroscientists have tackled for generations. Without consciousness, we feel no pain, as is evident from the effects of surgical analgesia. However, the relationship between consciousness of self (our capacity to "know we know") and pain remains elusive. Many scientists would agree that lower organisms (a snail, an ant, a worm) feel no pain and that higher organisms (gorillas, chimpanzees) do, but it remains unclear at what stage on the evolutionary ladder *felt* pain is present.

The classic model of pain describes three systems as active when we feel pain: the sensory discrimination system, the affective response system, and the cognitive evaluation system.[4] The sensory discrimination system is just what it sounds like—we detect painful stimuli in the environment via our senses. We sense pain through cells located in the skin and other organs called nocioreceptors, which detect noxious stimuli that can be smelled, tasted, touched, heard, or seen. In skin, there are at least three cell types that differ in how fast they can detect and send pain signals, the types of signals they detect, and the specific molecules they release. When stimulated, these cells send chemical messages to the dorsal horn of the spinal cord, where other cells send signals up to the brain. At the brain level, the release of more chemicals triggers a behavioral response to avoid the noxious stimuli, such as holding your nose, stopping eating, running, moving away, covering your ears, or shutting your eyes. In addition to the nerve fibers running up from the spinal cord to the brain, there are parallel fibers carrying messages from the brain down to the spinal cord to modify these pain signals. These descending pathways may *enhance* or *inhibit* pain, and in this way our brains can regulate our pain response through processes of affect and cognition. It is likely that these descending pathways are one means by which mindfulness modifies pain, as they are known to be influenced by attention, anxiety, depression, beliefs, attitudes, past experience, and other higher-order neural processes.[5]

A. D. "Bud" Craig is a neuroscientist at the Barrow Neurological Institute in Phoenix, Arizona, who is championing a new view of pain.[6] This new model suggests that a specific region of the brain, the insula cortex, shown in Figure 2, holds an internal image of the physiological state of the body, a thermostat of sorts to detect when the body is out of balance (homeostasis).

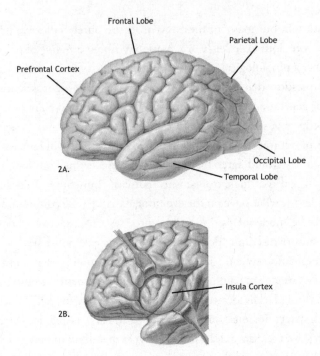

Frontal Lobe

Parietal Lobe

Prefrontal Cortex

Occipital Lobe

2A.

Temporal Lobe

Insula Cortex

2B.

FIGURE 2 External images of the brain with a view of the interior region of the insula cortex. Netter medical illustration used with permission of Elsevier. All rights reserved. Modified with permission.

Think of this as a "mini-me" of the entire body state (a re-representation) held in a virtual imprint in the brain. This *interoceptive* region of the brain exists in all primates but is enormously enlarged in humans, and it is not found among many other animals. The anterior part of this region of the brain, Craig believes, is the seat of consciousness itself, a region needed to have awareness of a "material me." He proposes that this is the region that differentiates a purely physiological pain response from one accompanied by *felt* pain. He thinks that the anterior part of this brain region and its connections to other parts of the brain are the key to keeping our sympathetic (fight-or-flight) and parasympathetic (rest-recover) systems in balance. Chronic pain and a host of other emotional disturbances (like depression, addiction, insomnia, and anxiety) arise when the balance between these two systems is out of sorts.[7] This idea about the role of the insula in maintaining this balance, and its relationship to felt pain, is relatively new and needs more investigation.

The finding that longtime meditators show differences in the insula cortex compared to nonmeditators suggests that mindfulness meditation has a direct impact on this brain region.

Conscious Regulation of Pain

An understanding of the biology of pain needs to account for the great amount of individual difference in pain response and the effect of phenomena such as beliefs and expectations on pain. Research has clearly demonstrated that people differ in their pain tolerance and pain sensitivity, yet what underlies these differences—genes, environments, beliefs, expectations, and so on—are only now being investigated. We know that changing states of consciousness can reduce pain, as is evident from the effects of anesthesia and hypnosis or the effects of substances, such as alcohol, that modify cognitive states and reduce the pain response. Conversely, thoughts, fears, and expectations can greatly enhance pain, as is evident for many of us when we face dental work, an immunization shot, or some other invasive procedure. The expectation of pain plays a role in the origins of torture, and the expectation that pain will be eliminated plays a role in the placebo effect in medicine.

Yogis and other meditative experts have been said to feel no pain while walking through fire, lying on a bed of nails, or undergoing a painful experience.[8] A recent study using functional magnetic resonance imaging (fMRI) in an advanced yogi helps explain such hard-to-believe phenomena. In one case, an experienced yogi was given a painful laser stimulation to the hand while undergoing an fMRI brain scan.[9] As expected, the regions of the brain known to be involved in feeling pain were activated, just as happened with other subjects undergoing this experiment. However, when the yogi was told to go into a meditative state and the pain task was readministered, certain previously highlighted regions (insula, anterior cingulate, and thalamus) were quietly silent, and the yogi said he felt no pain.

Because this was just one case study, we don't know whether it generalizes to others who practice meditation, but it suggests that with practice you can learn to control at will the brain regions that typically fire when your body detects pain. And as is evident in the case report, the insula cortex—that part of the brain thought to hold a re-representation of the body, the "mini-me," to detect changes in body homeostasis—is involved. Coupled with this finding is the observation that this part of the brain shows significant structural differences between longtime meditators and nonmeditators.[10]

The Placebo Effect

Scientists have long known that just believing a treatment works can be as effective as actually receiving treatment for a minority of patients. This expectation effect—called the placebo effect—routinely occurs and may provide insight into mind-body medicine in general. In pain studies, at least one-third of patients show a placebo effect—they experience a reduction in pain when they think they are being treated but are actually receiving a fake (placebo) intervention masked to look like the real stuff.

By studying the placebo effect, researchers are beginning to identify how expectation can modify pain. One finding reported by researchers at the University of Michigan is that the *expectation* of an analgesic effect increases the amount of opioids in the brain.[11] (Opioids are naturally occurring chemicals that have an analgesic effect like that induced by opium.) And the parts of the brain that become activated by the expectation of pain include the insula again, along with other regions thought to be involved in pain modulation.[12] But expectation can not only inhibit pain but *enhance* it. Which way you want your pain to go, up or down, may be partly under your control, and it may take nothing more than practice to regulate it.

Attention to Pain

How we attend to pain is a major factor in its perceived intensity. A toothache can be monumentally painful—unless you break an arm on your way to the dentist. A paper cut, hangnail, or canker sore can consume you—unless a stomach virus comes along to distract you. And a headache may send you home from the office and capture all your attention—until you trip and hurt your knee. Our chronic aches and pains get our attention when nothing more pressing takes it away.

It has long been recognized that pain is reduced when our attention is distracted from it, and now research is starting to show how this happens. At Oxford University, researchers studied eight adults in an fMRI scanner while a painful heat pulse was delivered to one of their hands (raised to a temperature that the subjects said was painful). During the stimulation, subjects were sometimes distracted by having to perform a mental task, and other times not. The brains of the subjects were examined to see which parts were activated during their experience of pain with and without attentional distraction. The findings showed that, when subjects are distracted, the pain regions of the brain *decrease in activity* and that the decrease corresponds with self-reports of pain.[13] Distraction away from pain is one way to lessen it, yet as we all know, when the distraction stops the pain may start again. Did you ever forget you had a backache or headache or toothache while at work, only for it to emerge full force as soon as you relaxed or lay down to go to sleep?

As you will see in the art and practice sections, mindful attention may be directly focused on pain, not distracted away. A mindful stance of curiosity and attention to pain—an ache, for instance, in the knee, the back, or the shoulder—may allow the pain to pass or to lessen. For example, according to a case report, a doctor who had suffered from severe headaches since childhood attended a mindfulness course and experienced an extreme headache at the beginning of a sitting practice. Rather than stop the practice, he observed the sensation of the headache and continued to meditate as instructed; then he noticed that the pain disappeared. He continued to practice, and within a week he was able to control his headaches by letting them appear and watching them disappear over a period of fifteen minutes.[14]

How might attention to pain help diminish it? Jon Kabat-Zinn suggests that the likely mechanism is through the role of "bare attention."[15] When you give pain bare attention, you are attending to the purely sensory experience of pain and disassociating that experience from the story you might attach to the sensation; you are adopting the stance of a "detached observer," or "impartial spectator," or one of "unentangled participation"—all terms for the same thing. In disassociating the sensation of pain from your narrative about the pain, you prevent the heightening of pain that can arise from the fear, thoughts, or emotions attached to it. Through practice with small pains (a foot cramp, a leg falling asleep or becoming numb, a stiff back), you can explore the difference between the sensation itself and the thoughts and fears that may exacerbate (or deaden) it. Through repetitive practice, this delinking (also called "disidentification") strengthens until the story and the sensations are no longer linked. In the disidentification, you may find that your pain lessens.

Mindfulness practice does seem to reduce the pain. In a study in Montreal, thirteen Zen meditators, each of whom had more than one thousand hours of practice, were compared to thirteen nonmeditator controls for pain response to heat stimulation on their calves. At the beginning of the study, the meditators required higher temperatures than controls to even feel discomfort; then, when asked to mindfully attend to the pain, their reports of pain went down. In contrast, the controls showed no decline in their pain response. It appears that using the stance of mindfulness to examine pain actually decreases it, but practice is needed—for the Zen practitioners, the more meditation practice the greater the pain decline.[16]

Mindfulness-Based Programs and Pain Reduction

Mindfulness practices were initially brought into medical settings specifically to help people suffering from chronic pain. Jon Kabat-Zinn created the secular program Mindfulness-Based Stress Reduction (MBSR) to help pain patients who had been given the final diagnosis, "You're going to have to learn to live with this."[17] In his initial study, fifty-one patients suffering from chronic pain (the largest group of whom had back pain) were put on a ten-week mindfulness program and examined for change. About half of the patients reported a 50 percent reduction in their pain levels. Although this initial study did not have a control group for comparison, it marked the way for mindfulness to be brought into medical settings and for researchers to begin to rigorously explore its efficacy in treating pain (along with a multitude of other conditions).

Studies of mindfulness to treat pain span a diverse sample of pain patients, including those with fibromyalgia, rheumatoid arthritis, migraine headaches, HIV, and cancer. Although most, if not all, studies show some benefit of mindfulness in reducing pain, few are of a quality that allows clear interpretation. Often no control group is included, and in some cases patients given a mindfulness program are compared to people given no treatment at all. Part of the problem with this sort of comparison is that mindfulness is taught in groups: The increased social support may be a source of pain reduction as well. Other factors that could account for the improvement are positive attention by the mindfulness instructor or the placebo effect. More studies are needed to tease apart these potential explanations.

In a later study by Kabat-Zinn and his colleagues, a control sample was drawn from their ongoing pain clinic and assessed before and after a traditional course of pain treatment. In that study, ninety chronic pain patients were given the MBSR course and compared to the controls on pain, body image, impairment, analgesic use, and psychological distress.[18] The MBSR participants experienced less present-moment pain, had less difficulty with physical activity, reported fewer medical symptoms, and showed improved mood and body image compared to controls. The effect was still evident at a fifteen-month follow-up. The study suggests that mindfulness may be a helpful complement to traditional pain treatment, but is it better than other psychosocial interventions?

In a study conducted at Arizona State University, 144 patients suffering from rheumatoid arthritis were randomly assigned to three treatment conditions—cognitive-behavioral therapy, mindfulness, or an education group—and compared on measures of pain as well as a physiological marker of pain response (interleukin-6: a molecule that increases with tissue inflammation).[19] All three groups showed pain improvement, improved mood, and improved ability to cope with pain. There was a slight advantage of mindfulness over the other two treatments for the subset of patients who were also depressed, but only the group given cognitive therapy showed a reduction in the biomarker of pain response. The data suggest that mindfulness may be comparable to cognitive therapy in pain reduction, but perhaps no better than cognitive therapy unless depression is present. An important point to remember when contrasting programs is the ease with which mindfulness can be accessed (it may be learned for free and is simple to do, although it takes effort to practice), while cognitive therapy is a therapeutic program taught by licensed clinical professionals.

If You Are Mindful, Do You Feel Less Pain?

Researchers in Bath, England, asked this question of 105 patients attending a pain management course.[20] They asked the patients to complete mindfulness questionnaires along with self-reported measures of pain distress. People with lower scores on mindfulness were those who experienced greater levels of pain, had more depression associated with pain, had more pain-related anxiety, and suffered more physical and psychosocial disability because of pain.

THE ART

One close friend of mine has struggled with a mysterious illness for many years. His symptoms range from extreme exhaustion to nausea, body aches, and intermittent fevers. The symptoms come and go, and no doctor has been able to diagnose it. He tells me that the only way he has been able to manage the pain and confusion is through his long-term mindfulness practice. He has struggled significantly with the pain, but every time I visit with him, he seems basically happy. He chalks this up to mindfulness. He says that the illness is his greatest teacher ever.

Let's now explore how these mindfulness tools can work to help reduce and manage pain. You will learn how to meditate with pain, and how to notice your reactions to pain as separate from the pain itself. You might find insight into how to deal with your personal physical challenges, and how to have a peaceful mind, even in the midst of pain.

Coping with Pain

We all have strategies for managing pain. Pain medications are one of the standard treatments for physical complaints. But what about when medications are no longer effective? And what if you want to use pain medications only in the short term, not for the rest of your life? Perhaps you have learned to manage pain through a variety of other means that are not too healthy—like numbing pain with alcohol or drugs, overeating, or excessive busyness. Maybe you have learned to turn your attention to something else in the midst of pain or know how to talk yourself through it. As we saw in the science section, distraction is an effective strategy, but temporary distraction inevitably comes to an end, and pain may return with even greater intensity.

People have a variety of attitudes toward pain. Some encounter pain and respond very stoically: *I'm fine. Not a problem. I can handle this.* A stoic may have a broken arm and refuse pain medication because she is sure she is fine. Others find even the slightest bit of pain traumatic. Perhaps you know the "catastrophizer" who gets a cut on her foot and immediately foresees gangrene. Or diagnoses a slight sniffle as cancer. She is apt to be up at 1:00 AM surfing the Internet for information about brain tumors because she woke up with a headache. And don't forget the self-blamer: *If only I had remem-*

bered to wear my jacket yesterday (even though it was eighty degrees out), I wouldn't have caught this flu—that was so stupid!

None of these responses in and of itself is a problem, but all of them are the type of response that can lead to mental suffering that increases physical pain. Our mental efforts can enhance or inhibit pain. The way people experience pain is not uniform; some have a higher tolerance for pain than others. From a mindfulness perspective, the significant factor to examine in understanding these differences is how you relate to pain. *The greatest difficulty in working with pain is not the pain itself, but how your mind reacts to the pain.* By applying mindfulness to pain, you can learn more about how you relate to pain and react to it, and this will teach you more about yourself in general.

Mindfulness of Pain

By applying mindfulness to pain, you can observe what actually is going on in your body, rather than get lost in thoughts, feelings, and concepts about pain, which tend to be a source of increased frustration. When you have a painful sensation, it is common to think that it is going to last forever (this is a thought associated with pain). You may feel angry about the pain (feeling). You may believe that it is monolithic—something huge, all-encompassing, and unchangeable (a concept about pain). When you perceive pain this way, it quickly becomes unbearable. Instead, when you bring mindfulness to the part of your body that is in pain, you begin to learn about the true nature of the painful sensation (without the thought associated with it).

When you have ideas about pain, you may be so caught in the ideas that you miss the reality of the experience (and this is true in general of bringing mindfulness to any experience). One of the most important observations that mindfulness can help you make is that pain comes and goes. It does not last forever. Even if you have chronic pain—which we can define as *pain that persists longer than the temporal course of natural healing*—pain is never constant. Pain waxes and wanes; it is not constant in its intensity, although emotionally you may feel as though it is. The pain shifts, it moves, it changes. However, many of us can be so positive that our pain isn't going to go away that we don't explore it closely at all. We just suffer from it or avoid it.

If you bring mindful attention (bare attention) to the part of your body that is in pain, you may discover the incorrectness of the belief that pain is constant. Indeed, it may be a belief in the constancy of pain that frightens, depresses, or angers you. But if you notice that pain comes and goes—that it shifts, lessens, increases, and decreases—you may notice that is not unchanging. This insight alone, based on observation, can be quite relieving. Even chronic pain does not always stay the same.

Taking Interest

If you can begin to take an interest in your pain and bring mindfulness to it as if the pain were an object in a laboratory experiment, you may see that pain is not such a monolithic experience; in fact, it really is quite interesting. That may seem hard to believe, but try it. Explore the bare sensation of a small pain for a moment—become aware of the actual sensations and notice the stories that may accompany it. This illustrates a key principle of mindfulness: Taking interest in a curious, open way (a key attitude of mindfulness) can give you a greater capacity to stay present with the experience—whether the experience is pain or anything else.

Here are some questions you might ask yourself: What does the pain feel like? Is it throbbing, burning, stabbing, itching? Is it big or small? Is it all in one spot or diffuse? Does it have a shape? A color? Is it pulsing or changing? Does it go into my body deeply or shallowly? Does it move?

As you begin to explore pain in these ways (you can start with the ice cube practice provided later in this chapter), you may discover pain as it really is: a changing set of sensations to which you may associate numerous thoughts and feelings. That is exactly what Stefan, a fifty-two-year-old author, discovered:

> I woke up with this very strong headache. Instead of going straight to the medicine cabinet, I decided to see what would happen if I were mindful of it. At first it was hard to do, but I breathed a little, and then brought my mindfulness to the headache. I found that it was sort of interesting. There were all these little spiky feelings along with a dull ache that was throbbing. It was about the size of an egg. It kind of moved back and forth. I kept feeling and observing the pain, and I realized that about twenty minutes had passed and I hadn't even felt that bad. I can't

explain—I was in pain, but I wasn't suffering. Being so curious about it made it tolerable and even interesting.

When Stefan could closely observe his pain with a compassionate mindfulness, he was able to get interested in it enough that it stopped being a problem and merely became the physical sensations of pain. And eventually the pain subsided.

The Past in the Present

One of the things you may discover about pain is how the past affects the present. For instance, if you carry a personal story about not being able to stand the cold—perhaps that you always get cold and have hated the cold since you were a child—you may really dread the ice cube exercise we will do in this chapter. If, on the other hand, you are an avid skier or cold-weather fan, you may rush ahead a few paragraphs to go straight to the exercise.

We often do not experience the present when the past impedes on it. Imagine meeting an old friend with whom you had a falling-out. Instead of seeing your friend anew, you may ruminate over old wounds (*How could he have done that to me?*). Even if he has changed for the better since the last time you saw him, you come into the encounter with biases from the past. The same is true when dealing with difficult bodily sensations. Here is how Corinne, a nineteen-year-old college student, tried to recognize the preconceived experiences and ideas that were having an impact on her present-moment experience of pain:

> When I was a child, my mother used to hold my head and rub it. Her hands and voice were so soothing. Now, as an adult, whenever I get a headache, I sort of relax and smile and remember my mother holding me, and I am rarely too upset by my headache.

A PRACTICE: THE ICE CUBE EXERCISE

Put an ice cube or two into a cup. Get in a comfortable seated posture. Close your eyes and follow your breath for a few minutes. When you feel relaxed and centered, put the ice cube in your hand or your fingers in the cup. Hold the ice cube for as long as you feel you can maintain awareness, but feel free to put it back at any time. Do not be overzealous about this exercise and do it in the spirit of play. You can try it for five minutes or however long you feel drawn to continue it.

Use your mindfulness to explore the ice cube on a few levels:

1. What physical sensations do you feel? Do they change or stay the same? Do they increase or decrease?
2. What reactions do you notice to the ice? *I'm scared . . . Yuck, I don't want to do this . . . This is stupid . . . I like this. . . .* Can you tease apart the stories you tell yourself and the direct experience of feeling the ice cube?
3. What patterns do you notice about yourself in relation to pain? Do you power through? Get fearful? Have globalizing (all-or-nothing) thoughts? ■

Suffering: Our Reactions to Pain

There is a famous adage: "Pain is inevitable, but suffering is optional." This anonymous saying sums up what you can learn about pain through mindfulness. You cannot avoid pain. Even if you are physically healthy now, at some point you may get sick, you may get hurt, and age and physical changes will occur. Pain is inevitable. It will come, and there is nothing you can do to prevent it—yet whether or not you *suffer* is another matter. Why is it that one woman can go through childbirth claiming that it was the most painful experience of her life while another declares it was the most transcendent? Along with other conditions, including the ease of delivery, the answer may lie in how we *relate* to pain. Clearly, sensory experiences are different, but how we relate to them—big or small—plays a powerful role as well.

Suppose we define pain as the pure physical sensation of the body responding to some negative stimuli, and suffering as our response to pain. From a mindfulness perspective, it is important to differentiate pain and suffering because however unavoidable pain is, we certainly have some leeway when it comes to suffering.

The biggest difficulty in working with pain is not the pain itself; it is how we react to it. With mindfulness, you can learn to see how your mental reactions to suffering function and how you can avoid being so caught in them. For example, Rachel wakes up every day utterly exhausted. Suffering from chronic fatigue syndrome, she is not sure she can get out of bed, and her first thought is how angry she is at having this illness. She remembers that she has been feeling tired for six months, but today, despite feeling a bit better yesterday, she feels worse than ever, the exhaustion is back, and now she is frustrated and angry. Her body has sensations of fogginess, achiness, and heaviness (pain). When she experiences these sensations, her mind kicks into action. It judges the pain, is discouraged by it, is frustrated, angry, or blaming—and all of these responses cause emotional turmoil (suffering).

Contrast Rachel's response with a mindful approach: She may note the pain itself, rather than her mind's reaction to it, and then practice attending only to the bodily sensations, releasing the story of their supposed permanence, the anger and frustration she associates with these sensations, and all the judging that normally accompanies them.

Perhaps at one time or another you have had one of these typical reactions to pain:

1. I am angry at the pain—it feels unfair. It is ruining my day; it is ruining my life.
2. I am scared of the pain—it feels frightening. It's making me anxious, and I imagine it getting worse in the future (this is called "catastrophizing").
3. I am discouraged and saddened by the pain—it feels hopeless and depressing. I find myself thinking, *I don't want to face it—not today, not ever.* I don't think I have the capacity to face it in the future.
4. I blame myself for the pain. I have thoughts like, *If only I hadn't worked so hard in my twenties, I wouldn't be dealing with this now.*

Of course, specific reactions are as varied as humans themselves, but generally they can be grouped into these categories. Unfortunately, we often don't notice them well enough to separate them from the painful experience, and that is how our reactions take on a life of their own. The blame builds on itself, the fear and worry intensify, and before we know it, we are sure that we will end up in a severe crisis. These are all "suffering-based" reactions, and they are superfluous to our actual physical experience of pain. Often it is these types of thoughts that cause us to suffer even more than the pain itself. However, it is bad enough to feel pain—why add an extra layer of blame, anger, rage, shame, or judgment for feeling the way you do?

One reason why pain can become unbearable is the tension you may feel around the pain. You don't want to feel it, and you're having lots of emotions about it, so your body tightens and the original pain increases. With mindfulness, you can learn to separate out your reaction to pain (the suffering) from your actual experience of pain. If you can learn to relax in the midst of pain, perhaps by breathing into the pain, you can tolerate it better. When you do this, you get a little bit of space and freedom. You start to relax around the pain instead of tensing up and making it worse. Then you can see the emotions that are causing your suffering—the layers added to the simple experience of painful sensations.

Can you be with your pain without adding suffering to it? Yes, and mindfulness is a means of doing so. When you notice your mind heading off in the direction of catastrophizing, blaming, worrying, judging, and so on, you can practice to simply notice that you are having these thoughts or feelings and remind yourself that they are not purely the pain.

Can you just feel the pain as painful sensations rather than taking it so personally, scheming to get out of it, worrying, imagining that you are going to end up in the hospital, and so on? Can you detect the additional layers of suffering on top of your painful experience? Ian, a twenty-nine-year-old musician, explains it this way:

> I woke up in the middle of the night with a toothache. Immediately my mind went into a panic. *What's wrong? Why did this happen? What if it gets worse?* Our family was planning a vacation, and I worried we wouldn't be able to go or that it would ruin the vacation. I got so fearful I imagined I would need tooth implants, and then at a certain point I realized, wait a minute, it's just a toothache. I don't know what is really going on. I began to relax. When I breathed for a moment and concentrated on the pain itself, I saw it was throbbing and aching, but that was about it—it was just a toothache.

Often people wonder, *If I am mindful of the pain, will that make it go away?* Sometimes this happens, but you have to be careful with this attitude. If you are paying attention to pain in order to get rid of it, then you have a subtle aversion to the pain—you are not fully present with it. Another approach is to know that you can be mindful of the pain in order to understand yourself and the pain and to learn to be present with a sense of peace even in the midst of challenging sensations.

Meditating with Pain

When you are meditating with your breathing, you may notice pain in your body, whether from sitting in an unfamiliar position or from an existing pain. If the pain becomes obvious and pulls your attention away from your breathing, focus on the pain. Bring your mindfulness to it, explore it, sense it, and see what happens to it as you notice it. When it no longer holds your attention, return to the breath.

Additionally, in both your formal meditation and your experience of pain in daily life, try these three techniques:

1. *Breathing with pain.* Often when we feel pain, we are tense, wound up, and trying to push it away (distracting ourselves from it or avoiding it). Use a mindful approach instead: Relax, take a few slow breaths, and imagine your breath going into the area of pain and softening it.
2. *Mindful distraction.* Trying to distract yourself from pain is not always an unmindful way to lessen it (remember the discussion of the success of distraction from the science section). To mindfully distract yourself from pain, find a pleasant (or neutral) part of your body that you can return to as necessary while being aware of the pain. Most people choose their hands or feet. If you have a bad headache, don't focus only on the headache pain but bring your mindfulness to your feet, let your mind rest and relax a little, and when it feels at ease, return your attention to the painful place for a short time and notice what has happened. You can move your attention back and forth without losing the stream of mindfulness and changing the focus of attention to make the process easier.

3. *Bringing kindness.* It is helpful to hold a gentle, caring attitude toward pain while exploring it (or throughout the day). Feeling pain is very difficult, and it can be exhausting, overwhelming, frightening, and frustrating. Learning to be as kind as possible to yourself in the midst of pain can help you learn to be more mindful of it. You might even imagine holding the painful part of the body with care and kindness, as if you were holding a small child, a puppy, or someone you love. For further instruction on kindness practice, go to Chapter 7.

Learning from Pain

Ultimately pain can be a fascinating area of self-discovery and exploration. It is a means of discovering ancient habits you may have, such as a tendency to criticize yourself whenever you are in pain, or to power through pain, not wanting to face it. As you explore your relationship to pain, you may recognize your coping strategies and discard them if they are no longer useful. You may even discover how you relate to difficulties in life in general, the physical body being just a very real example of it. Cate, a thirty-three-year-old shopkeeper, saw how this worked during her pregnancy:

> I am pregnant and have had morning sickness for three weeks now. I shouldn't call it morning sickness, because I'm sick all the time. I feel nauseous, hungry, emotional. I hate feeling nauseous; it's my least favorite feeling in the world. I am now trying to apply mindfulness to the nausea, and when I just relax the best I can and feel the sensations, I notice, my mind makes it way worse than it is. I never realized how out of the present pain takes me. It's like my mind goes straight for the worst possible scenario. I tend to feel so sorry for myself. If I can remember sometimes to bring mindfulness to the pain, I am able to breathe through it and trust I will get through it and open to the possibility that this pain will help bring me my beautiful baby.

If you approach pain in these ways—attending to the direct experience of the sensations themselves, noticing the changing nature of pain, observing your reactivity and preventing future reactivity—then your pain may lessen, and most importantly, you will find a much more renewed sense of well-being in the face of the inevitable pain of life.

THE PRACTICE:
MEDITATING WITH PAIN

Use this practice if you are experiencing any physical pain.

Try to get as comfortable as you can in your sitting posture. If the pain is really bad, you may wish to lie down. Find the most comfortable position to practice.

First take a few breaths and allow yourself to connect with the fact that your body is sitting (or lying down). Notice your posture and body shape. Now find a part of your body that is not in pain and bring your attention to it. Find a part that feels pleasant or neutral, at the very least. Explore whether your hands, feet, or legs feel relaxed and pleasant. Let your attention stay at this pleasant area for a few moments. Now bring your attention to the area of pain. What do you notice? Is the pain sharp or dull? Burning? Stabbing? Fiery? Clenching? Is it moving, or does it stay in one place? How deeply does it go into your body? Get very curious about the changing set of bodily sensations.

After thirty seconds or so (you can choose any short amount of time), bring your attention back to the pleasant area of your body. Let yourself stay present, aware of the pleasant or neutral sensations for the next few minutes. Notice if you have an attitude toward the pain. Do you hate it, fear it, resent it, blame yourself for it? Can you notice how it is that you feel or think about the pain? Do you feel an accompanying body sensation like a clutching feeling in your gut or vibration in your chest? Notice this reaction, breathe, and let it be there. There is nothing wrong with a reaction. If you have no reaction or the reaction stops, feel free to investigate the painful area one more time.

Return your attention to the pleasant area, and once again rest there for a minute or so.

Now, for the last time, return to the painful area. What do you notice? Breathe. Feel whatever is present on the physical level. Offer yourself a little bit of kindness in a way that makes sense to you. You can imagine holding that part of your body with care and compassion, or just offer this attitude to yourself. Notice what happens.

Return your attention to your whole body, sitting or lying and present. Open your eyes when you are ready.

Whenever you are meditating and encounter pain, you can try this practice as written, feel freeing to vary how frequently you move back and forth between painful and neutral sensations.

6

FEELING BAD

Dealing with Negative Emotions

To fly, we have to have resistance.
—Maya Lin

The difficulties in life go beyond physical pains to include emotional ones as well—from mild irritants like traffic jams and missed appointments to major challenges like job loss, divorce, or the death of a loved one. The feelings associated with such stressors are ones we call negative emotions—anger, sadness, fear, anxiety, greed, envy, pride, and other subtler sorts of emotional states.

Mindfulness is about being present in a curious manner with *whatever* emotion arises—good or bad. It is about experiencing things as they are and in that process increasing your awareness, including your discriminating or investigative abilities. Mindfulness is a means of investigation, but who really wants to dig into negative feelings and to experience them as they are? Who wants to get curious about that feeling of envy around a close friend's success? Or curious about a twinge of greed? Or anger at your spouse's inattention or the sadness you feel when your child is disappointed? Ugh. How uncomfortable.

Yet, with mindfulness, negative emotions may become a little less negative—by which we mean that they will be more easily recognized and understood, and some may even diminish in intensity. When you see an emotion for what it is—whether bad or good—you're better able to detect the source of the emotion and to let go of tendencies either to want things to change or to want them to stay the same.

THE SCIENCE

We all feel bad at times—whether we're sad, anxious, irritable, envious, or angry—and these emotions wax and wane throughout our lives. No one is immune to negative emotions, and how we deal with them can prevent, modify, or reduce their severity. In the extreme—when mood, anxiety, or other negative emotions persist and cause impairment—they can lead to a psychiatric disorder. Half of the adults in the United States, at some point in their lives, have met the criteria for such a disorder, and the rate among children is up to 20 percent and rising.[1] Science has demonstrated that psychiatric illness differs by degree from our normal variation in feelings: Sadness has at its extreme depression; phobias and panic disorder are extremes of anxiety; and mild mood swings are probably at one end of a spectrum that has bipolar illness at the other. This chapter is about how we relate to negative emotions across the range of severity.

The old nature-versus-nurture debate about behavior has been replaced today with the view that nature and nurture, far from being mutually exclusive, are inextricably intertwined. Most human feelings arise from a combination of genetic blueprints interacting with environmental experiences. For example, suppose that you carry a gene variant that affects serotonin* transport (a molecule that helps move released serotonin back into cells). People with a variant of this gene are at increased risk for depression, but only if in childhood they experienced trauma or a severe lack of social support.[2] Our genes influence our mental health *as a function of the environments in which they are expressed*. Scientists are now searching for these specific gene-environmental relationships. Mental training, such as mindfulness meditation, appears to influence some gene regulation, suggesting that we can alter our internal body states through lifestyle changes, including mental training, and in turn regulate our gene expression.[3]

---

*Serotonin, a neurotransmitter found widely in the gut and the brain, is involved in a variety of behaviors, including social relating, aggression, mood, sleep, and appetite.

Emotions and Feeling

Emotions arose in evolution to aid biological survival. Emotions are *physiological responses to environmental stimuli*, such as danger or competition over resources. Feeling is the conscious or *subjective experience* (sad, happy, disgust) of emotional responses, which are the biological reactions our bodies and brains undergo *unconsciously* all the time. Like thought, emotions can arise either unconsciously or consciously, and a great many do so without our awareness, although feeling and emotion are thought to reflect a common underlying system. Because the brain circuitry of the emotional system is much older in evolution than the circuits associated with thinking, there are stronger connections from the emotional centers to the thought centers than the other way around.[4] That explains why it is much harder to be happy in the aftermath of a breakup by just telling yourself to be happy than it is for all logic to disappear in the midst of the arguments that may have led up to it.

When we are not reacting emotionally, we are in a different physiological state of balance. We all know that balanced feeling—not high or low, not fear or joy, not anger or love, but simply nonreactive. Recognizing your bodily and mental experience in this state of not reacting emotionally is like recognizing the space between the words printed on this page, or the background elements of a Picasso painting, or the space within a Frank Lloyd Wright building that makes it an architectural masterpiece.

Mindfulness is a tool for improving your discernment of emotional states (and the bodily changes that accompany them) when they arise. You can become a Sherlock Holmes of your feelings and their associated physiological changes. Through investigation, you can detect them earlier and with finer resolution. Lao-Tzu wrote in the *Tao Te Ching*, "Deal with a thing while it is still nothing."[5] We all remember times when we could have stopped a situation from evolving into a big mess by catching ourselves—whatever it was we said or did—before the situation escalated. Catching your emotional reactions early, when they are still small, is a way to alter your actions to keep them from fueling difficult situations. Think of a time when you reacted emotionally and that led to big problems; later you probably saw how easy it would have been to just say or do nothing (just "act like a log"). When you pause between emotion and action, your words and actions are less likely to hurt yourself or others because you're able to circumvent or at least lessen your emotional reaction. And because we are only aware of the tip of the iceberg of emotional responses (a huge number of emotional reactions occur unconsciously), the process of discovery is likely to be never-ending. There is *always* an emotional reaction we are likely to miss.

The Biology of Emotion

Our bodies—like those of other animals—are constantly reacting and responding to the environments around us and changing accordingly. For example, a recent study in mice suggests that just the *smell* of coffee triggers a turning up or down expression of some seventeen genes in the rat genome.[6] (Imagine what *drinking* the coffee might do.) We react emotionally to stimuli or triggers in our environments, whether the trigger is the smell of smoke, a food we eat, a job loss, a hurt child, a lost wallet, a long line at the DMV, or a catastrophic event such as September 11, and much of the time we are unaware of the triggers. The biology of emotion had a vast evolutionary past in which to tweak and perfect its function well before consciousness (and feelings) entered into the equation.

Scientists no longer consider one brain region the "emotional brain," as in the past, but rather recognize that emotions arise through complex interactions within the neural circuits that connect regions of the cerebral cortex (outer layer of the brain), such as the prefrontal cortex, to subcortical brain regions, including the cingulate cortex and amygdala.[7] A brain depicting these different regions can be seen in Figure 3.

The Multitude of Emotions

How many emotions do we experience? Paul Ekman, a psychologist and expert on human emotions, says that humans recognize six basic emotions from facial expressions: surprise, happiness, anger, fear, disgust, and sadness. Other scientists think that there are between four and eight emotions. In 1958 the psychologist Robert Plutchik proposed that the wider range of human emotions comes from a core set of eight emotions, in the same way that all the colors of the rainbow arise from mixing the primary colors of red, blue, and yellow.[8] On Plutchik's emotional wheel, joy and acceptance create love, fear and joy create guilt, and so on.

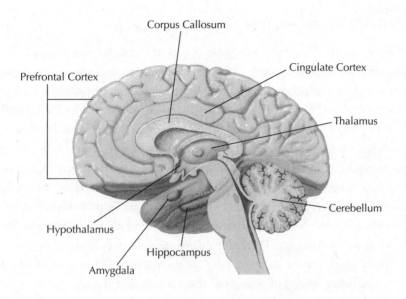

FIGURE 3 An interior image of the brain. Netter medical illustration used with permission of Elsevier. All rights reserved. Modified with permission.

Humans are not alone in experiencing emotion. Depending on the species we study, the variety of emotions differs (shame is not part of a rat's repertoire), but some emotional systems (such as fear) are essentially the same across species because they provided a useful function for adaptation early in evolution. If you peruse the lists of basic human emotions, you will see some that are associated with feeling "bad" (anger, fear, disgust, sadness) and others that are associated with feeling "good" (happiness, joy). Emotions evolved to help us adapt to hostile environments, so it is no wonder that many of them are associated with negative feelings. In our evolutionary past, they probably represented physiological solutions to challenging situations, such as danger from predators (fear), competition over food and mates (anger), and illness caused by poisonous foods (disgust). Many negative emotions correlate with behaviors of self-survival and division or competition (fear, anger, envy, greed, hatred), while positive emotions correlate with behaviors that promote social connection and cooperation (love, compassion, joy). We turn to these latter emotions in the next chapter.

Fear, Anxiety, and the Stress Response

Anxiety is one of the most prevalent sources of bad feelings in the world to-day. It is an unpleasant sense of apprehension often accompanied by symptoms such as headaches, perspiration, heart palpitation, stomach discomfort, and restlessness. About one in four adults suffer from extreme anxiety, while one in three report that they experience extreme stress every month. Anxiety disorder is the most common mental illness in the United States, affecting 40 million adults, and it has increased in severity over the past forty years.[9] For example, children who were considered "not anxious" in the 1980s score higher on anxiety scales than did child psychiatric patients in the 1950s.[10]

Anxiety is the feeling associated with stress, and stress is on the rise. According to the American Psychological Association, two-thirds of all visits to a family physician are due to stress-related symptoms, 43 percent of us suffer from health effects of stress, and stress is linked to the six leading causes of death.[11] Furthermore, half of Americans report that their stress levels have increased in the last five years.

The Biology of Anxiety and the Fear Response

The best biological model of anxiety is the fear response, and the neuroscientist Joseph LeDoux at New York University is a leading expert in it. In his book *The Emotional Brain,* he explains the biology of fear and how we learn to fear even in the absence of any immediate threat. While fear is an acute stress response to immediate danger, anxiety is a stress response when no danger is present. We all know that when faced with fear the body goes into a fight-or-flight response pattern. This physiological state (fight-or-flight) is easily triggered by certain unconditioned stimuli, such as fire or a shock (pain), but it can be learned when it is paired with a conditioned stimuli (like the bell in Pavlov's dog experiments). This "learning" is called fear conditioning, and it arises through the pairing of an unconditioned stimulus (US) with a conditioned stimulus (CS), eliciting the fight-or-flight body response; fear conditioning is the learning that takes place from CS-US pairings. Some pairings are easier to learn than others. Apparently, through evolution, we have encoded in our DNA the heightened threat of certain stimuli, such as snakes and insects, so that we either "learn" them very fast or the fear is inherently present.[12] Today the remnants of these readily made fears are evident by the disproportionate number of phobias that people have toward snakes and spiders compared with things to which they are exposed far more often, such as kittens or toothbrushes.

There are lots of different CS-US pairings in the world associated with our fear response. Most of us have paired appropriate CSs with the fight-or-flight response so that we avoid lions (except behind moats at a zoo), are careful to watch for snakes while hiking mountain trails, and don't wander across busy freeways on foot. But some people "fear" too much in the absence of real danger. The human capacity to project our selves through space and time has led them to imagine "what if" in the absence of any real threat, creating anxiety when it is not warranted for survival.

Why, in the evolutionary past, did humans develop anxiety in the absence of any imminent threat? One theory is that anxiety may have reinforced group living for our hominid ancestors. If you were on your own in the days of wooly mammoths and large predators, with merely your hands for protection, group living was an important way to keep down the risk of getting killed. Selection for group living may have unfolded if an individual's heightened physiological state (anxiety) was calmed in the presence of a group. Whether that is the means by which anxiety evolved, it is clear in the twenty-first century that the ancestral sources of fear (large predators, snakes, insects) are fairly obsolete and that group living is well established. The peculiar fears and phobias we have today can seem quite strange at times. Gary Larson captured that point in his cartoon of a man in socks running around a kitchen table being chased by wolves with the caption, "Luposlipophobia: Fear of being chased by wolves around a freshly waxed kitchen floor while wearing only socks on your feet." Phobias and other anxiety disorders all share some element of fear conditioning gone awry.

Conscious and Unconscious Learning

When you learn to pair a CS with a US, your brain encodes this information in an unconscious way through a brain circuit that goes from the sensory stimuli (visual, auditory, tactile, and so on) to the amygdala, an important part of the brain where fear is concerned (see Figure 3 for its brain location). The amygdala is a small, almond-shaped region of the brain with a set of cells that respond to traumatic stimuli by a series of chemical and electrical changes (see Figure 3). The pairing of a CS with a US, via the convergence of sensory connections in the amygdala, leads to the formation of an association between these stimuli. This association does not require conscious awareness. *You can learn to fear without any knowledge of it happening.*

There are two routes by which such associations are formed.[13] One, which LeDoux calls the low road, involves the transmission of CS and US information directly to the amygdala without going through the cortex. The memory of the connection of CS to US encoded via this route is extremely strong but not very specific—the amygdala can't tell the difference between a stick and a snake through this route, so fear responses are generalized to any objects that are similar in some way, such as in their shape. The association is pretty resistant to change. There is also a second brain pathway involved in fear conditioning that includes further processing of it by cortical regions (medial prefrontal and lateral prefrontal regions). This pathway, which LeDoux calls the high road, allows much more precise and detailed information to activate the amygdala, potentially preventing overgeneralization. The fear response you express will depend on whether the information from the low and high roads is synchronized in the amygdala. Thus, activation of the amygdala by the low road, independent of the high road, leads to fear responses that do not necessarily match your conscious experience of the world and that cannot easily be controlled by consciousness.

To illustrate these two pathways and their influence on human behavior, consider a person with a fear of flying in an airplane, a fear shared by up to 40 percent of people.[14] A fear of flying can be extinguished using a therapeutic approach called "systematic desensitization." In this method, a person is exposed, in a safe setting, to the CS—for instance, with a picture of an airplane or a thought about flying—and then gradually, with repeated practice, is able to extinguish the learned association of "plane" and "fear" (probably through the high-road route). But these processes do not erase the amygdala memory, and the fear may reemerge when the person is in a heightened state of distress or perhaps when he or she is exposed to a stimulus similar to the first (for instance, while traveling "up" in the sky over a bridge).

Mindfulness and the Stress Response

Evidence that mindfulness reduces the stress response emerges from numerous studies using the Mindfulness-Based Stress Reduction (MBSR) program.[15] More than fifty studies using MBSR or other mindfulness-based programs show that it can reduce stress and anxiety among the general population as indexed by a wide variety of measures, including self-report scales, neuro-physiological markers (heart rate, skin conductance, fMRI imaging of amygdala activation), cortisol levels reflecting activation of the stress response, and tools that have been developed to elicit fear in the lab (for example, giving a speech in front of a group of strangers).[16] However, among individuals with anxiety disorders, findings are less conclusive, owing in part to the paucity of studies adequate in size and with appropriate controls to interpret results. In several studies with reported positive findings, a lack of control subjects makes interpretation difficult. (For example, the social support afforded by a group setting may also influence changes in anxiety.)[17] In one study of social anxiety, researchers compared MBSR with a first-line psychological intervention and found that, although both programs helped patients, the standard intervention worked significantly better.[18] Perhaps mindfulness will need to be tailored more specifically to symptoms and underlying mechanisms for greater efficacy within clinical anxiety. A mindfulness-based program that does that for the treatment of obsessive-compulsive disorder (a type of anxiety) seems to help people with their symptoms and also modify specific brain functions, suggesting a targeted influence on the underlying neurobiology of this condition.[19]

A primary component of psychotherapy in treating anxiety disorders is the use of exposure (to the anxiety-provoking stimulus) and response prevention (preventing a response, like avoidance). Lobsang Rapgay, a clinical psychologist specializing in anxiety disorders and an expert in mindfulness at our center, suggests that many mindfulness programs may need to have more explicit instruction and practice on focusing attention on the direct experience of anxiety-provoking stimuli to increase their efficacy in treating anxiety disorders.[20] It is likely that more work is needed to tailor mindfulness-based programs to the treatment of anxiety disorder, but the emerging positive findings to date suggest that additional studies are highly warranted.

Emotional Sensitivity and Regulation

How people react to stressful stimuli in the environment differs from one person to the next—again, as a consequence of their genetic makeup and past experiences. For some, a comment greeted with a slight roll of the eyes from a friend may trigger anxiety or sadness. For others, only a screaming fistfight elicits a reaction. The term "emotional sensitivity" describes our individual differences in responding to emotional stimuli. Judith Piggot at UCLA studies emotional sensitivity, particularly in individuals with autism. She has developed a clever way to measure response differences to facial emotions: She has digitized standard facial images in order to be able to morph their emotional expressions, changing them from neutral to sad or neutral to happy, in a continuous sequence. Then, using equipment to measure EEG, heart rate, skin perspiration, and breathing rate, as well as fMRI, she detects body changes in research subjects watching a video of the changing facial expressions *in real time*. While research subjects watch the video showing subtle changes in facial emotion, Piggot assesses their emotional sensitivity by measuring differences in their body and brain response. (You and I, for instance, probably don't detect a grin or a frown at the same rate.)

Humans differ not just in their sensitivity to emotion but also in their ability to regulate it. Psychology and neuroscience play big roles in explaining these differences. The psychologists Oliver John of the University of California at Berkeley and James Gross of Stanford University have shown that emotion regulation is complex, but that at least two regulatory strategies contribute to differences among people: cognitive reappraisal and expressive suppression.[21] Cognitive reappraisal is changing the way you think about the emotional stimuli so that it loses some of its potential threat—in other words, you try to find a way of thinking about the "event" that recognizes and validates your reaction but then helps you adopt an adaptive and hopeful approach. Let's say that when you and a friend meet for lunch, she casually remarks, "Are you okay?" which you take to mean, "Oh, thanks, do I look that bad?" and you begin to feel twinges of anger. Cognitive reappraisal enables you to change your way of thinking by remembering how often you yourself say, "Are you okay?" to others without intending anything sinister. This reminder converts your friend's comment to a neutral attempt to just say hello. Or perhaps you focus on the caring aspect of the remark, your friend having expressed an interest in how you are feeling. Expressive suppression is just what it sounds like: You let the emotion arise but outwardly suppress it. At lunch with your friend, you grin and answer, "Yes, I'm fine," letting anger simmer and even begin to boil while your smile remains the same.

Most people adopt these two strategies to varying degrees all the time in dealing with emotions. Cognitive reappraisal works much better than suppression.[22] It reduces negative emotions more quickly at both the physical and psychological levels. Mindfulness may improve emotion regulation by increasing cognitive reappraisal, reducing suppression, and/or increasing meta-cognitive awareness (described further subsequently). One study showed that mindfulness practice does reduce suppression,[23] while other research shows that it increases positive reappraisal[24] and that it is associated with aspects of emotional labeling (a sort of cognitive appraisal).[25] As we saw in Chapter 1, people who score as more mindful on mindfulness scales have greater frontal brain activation (and a quieting down of amygdala firing) during an emotional labeling task than do less mindful people. But meta-cognitive awareness appears to be a very important component of the success of mindfulness practice on emotion regulation, as the following research demonstrates.

Cognitive therapy (CT) and cognitive-behavioral therapies (CBT) are widely used nonmedication approaches to treating negative emotions. Both of these approaches help people use more adaptive "cognitive appraisals" (and behavioral responses in the case of CBT).[26] They work by changing the cognitive sets that people use to interpret their experiences (as in the example of reappraising your friend's lunchtime comment). Another example might be a teenager who is highly motivated to be successful in school but develops anxiety around exams and is flooded with negative thoughts such as *I'm going to fail so there is no point in studying.* The thought might interfere with the teen's ability to study, lead to a poor grade on the exam, and contribute to a spiral of increasingly negative thoughts, self-defeating behavior, and depressive symptoms. In CT, the therapist would work with the teen to identify alternative thoughts about the situation that are more helpful (cognitive reappraisal)— for example, *Exams are tough, I am anxious, but when I put my mind to it and focus on the work, I have usually done pretty well. Let me just pull myself together, sit down, and focus on the math problems in this first chapter.* These more helpful thoughts might enable the teen to become more focused and to respond with more studying and less worrying. Mindfulness strategies incorporated with

CT help individuals observe and accept their thoughts in a neutral, not critical, way and thus create a more peaceful emotional state that is conducive to adaptive cognitive and behavioral responses.

John Teasdale, a psychologist at Cambridge University, and his colleagues proposed that CT enables change, not by changing beliefs per se, but by a mechanism of increased "meta-cognitive awareness."[27] Meta-cognitive awareness refers to a de-centered relationship of self to thoughts and feelings—the idea that you can be a neutral observer of your own experiences, whether these are sensory experiences or thoughts or feelings. Many terms are used to describe this meta-cognitive stance. We have already used the words "de-linking" and "disidentification"; others use terms such as "reperceiving," "de-centering," "defusion," and "distancing."[28] Still others use terms such as "detached discerning ability."[29] More descriptive terms for the attentional stance of a person witnessing his or her own experiences include "impartial spectator," coined by Jeffrey Schwartz, a psychiatrist and expert on consciousness and the brain,[30] and "unentangled participation," a term used by Ajahn Amaro, a Buddhist monk and co-abbot at the Abhaygiri Monastery in California.

Mindfulness and Depression

Teasdale and his colleagues developed mindfulness-based cognitive therapy specifically to enhance the meta-cognitive stance.[31] In testing its efficacy, they compared traditional cognitive therapy to mindfulness-based cognitive therapy in a sample of clinically depressed patients in remission. They found that the relapse rate into another depressive episode differed dramatically: 62 percent of patients given traditional cognitive therapy relapsed, but only 36 percent of those given the mindfulness-based version relapsed. To understand what led to the difference, the researchers measured "meta-cognition" in the patients and found that those who showed the strongest meta-cognitive awareness were the ones least likely to relapse.[32]

These data lend support to the idea that mindfulness does work, in part, by increasing meta-cognitive awareness and that a mindfulness-based version of cognitive therapy is more effective than traditional cognitive therapy for depression. The program also works to improve mood for depressed patients even when they are not in relapse but in a full-blown depressive episode.[33] And mindfulness in general (not necessarily as part of a clinical therapy) improves mood for the general population, as we will see in the next chapter.

What About Anger?

The majority of studies using mindfulness to deal with negative emotions have focused on mood and anxiety, although aggression, anger, and malevolent behavior are other sources of "feeling bad" that may benefit from mindfulness. Very little research has been conducted on reducing violence, aggression, or anger with mindfulness, but a few reports suggest that this is a viable route for future research. Specifically, in one study a mindfulness exercise (mindfulness of the feet) was taught to three highly aggressive teens, and after learning and practicing the exercise for several weeks all three showed reduced aggression and an increased capacity to calm themselves in the midst of intense internal anger.[34] In a study of 175 undergraduate students at the University of Georgia, researchers found that higher self-reports of mindfulness corresponded with lower levels of aggressiveness and perceptions of hostility from others. Furthermore, with training in mindfulness, people displayed less aggressive behavior than those who had not been given training when they were put into an experimental condition of social rejection. (The scientists simulated an experience that led to a feeling of rejection and then watched how people dealt with it.)[35]

If a simple mindfulness practice helps people regulate negative feelings of anger and aggression, it might change the behavioral outcomes of violence; mindfulness might be a viable tool to help reduce violence in our country and the recidivism of criminals. The Insight Prison Project at San Quentin State Prison in California incorporates mindfulness instruction into its violence prevention classes. One prisoner wrote of the experience: "I've learned about early warning signs and about recognizing when I am about to get into trouble—and then how to come back to myself. This stuff really works; I know what to do because I have choices now."[36]

Additional evidence that mindfulness can reduce violent behavior comes from a recent study of mindfulness in treating "externalizing behavioral disorders" in adolescents. Externalizing behaviors include hyperactivity and irritability as well as behaviors such as lying, truancy, stealing, or setting fires. Children and adolescents who exhibit such behaviors are at increased risk for antisocial behavior, including crime, in adulthood.[37] Researchers at the

University of Amsterdam found that a mindfulness-based cognitive therapy program improved children's self-report measures of externalizing behaviors, their self-control, and their quality of life compared to the children who did not get the program (the "wait-listed controls").[38] The study was small, and since no active control was used—it was compared to a wait-list group rather than an alternative treatment—the strength of the findings is limited until further work is completed.

Based on the science, mindfulness is proving to be a viable tool to deal with negative emotions. Its effects seem to be due to increased meta-cognitive awareness, and it appears to be useful across a wide range of emotional experience—including depression, anxiety, stress, anger—yet the strength of these effects need more research.

THE ART

I have often wished that Emotions 101 was a class offered in grade school. Imagine if all children were required to attend a class that taught them ways of managing anger, dealing with stress and anxiety, and coping with pain and suffering. This may be a distant dream, although Daniel Goleman's 1996 groundbreaking book, *Emotional Intelligence*, has had an impact on school curricula and teacher training programs across the country. However, programs to promote emotional intelligence are still a long way from being core curricula in most school systems.[39] Despite the fact that every day people are disturbed by, overwhelmed by, and impaired by difficult emotions, most of us do not have the skills to find perspective amid strong emotions. Mindfulness can be a key to learning how to relate to emotions in healthy and useful ways.

Unskillful Approaches to Emotions

Most adults have poor skills for working with emotions because they were not explicitly taught how to deal with emotions as children. Instead, they learned how to handle their emotions in other ways, primarily by osmosis and by observation in their families of origin. Teachers, peers, and the media may also influence them.

For instance, if you grew up in a very loud family (did you ever see the *Saturday Night Live* skit from the late 1970s?) in which emotions were expressed frequently and often at the top of the lungs, you may have grown up to be an "expresser." Or you may have rebelled against such overt emotionality and learned to be a "repressor"—someone who is mild in expression or holds in emotions. As we saw in the science section, a multitude of factors, both genetic and environmental, enter into how you sense and respond to emotions. In my own family, most emotions were acceptable, except for anger. Whenever someone got angry, everyone else in my family got very uncomfortable. I learned that the appropriate response to anger is to avoid it at all costs. I struggled hard to be a good girl and to avoid anger, but in doing so I cut off an aspect of my full range of normal human emotions.

Our relationship to emotions can elicit a variety of responses. Many of us get strongly caught up in them ("I'm so sad, this sadness is never going to go away"). If you're like this, life may feel like a series of dramas, with yourself always at the center. Or you may have a friend for whom life is one emotional crisis after the next. She may tend to be very vocal about the maelstroms of emotion or to blame others for her problems. At the other end of the spectrum are those who are emotionally avoidant: They appear to be fairly unemotional, even when that response is surprising, and they might report a sense of being distant from their emotions or an inability to express them.

Some of us are not at the extremes of the emotional spectrum but still express our emotions in unskillful ways: "I was feeling utterly depressed about my possible work termination, and I yelled at the woman at the post office when she brought me the wrong stamps. I couldn't believe I was so rude." Such "acting out" of emotions can be harmful to ourselves and others. In observing my students over the years, I have seen a wide range of responses to emotions, from expressive to repressive, and we all fit somewhere along the spectrum.

The Mindful Approach to Emotions

The mindful approach to emotions is neither expressive nor repressive per se; the mindful approach is to recognize your emotions, feel them fully, and then let them go so that they don't control you or lead you to act in ways that are harmful to others. You can learn to relate to your emotions from this mindful perspective.

Using this perspective, you can think about emotions as "energy in motion." In other words, emotions are a kind of energy or force that is constantly in motion, moving through you. You have had millions of emotions throughout your life, but where are they now? They are no longer with you, are they? Emotions are a temporary set of experiences—physiological changes that we associate with thoughts and feelings and body states—passing through us, almost like weather patterns. Sometimes inside us it is stormy, sometimes mild and cloudy, sometimes sunny.

These emotional "weather" patterns change all the time, yet when we are in the midst of them, we think they are going to stick around forever. To approach them mindfully is to notice their transient nature. And with practice, you can learn to neither indulge nor cut off your emotions, but to be present with them with care and attention.

RAIN

To help you learn the basics of working mindfully with emotions, we offer an acronym, often taught in Buddhist insight meditation circles, that you can apply when working with emotions: RAIN, which stands for Recognition, Acceptance, Investigation, and Non-identification.

Recognition

Recognition is the first step to being mindful in the midst of your emotions. Have you ever been so caught up in your feelings that you felt overwhelmed or unable to see or think clearly? Maybe several emotions were exploding inside you at once. With recognition (R), you gently recognize and label your emotion, such as "fearful," "angry," or "sad." We learned in the science section that labeling a feeling is a means of regulating it; just labeling an emotion can lead to prefrontal cortical calming of the emotional centers. In labeling your emotions, you begin the process of cognitive appraisal, which helps you calm down.

In the midst of an emotion, you may find that by identifying and labeling it you are not so overwhelmed by it. You don't have to be precise with the wording of the label; for instance, you don't need to struggle to figure out whether the label is "sad," "depressed," "blue," or "unhappy." A close approximation is enough: "Sad" should do the trick. However, if you are sad and you label that emotion "potato," labeling is not going to be as effective.

Acceptance

Acceptance is an interesting aspect of this process. Mindfulness, in general, brings to your experience a kind and accepting attention. From the perspective of mindfulness, *whatever you are experiencing is okay.* To be clear, the feeling itself is natural, but what you do with the emotion is another story. As a human being, you have had every possible emotion run through you—fear, terror, joy, grief, envy, shame . . . the list is endless. Everyone has had murderous rage inside them at some point. Yes, even murderous rage. From the perspective of mindfulness, however, all emotions are okay, because they are true, real, what is happening in the moment, and part of the human experience. Of course accepting that your emotions are okay doesn't mean it is okay to act on every one of them, but you can become mindful and accept that they are passing through you. Steven, a thirty-seven-year-old salesman, reported:

> I was meditating the other day, and I felt a huge surge of anger. I remembered what you said, that all emotions were okay, and I thought, *Can I accept this emotion?* and well, I said, *Sure, why not, it's just an emotion.* Suddenly I felt this enormous sense of relief. That anger is real, it's part of me, it's natural. I think in my entire life I have never once acknowledged and been okay with my anger.

Mindfulness encourages you to be present, without shame or blame or fear, to what is truly happening. Being present this way allows you to be with your emotions with compassion, almost the way you would be present with a child's emotions. Let's say a child falls down and hurts himself and begins to cry. Most of us would not judge the child, blame him, and reprimand him for crying. Instead, we would hold him, comfort him, and say, "Yes, I understand you are sad, and I'm here for you." In a sense, that is what you are learning to do with yourself and your emotions.

Although the idea of accepting your emotions is fine and good, in practice you may find it very hard to accept some of them. You may fear, judge, be embarrassed by, or feel an aversion to particular emotions. *Yuck, I don't want to feel this emotion* is a very common response. If that is the case, as you practice mindfulness with emotions, bring your attention to your reaction to the emotion, which has become an emotion itself.

For example, if you are mad at your child, but ashamed of yourself for being mad, the emotion to work with is actually the shame, since, as the most dominant emotion, it's preventing you from clearly seeing and accepting the anger. You can label and try to accept the shame, then move on to the next step in the RAIN process. If you cannot accept the emotion, then you are simply aware of not being able to accept the emotion, which is the truth of the moment. Learning to be mindful of emotions can be a slow process, so please don't be discouraged (another emotion); just be patient and continue to explore the process.

Investigation

To investigate an emotion is to feel it in your body, discovering how it manifests itself. As discussed in the science section, a physiological response is associated with the experience of an emotional feeling. One of the best ways of being present with an emotion is to attend to these physical sensations. When you are caught in a difficult emotion, you may get lost in the story about it, which feeds the emotion and intensifies it. For example, if you are worried about finances and keep thinking about the rapidly decreasing sum in your 401(k), you are likely to continue to feel more worried. (Some people have a mistaken internal belief that worrying about something will prevent it from happening. One friend jokingly calls it "prophylactic worry.")

Worrying about the future doesn't necessarily prevent an event from occurring, but it will certainly make you more worked up about it. Similarly, thinking about any emotion and the story behind the emotion tends not to lead to relief from the emotion. The key, then, is not to keep dwelling on the story behind the emotion, but to feel the corresponding sensation of the emotion in your body. Tuning in to the bodily sensation can calm the emotion and show you that it is not as difficult as you may have thought: It is just a set of complex bodily sensations and the thoughts surrounding them.

What do you notice in the midst of an emotion? Check out your stomach, where you might notice a tightness, clenching, heaviness, or burning. Or your chest: Do you feel vibration, movement, or tightness? Is your throat clenched or stopped up? Perhaps there is heat in your face, or tightness in your jaw.

When you feel an emotion, investigate this emotion's manifestation as sensation in your body, as Janice, a fifty-nine-year-old internist, did:

> I had been walking around for a couple of days in dread of a yearly visit from my brother, who was flying in from New York. He has a history of being inattentive to my time and scheduling and has taken me for granted. This year he was diagnosed with cancer, for which he received timely and successful non-invasive surgery. It was a wake-up call for him, and he has been better about staying in touch. I was expecting him to call me, but by the fourth day of his arrival to stay with other relatives, he still had not contacted me; I realized that he had not changed. I was getting very annoyed and dismayed at his not contacting me and noticed how this was affecting my state of mind and emotion. I was aware of a tight feeling in my chest—around the heart—and noticed how this tapped into the "out of the loop/lonely" feeling I occasionally feel with my siblings. The feeling was floating in me like a small oily surface on a pool of water. My belly was tight, my chest felt contracted. But I remained a witness to its power and allowed it to just be, without letting it "get me down." I then decided to give him a call, at which he sounded very pleased to hear from me, and we had a good honest talk—minus any attachment. Being aware of the effects of even slightly annoying emotions and allowing them to be without diving into a pool of intense interpretation has been very helpful.

Not everyone can feel emotions inside their bodies. If you are having trouble connecting with any bodily sensations, just relax, take a few breaths, and try to notice the general sense of the emotion, like, *I'm feeling fear.* You might ask yourself, *Where do I think I feel the emotion?* Over time, as you practice conscious embodiment and self-awareness, your ability to feel emotions in your body will become more pronounced and accessible.

Sometimes people make the mistake of thinking that "investigation" means to think about the emotion. They want to know why they are having the emotion, where it is rooted in their past, and so on. This is a helpful way to explore emotions, and very typical of some therapeutic approaches, but different from the mindful approach. To be mindful of an emotion, simply investigate in your body; notice sensations in your body, and explore the bodily response with curiosity. It is possible that as you do this some insight will arise as to its origins. You may have a sudden flood of memory, or some understanding may come. The point of being mindful of emotions, however, is not to have a particular experience—you are not trying to make the emotion go away or to have a deep insight into your childhood—but to become aware of emotions the best you can, particularly to see how they manifest through your body in the present moment. In this way, you can find yourself at the next step.

Non-Identification

If you have gone through the first three steps, it is likely that some non-identification (also known as "disidentification," "de-centering," and "de-linking") will have occurred for you. Non-identification means not taking your emotions so personally, having some space around them. Noticing the truth of emotions—that they come and go and that "this too shall pass"—is a way of disidentifying from them, or developing what was discussed in the science section as "meta-cognitive awareness." With non-identification, you have come to the point with your emotions where they have stopped being *your* emotions that are causing you so much suffering and become instead *the* emotions—that is, something that is passing through you ("energy in motion").

Non-identification is a difficult concept to understand. Perhaps you have had a moment in life when you were in the midst of some challenging emotion (fear, grief, anger) and a part of you, even if only a very teeny tiny part, knew that in spite of the emotion, deep down you were okay. In other words, you were disidentified. Non-identification does not turn you into a zombie without emotions. It does not divorce you from your negative emotions so that you are happy all the time. It just gives you a little space and some wisdom about the emotions; it helps you to not take them so personally and to see their changing nature. You become able to reflect in the midst of an emotion, as Janice did, that you are not the emotion. As you become more skillful with your emotions, you can affect others, as John, the twenty-seven-year-old father of a young son, saw:

> I was so inspired by learning how to be mindful of my emotions that I decided to teach it to my six-year-old. So when he said, "I'm angry," I taught him to say, "I have anger." We talked about how his emotions come and

go. It has been very interesting to watch him be less frightened by his own anger and to feel like it is a part of him rather than wholly him.

Non-identification is not always an easy thing to do. Sometimes your emotions may be so strong that you have no space from them whatsoever. This is quite normal, and it is likely to happen often as you learn to practice mindfulness with emotions. Sometimes you may find yourself only aware of your emotions after several hours or even days have passed, when you realize that you have spent the whole time stewing in anger or grief. But then your mindfulness kicks in and you say, *Oh, I've been really angry.*

As you practice with RAIN, you will get faster at identifying and investigating the emotions, so that it will not be many hours later that you recognize an emotion but much sooner; recognition will also happen more frequently and more easily. At times you will even be mindful right in the midst of an emotion and act in ways, because of your mindfulness, that you never would have expected. Melissa, a forty-six-year-old mother and therapist, told us:

Normally when my husband comes home from work, I immediately lay into him with a list of all the things he'll have to do that night. He's asked me to back off, to even e-mail a list to him so he has time to think it over. But I feel like it is out of my control, something kind of takes over me, and I just start telling him what to do. One day I decided to investigate what was going on with mindfulness. He came home from work, and I meditated for ten minutes before he walked in the door. As he came through the door I noticed myself gearing up to tell him what to do that night, but instead I connected to the sensations in my body. Boy, was I anxious. So I stopped, took a breath, and let myself feel the anxiety. He walked past me and asked why my eyes were closed, and I said, "I'm practicing mindfulness." He said, "Thank God for your meditation class," and we both started laughing. I saw I don't have to impulsively tell him what to do out of my own anxiety.

You may be wondering whether these practices will work even when you are suffering from a long-term chronic emotion. Can you use RAIN in the face of severe distress or suffering, such as the death of a loved one? Mindfulness of emotions is a tool among many tools that can be helpful for working with emotions. If you are facing grave emotional distress, please know that there are many other approaches as well that may help you, including therapy, journaling, medication, talking with friends and family, ritual, and spiritual counseling.

THE PRACTICE:
MINDFULNESS OF EMOTIONS

In your daily meditation practice, you may notice emotions coming and going. If so, simply become aware of them, using a label if it is helpful. If an emotion is strong and persistent, you can try this guided meditation.

Relax into your meditation posture. Feel your body present. Notice any pressure, movement, or places where your body makes contact with the floor or the chair. Find a place in your body that feels relaxed, pleasant, or neutral. Most people find this place in their hands, feet, or legs. Let your attention go to this pleasant area. Let it rest there. Notice the pleasant or relaxing sensations.

Now bring your attention to the emotion you are feeling. First *recognize* it. What is its label? Softly give it a mental label (fear, sadness, regret . . .). Now return your attention to the pleasant area of your body and let your mind relax there for a while, still maintaining your mindfulness.

Now is it possible for you to *accept* the emotion? Ask yourself, *Is this emotion okay for me to feel?* If the answer is yes, move on to the investigation. If the answer is no, then ask yourself: *How do I feel about this emotion?* You may be angry, scared, resistant, or judgmental. If so, then continue the practice with that emotion—the anger or fear or resistance or judgment that you are feeling toward the original emotion. Now, once again, spend some time (thirty seconds or so) with the pleasant area of your body. Make sure to breathe.

Moving on to the *investigation*, where do you feel the emotion in your body? Check your belly, chest, throat, and face. Keep breathing. After several seconds, return your attention to the pleasant part of the body. Stay connected to these sensations for at least half a minute. Now, once again, gently bring your attention to the place where you feel the emotion in your body. What are the sensations? What happens as you notice them? Do they increase, decrease, intensify, lessen? Do they change into some other sensation?

Notice these sensations in as kind a way as possible. If the experience of attending to your emotions gets too intense, return to your pleasant area. You can go back and forth as necessary.

Going to the last RAIN step, explore whether there has been any space or sense in this process of not being so caught in the emotion. Have you experienced some relief? Ask yourself, *Do I feel like it is* my *emotion or* the *emotion?* The answer may not be intuitively obvious. It may take some time before *non-identification* becomes possible.

When you have practiced this meditation for a little while, return for the last time to the pleasant part of your body and let your attention rest there. Allow the pleasant sensation to spread, if possible, throughout your body. Now try to bring some loving-kindness to yourself for whatever you're feeling right now. Hold yourself with kindness.

7

FEELING GOOD
AND FINDING HAPPINESS

Most folks are about as happy as they make up
their minds to be.

—ABRAHAM LINCOLN

A 2008 scientific study by the sociologists James Fowler and Nicholas Christakis showed that happiness can spread through social networks somewhat like a virus. We literally can "catch" happiness from friends and loved ones, although to varying degrees. For example, Fowler and Christakis showed that you can contract happiness about 25 percent of the time if a friend who lives within a mile of your home becomes happy, 34 percent of the time from a next-door neighbor, 14 percent of the time from a brother or sister living within a mile, and only 8 percent of the time from a live-in husband, wife, or partner.[1] The data show that happiness can spread, but the mechanism for how that happens is not yet known. Along with that question are a host of others that scientists are now asking, and chief among them is this one: What is happiness anyway?

Bliss, joy, and exuberance are words that describe states of extreme happiness, which is a feeling we all experience at times, triggered by events like the birth of a child, a marriage, an unexpected job offer, or a creative burst. Are these blissful states the same as happiness in day-to-day life? Why are some people happier than others? How can we increase happiness? As scientists turn their attention to these questions, using tools of brain imaging and genomics, they are asking also whether mindfulness meditation and loving-kindness practices increase happiness, and if so, how.

THE SCIENCE

Extreme exuberance may be induced by a variety of experiences, including drugs, psychiatric illness, brain injury, nature, and religion. Aldous Huxley described the effects of mescaline as one means of discovering a world of "visionary beauty."[2] The psychologist Kay Jamison, a sufferer from manic-depressive illness, described exuberance as an "important phase of acute mania" and a "pathological enthusiasm" with a "dangerous undertow."[3] Jill Bolte Taylor described the bliss she experienced when a brain hemorrhage rendered her left hemisphere nonfunctional as "my spirit was free to catch a wave in the river of blissful flow."[4] Niko Tinbergen and Narghanita Laski are ethologists (scientists who study animal behavior), and they suggest that being in nature is the most common experience of "transcendent ecstasy," evident in the words of George Copway, who said: "And wherever I see her [Nature], emotions of pleasure roll in my breast, and swell and burst like waves on the shores of the ocean."[5] William James described religious ecstasy in the experiences of both saints and laypersons. Here is a representative example:

> The ordinary sense of things around me faded. For the moment nothing but an ineffable joy and exultation remained. It is impossible fully to describe the experience. It was like the effect of some great orchestra when all the separate notes have melted into one swelling harmony that leaves the listener conscious of nothing save that his soul is being wafted upwards, and almost bursting with its own emotion.[6]

A shared feature of these various states of bliss is a sense of *self-transcendence*, a rising above the traditional day-to-day, self-centered view of the world. In ecstatic experiences, there is a shift from a view based on a self-centered "I" acting as an independent agent in the world to a view based on an intuitive sense of interdependency and "oneness" with the object of experience, whether that object is music, art, nature, another human being, or the universe at large. Teilhard de Chardin described the intuitive experience of being one with the universe as the "universal unity of being."[7] One way to think of this state of self-transcendence is to consider it one end of a continuum of how we relate to the universe at large, ranging from a self-centered, independent perspective at one extreme to a self-transcendent, interdependent perspective at the other.[8] Psychologists have used other terms to describe this range from self-centered to self-transcendent. As mentioned in Chapter 5, Mark Leary at Duke University calls the self-centered experiences "hyper-egoic" and the self-transcendent experiences "hypo-egoic,"[9] while Mihaly Csikszentmihalyi, a leading expert on creativity, calls the self-transcendent experiences "flow."[10] Self-transcendent experiences are often affiliated with feelings of bliss and joy, as well as creativity, freedom, and distortions of time.

The Emergence of "Positive Psychology"

Positive psychology is a relatively new field of psychology that centers on the investigation of "authentic happiness," a field of study that began in a garden. Martin Seligman, a psychologist well known for his work in depression, is considered the godfather of the field of positive psychology, which was born, as he describes it, when he was gardening with his five-year-old daughter Nikki. As she pulled weeds, threw them in the air, and danced, he became angry; wanting to get the job finished, he yelled at her. Nikki reminded him that if she could give up whining at age five (which she had done), then he could give up being a grouch. In that moment, he had an epiphany: He would turn his attention from the narrow focus of psychology on mental "illness" toward a broader focus that would include *enhancing* well-being through research on human strengths and virtues.[11] The landmark publication in this emerging field was a new manual of sorts, the *Handbook of Positive Psychology*, intended to complement the *Diagnostic and Statistical Manual*, the handbook for diagnosing psychiatric disorders.[12] The new classification manual of human strengths provided a foundation for more formal research on the components of happiness.

Models of Happiness

Psychologists suggest that happiness arises with a sense of fulfillment, with living a *meaningful* life. Tools that promote meaning will therefore promote happiness. Under this model, there are four key components of meaning: purpose (a connection to future events), values (ideas that enable you to decide whether actions are right or wrong), a sense of efficacy (a belief that you can make a difference), and self-worth (a belief that you are good and worthy). Happiness is increased by strengthening these components, while sadness and despair occur with their demise.[13] Positive psychology research includes the investigation of the tools that promote these four components, and research shows that happiness can be enhanced. For example, Seligman's group investigated five different happiness exercises and found that all improved happiness but that only two continued to have an effect after six months. These initial studies support the idea that tools can be developed to increase happiness through specific targeting of the four components of meaning.

In contrast to a meaning-based model of happiness, Robert Cloninger, a psychiatric geneticist at Washington University in St. Louis, argues that authentic happiness arises only with *coherence of personality*, which ultimately requires *intuitive awareness*. Under Cloninger's model, an individual with a coherent personality is someone who not only has a sense of meaning, purpose, values, and self-worth (the four components of the meaning-based model) but is also integrated in intuitive awareness. This model has a parallel in the ancient Greeks: Plato's concept of happiness held that a nonrational mode of knowing (intuition) leads to a fundamental understanding or insight into the nature of reality. Plato called this insight "the Good." In contrast, the meaning-based models of happiness, which do not require this intuitive awareness, are more in line with Aristotle's view of happiness as arising through virtuous action.[14]

Coherence of Personality

The coherence of personality model proposed by Cloninger evolved over several decades, expanding from an initial model of temperament to one including character development to one also including intuitive awareness leading to coherence.[15] *Temperament* is defined as our biological response patterns to the environment, including avoidance (how we respond to painful stimuli), approach (how we respond to novel stimuli), reward dependence (how we respond to varying degrees of reward), and persistence (our stick-to-it-ness). Specific brain circuitry is associated with temperament traits.[16] *Character* describes our subject-object relationships—how we relate to ourselves (self-directedness), how we relate to others (cooperativeness), and how we relate to the universe at large (self-transcendence).[17] Coherence arises when an individual, of any temperament, achieves heightened character development with the emergence of an intuitive understanding of our dependent nature (the awareness that we are inextricably intertwined and connected).

Research on thousands of individuals using a self-report measure of personality shows that overall happiness is strongly associated with being in the upper half of the population on all three character domains: self-directedness (S), cooperativeness (C), and self-transcendence (T) (see Figure 4).[18] (Uppercase letters S, C, and T reflect that a person scored in the upper half of the population distribution, while lower-case letters s, c, and t reflect that a person scored in the lower half of the population distribution on the specific scale.)

Mindfulness is associated with character traits: Individuals who score higher on mindfulness scales or subscales score higher on self-report measures of character.[19]

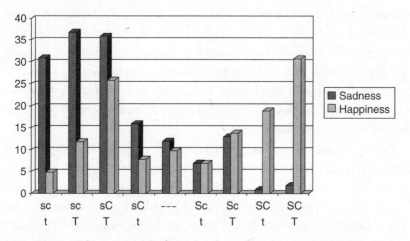

FIGURE 4 The percentages of people who are happy or sad according to their TCI character configurations (from Cloninger, C.R, Feeling Good: The Science of Well-being, COPYRIGHT NOTICE included in licensed material; Reproduced with permission of the Licensor through PLSclear.).

The Character Traits of Personality

Self-directedness refers to how we see ourselves (the self-self relationship) measured by items such as "my behavior is strongly guided by certain goals I have set for my life."[20] If you are highly self-directed, you feel responsible for your actions, purposeful, accepting, resourceful, and hopeful; in some ways self-directedness is associated with measures of how well you self-regulate—that is, how well you monitor and modify your actions, thoughts, and feelings to obtain goals or adapt to environments.[21] Low scores on this dimension are associated with poor self-esteem and risk for a variety of psychiatric illnesses. For example, adults who score in the lowest tenth percentile of the population on this scale (and on the cooperativeness scale) have a very high risk of having a personality disorder.[22]

Cooperativeness describes how you relate to others (self-other relationship) and is measured by items such as "I can usually accept people as they are even when they are very different from me."[23] Individuals who score in the upper range on cooperativeness have qualities of tolerance, forgiveness, empathy, helpfulness, and giving (charitable). The recently discovered mirror neurons—brain cells that are important in the development of imitation, empathy, and social behavior—are likely to play a role in this aspect of character. Mirror neurons provide a cellular mechanism for how you know what another person is feeling; they fire when you see another person experiencing or doing something, as if you yourself were experiencing it or doing it. If you see someone accidentally hit his or her hand with a hammer while hanging a picture on a wall, your brain's pain-sensing regions light up as if you had hit your own hand. This shared experience—an attunement to others—probably contributes to empathy and cooperation.

Self-transcendence (self-universe relationship) refers to something larger or beyond yourself and is the construct most closely tied to spirituality. Items reflecting this dimension are ones such as "Often I have unexpected flashes of insight or understanding while relaxing" and "Sometimes I have felt like I was part of something with no limits or boundaries in time and space."[24] Individuals who score high on this dimension are sensible, idealistic, transpersonal, faithful, and spiritual. Elevated self-transcendence appears to be an important protective factor in the face of severe illness, grief, becoming very elderly, and the dying process.[25]

Character traits work in concert with one another. For example, individuals who score in the high range on self-transcendence but in the low range on self-directedness are not necessarily happy (see Figure 4); in fact, they are at increased risk for psychiatric illnesses such as mania, schizophrenia, and other psychotic illnesses. Self-transcendence alone may correspond to momentary states of exuberance, but an individual's failure to function well in society, as reflected by low scores on self-directedness and cooperativeness, is associated with depression and a poor quality of life. Cloninger suggests that coherence of personality (and ultimate happiness) may be measured by the positive development of all three aspects of character: self-directedness, cooperativeness, and self-transcendence.[26]

Happiness and Intuition

Although science has yet to uncover the ultimate cause of happiness, the question of whether or not intuitive awareness is essential poses a challenge to science. Does authentic happiness *require* an intuitive process? The answer may be beyond the scope of science. If ultimate happiness requires intuition, a nonrational mode of knowing, is it feasible for science, a rational mode of knowing, to ever uncover it?

"Intuition" has often been a bit of a bad word in science, since scientific knowledge is based on reason; intuition, by definition, is a nonrational means of knowing. Yet throughout history intuition has spurred discoveries that catapulted science forward.[27] We are all familiar with "Aha!" moments—those times when ideas or answers do not follow the rational mode of uncovering knowledge but pop out of the blue. Archimedes had his "Aha!" moment in discovering buoyancy while floating calmly in a bathtub. Richard Feynmann, the Nobel Prize–winning physicist, made his discoveries in quantum thermodynamics by watching a dinner plate spin and wobble on the table in front of him at a routine cafeteria lunch. Feynmann reportedly said, "I continued to play with it in this relaxed fashion and it was like letting a cork out of a bottle. Everything just poured out and in very short order I had worked out the things for which I later won the Nobel Prize."[28] Creative bursts like this are key to moving humanity forward. They have been given many names—besides "intuition," they are also called "insight" or "creativity"—and are recognized by scientists and laypersons alike as a key to discovery—and perhaps to authentic happiness. Jonas Salk, discoverer of the polio vaccine, once said, "Intuition tells the thinking mind where to look." He described his own intuitive (and transcendent) experience that shaped his scientific research:

Very early in life I would imagine myself in the position of the object in which I was interested. Later when I became a scientist, I would picture myself as a virus, or cancer cell, for example, and try to sense what it would be like to be either. I would also imagine myself as the immune system, and I would try to reconstruct what I would do as an immune system engaged in combating a virus or cancer cell. . . . [Then] I would design laboratory experiments accordingly.[29]

The Study of Intuition

Scientists have recently turned their attention to intuition, in part because intuition may be superior to the use of reason when we need to make a decision in the face of excessive information.[30] Studying intuition or insight in the lab is challenging because it does not unfold in a linear way but rather "out of the blue." The anagram task is one way, however, in which scientists have begun to study intuition. Anagrams are scrambled letters that make a word, such as:

A D S N I N D L Y E*

In solving an anagram, people use two approaches—a linear trial-and-error process of sorting letters in every possible combination until a solution is found, or a nonlinear approach in which the full "image of the word" pops into the mind. The insight method uses much greater activity of the right hemisphere (anterior superior temporal gyrus) coupled with a sudden high-frequency gamma wave band of EEG activity (see the more detailed description of EEG later in this chapter).[31] As we uncover the biological clues to insight, we may further our understanding of the conditions that foster it and the benefits it affords the individual and society.

Some of the great rational minds recognized the importance of intuition. Albert Einstein wrote, "The intuitive mind is a sacred gift, the rational mind a faithful servant; we have created a society that honors the servant and has forgotten the gift."[32] Thomas Paine, the proponent of reason whose writings helped shape the founding documents of the United States, wrote:

---

*The solution is DISNEYLAND.

There are two distinct classes of what are called thoughts—those that we produce in ourselves by reflection and the act of thinking, and those that bolt into the mind of their own accord. I have always made it a rule to treat these voluntary visitors with civility. . . . It is from them I have acquired almost all the knowledge that I have.[33]

Two Sides of the Same Coin

When you meditate or practice mindfulness, you have an opportunity to increase your intuitive awareness, which may be crucial for authentic happiness. One way to think about reason and intuition and their integration is to consider them as two sides of a coin. To keep a coin rolling, you cannot place too much emphasis on either heads or tails; if you do, the coin topples over and comes to a stop. A perfect balance is having both intuition and reason guide you through life.

Many times in our lives we tip too far one way or the other and get stuck, like the coin on its side. With practice you can integrate both intuition and reason into your daily life, recognize when you have let the coin fall to one side, and learn how to pick it up and start rolling again.

Mindfulness and Happiness

Although a complete understanding of causes of happiness is still elusive to science, there is overwhelming scientific evidence that practicing mindfulness can enhance it. We saw in the previous chapter that mindfulness can help individuals shift from depressed (low levels of happiness) to less depressed states, as well as help prevent relapses of depression. At the other end of the spectrum, mindfulness appears to enhance a steady-state of happiness, defined as a state of well-being, a steady-state of contentment, or what can be called equanimity (balance or even-mindedness) or peace of mind.

The positive relationship between well-being and mindfulness, both at the trait level (among people without any formal training) and as a state change (with formal training), is perhaps one of the most consistent findings in mindfulness research to date. For example, in a study of self-reported mindfulness and a variety of measures of well-being in college and community samples in the northeastern United States, there was a strong positive relationship between scoring high on mindfulness and feeling good, as measured by positive affect and life satisfaction.[34] Studies with samples drawn from high schools, colleges, medical schools, and other communities also show that mindfulness instruction increases well-being and mood.[35] A biological mechanism associated with such change is not yet completely understood, but brain imaging studies support the idea that increased brain coherence may be part of that mechanism.

A Brain in Harmony

Brain coherence, which can also be called brain synchrony, is the synchronized electrical firing of cells across brain regions. Shared electrical firing of cells—a measure of cell communication—occurs not only in adjacent regions of the brain but across larger distances as well. In fact, it is synchronized cell firing that enables specific EEG patterns to be realized at all. An EEG pattern is a specific electrical charge arising in the brain that can be measured by electrical signals on the surface of the head. When a brain cell fires, an electrical charge is associated with it, and electrodes placed on the surface of the head can detect it. The electrical charge depends on the number of cells recruited to fire together, their location, and what we are doing, thinking, or feeling at the time.

Several known EEG patterns correspond to specific brain states. In general, the EEG pattern called "beta" reflects a highly active brain state—as when you are doing a crossword puzzle or math problem. The "alpha" pattern reflects an alert brain state at rest and not doing anything specific; the "theta" state reflects a calm, inactive brain state; "delta" is a sleeplike state; and "gamma" is a state of intense hyperactivity. If cells within a particular pattern recruit other cells to fire in that same pattern and to synchronize in phase, we say that there is greater coherence across the brain.

Since the 1960s, when the hippie movement made meditation a household word, EEG studies have been under way to see how the brain changes with meditation. A survey of EEG studies of meditation suggests that it does influence brain electrical patterns, specifically by increasing certain relaxed state patterns (theta, alpha) and hyperstates of activity (gamma) and by increasing coherence.[36]

Richard Davidson's group at the University of Wisconsin has conducted perhaps the largest number of studies on meditation and brain coherence in the last decade. Antoine Lutz in Davidson's group has reported increased gamma wave coherence during meditation in longtime meditators. (Remember that gamma waves are associated with insight in problem-solving studies.)[37] Another study from Davidson's group, led by Helen Slagter, shows that increased theta wave coherence arises with meditation training and with improved attention.[38] Coherence is thought to play an important role in engaging the brain to work effectively, somewhat in the manner of orchestra instruments coming together to play a symphony. Coherence pulls together the various brain networks, as though they were the sections of an orchestra, to coordinate cognitive and affective functions. The bottom line is that meditation seems to create greater harmony in the brain: Cells are more in sync with one another and are firing together, as if they recognize one another as part of a whole.

Stephen Strogatz, a physicist at Cornell, has been studying synchronicity in nature for many years.[39] Nature tends to move toward synchrony. Fireflies tend to light up together, people running around a track tend to run together, and women living together tend to menstruate together; clocks even tend to align their ticking when housed together. Brain cells show this tendency too, and meditation seems to heighten it. Like musicians tuning up together to play a symphony, our brains seem to attune as we attune to ourselves, to others, and to the universe at large.

To attune is to bring into harmony or to make aware. Attunement can be used to describe our relationships—to self or others or the universe at large (corresponding to the character scales for self-directedness, cooperativeness, and self-transcendence). Daniel Siegel, a child psychiatrist, expert in interpersonal neurobiology, and codirector of our center, uses attunement to describe how a person focuses attention on the internal world of another, as a parent does with a child; this kind of attention corresponds to a sense of being "felt" by the other and is a key to healthy *inter*personal relationships. The same applies to attunement with yourself in the *intra*personal relationship of self to self (purportedly measured by the scale of self-directedness). Siegel argues that mindfulness does for oneself what secure attachment (such as mother to child) does interpersonally.[40] And we suggest here that mindfulness enhances attunement not only to your own self and to others but to the whole universe (and your place in it). As you bring into harmony the various ways in which you relate to yourself, to others, and to the universe, you may experience a corresponding increase in coherence of personality and brain state. Perhaps well-being is the feeling associated with the physiological and subjective states of such increasing synchrony.

Although we have yet to understand how brain synchrony relates to emotion per se, data on emotion and brain coherence show that they are related. Andrew Leuchter, a psychiatrist at UCLA, has demonstrated a relationship between depression and *decreased* coherence, particularly in posterior brain regions.[41] Whether depression causes the decreased coherence or decreased coherence causes the depression was addressed by a study of the offspring of depressed parents. In a study of forty-one teen girls who were the daughters of depressed mothers but who were not themselves depressed, the researchers found reduced brain coherence in the temporal lobe regions.[42] This finding suggests that reduced coherence may be inherited to some extent, creating a risk for depression. It appears that as the brain shifts from less to more coherent, we may shift from sad to happy.

Synchronized Individual Transformations

We speculate that people who meditate together not only find their individual brains becoming more coherent but also share that coherence with others, through synchronizing. If happiness spreads, perhaps mindfulness does too. If increased brain coherence synchronizes among members in a group mindfulness practice, perhaps synchronized individual transformations (SITs) (an acronym apropos to the activity) take place. As far as we know, there are no scientific studies testing such a hypothesis that brain coherence increases more rapidly in group meditation than in isolation, but it seems worthy of further investigation. Perhaps the more mindful you are, the more mindful your friends are too, as mindfulness, like happiness, may spread through social networks.

Self-Compassion and Happiness

Mindfulness may be one route to enhancing well-being, but self-compassion appears to be another. Mark Leary at Duke University suggests that self-compassion has three components: kindness, mindfulness, and "awareness that you are part of the human condition." Studies of self-compassion training among college students suggest that increasing self-compassion increases happiness.[43] Unlike self-esteem, which is important in happiness but if too elevated can lead to narcissistic behavior, self-compassion in its extremes appears only to enhance a person's health and well-being; there is no downside to it. We can boost self-compassion through practice, and loving-kindness meditations are one way to do that (see the art section). A study conducted at Stanford University found that teaching loving-kindness to college students using guided imagery increased kindness among them compared to students given a neutral imagery instruction.[44] In just a short seven-minute session, students given the loving-kindness exercise rated strangers in a more positive light (as brilliant, as loyal) and as warmer and more similar to themselves than did students given the neutral task.

What happens to the brain during loving-kindness exercises? The study by Antoine Lutz in Wisconsin found that the brain regions involved in feeling, planning, positive emotions, and maternal and romantic love were activated during such exercises much more among long-term meditators than among nonmeditators.[45] Furthermore, the more meditation practice the person had done, the bigger the effect. These data and that of others suggest that kindness is a flexible skill that can be taught.

Body to Mind, Mind to Body

When you meditate on kindness, your body may change accordingly; conversely, your body can change to create feelings of kindness. We saw previously that if you feel warm, you act warmly toward others (with kindness and compassion), in contrast to when you feel cold.[46] Remember the experiment that showed just holding a hot cup or a cold cup of liquid changed whether or not students viewed strangers as kind? There are other examples of the body leading the mind, much of it coming from studies of facial expressions on feelings and how people see the world. Scientists tricked college students into smiling to see what effect the physical expression of smiling has on how an individual feels (happy, sad, neutral). They tricked the students into smiling by telling them that by participating they were helping to figure out methods for assisting disabled populations; to this end, the researchers asked the students to hold a pencil between their teeth in various configurations. The physical appearance of smiling—lips curled upward and teeth showing—was compared with no-smile facial configurations while the students watched video clips that evoked positive or negative feelings. During pleasant scenes, such as humorous cartoons, the students who were "smiling" reported more pleasant experiences (measured by their own report and by body changes in arousal) than students without a "smile."[47] This study and others like it support the idea that a simple facial expression—a smile—can lead us to experience the world in a happier way.

THE ART

This story, from an anonymous source, sums up how our minds work:

> One evening a Native American elder told his grandson about a battle that goes on inside people. He said, "My son, the battle is between two 'wolves' inside us all. One is anger, envy, jealousy, sorrow, regret, greed, arrogance, self-pity, guilt, resentment, inferiority, lies, false pride, and superiority. The other is joy, peace, love, hope, serenity, humility, kindness, benevolence, empathy, generosity, truth, and compassion." The grandson thought about it for a minute and then asked his grandfather, "Which wolf wins?" The elder simply replied, "The one you feed."

This story reminds us that the development of positive emotion is rooted in an underlying principle borne out by the science of neuroplasticity (discussed in Chapter 1): What you practice you will cultivate. Simply, if you practice being mean and nasty, you will get meaner and nastier; if you practice being kind and caring, you will get kinder and more caring. It is an obvious equation, but people tend to overlook the sheer simplicity of it and don't consider the ramifications of their behaviors, habits, and actions, especially when they are in the midst of them.

Additionally, people tend to limit their belief in themselves. They assume that if they were born a certain way, they will always be that way. So when they attempt to be more compassionate or more altruistic, they may dismiss their own efforts, thinking, *Well, there is Mother Teresa, and then there is me.* This is unhelpful thinking. If you are motivated to develop compassion and kindness toward yourself or toward others, you can do that; all you need to do is put effort in that direction. This effort may not be easy, but you can in fact change your brain and your behavior. (We have seen that you can even change your gene expression!) This section focuses on practical tools you can use to cultivate positive emotions, specifically equanimity and loving-kindness.

Mindfulness with Positive Emotions

In the previous chapter, we discussed how to work mindfully with difficult emotions. People often wonder, do the same principles work with positive emotions? What about joy, excitement, connection, transcendence, pleasure, compassion, and ease? Can we be mindful of them too? Does it make sense to apply RAIN—Recognize, Accept, Investigate, Non-identification (described in Chapter 6)—to positive emotions? Do we want to disidentify from them too?

For some people, negative emotions feel more familiar than positive ones. Many of us feel comfortable when our inner and outer lives are chaotic. Depression or anxiety may feel like the norm, and it can be hard to imagine living any other way. If this is your experience, then your task is to let yourself feel and cultivate positive emotions. And when you do experience positive emotions, make sure you practice the RAI portion of RAIN. When you recognize, accept, and investigate, you will feel positive states more deeply.

Perhaps, like many of us, you tend to be like Teflon with positive emotions—they slip by you and don't stick to you. When you tap into a moment of joy or peace or ease or calm, whether it comes from meditation practice or arises spontaneously in life, you can mindfully attend to this emotion and let it be present. You can begin to familiarize yourself with how this emotion feels in your body and how it works in your mind. Positive feelings might be subtle at first, not easily recognizable and unfamiliar to you, but over time, with practice, they will become more and more who you are. Further, as you will see in this chapter, you can deliberately increase and cultivate them.

On the other hand, perhaps you have a tendency to get caught up in your positive emotions—to "live for the highs" and get depressed or feel lost when they disappear. If this sounds like you, it may be useful to practice the N in RAIN—to bring the aspect of non-identification to the process of working mindfully with positive emotions. Can you see that positive emotions, like difficult emotions, are also transitory? They are beautiful and feel wonderful in the moment, but they too will pass. If this is your situation, learning to disidentify can be helpful. William Blake sums it up nicely:

> *He who binds to himself a Joy*
> *Doth the wingèd life destroy;*
> *But he who kisses the Joy as it flies*
> *Lives in Eternity's sunrise.*

Equanimity

As we saw in the science section, the most consistent finding in mindfulness research is that mindfulness is related to reported feelings of well-being and ease. We might ask what this is like experientially and how more and more well-being can be cultivated.

"Equanimity" is a word not frequently heard in everyday speech. It means even-mindedness or balance; experientially, equanimity feels like what we term "well-being." *Merriam-Webster* defines it as "evenness of mind especially under stress."

When your mind is relaxed and at ease and you feel impartial and balanced, then you are experiencing equanimity. We have all had the experience of being in the midst of a difficult situation that would ordinarily cause us a lot of pain and yet, in spite of the conditions, deep down we somehow feel okay about the situation. This is a feeling of equanimity. Many people report, for example, that they have occasionally received bad news with surprising calm and centeredness. With equanimity, rather than being tossed and turned by the ups and downs of life, your mind feels balanced and even and you are not overreactive—neither suffering nor bliss overwhelms you. Equanimity is a very pleasant state of mind characterized by a sense of "okayness" and well-being.

Equanimity is not a state of disassociation or dispassion but in fact a very connected state of mind. It is a misconception that equanimity places you above worldly concerns or makes you apathetic; neither is the case. With equanimity, you are very engaged in life and not the least bit apathetic. You care passionately about a situation, yet your happiness and well-being are not tied to the outcome of the situation. Somewhere deep inside you recognize that you have preferences, but that your happiness does not depend on fulfilling them. So you stand up for yourself and what you believe in, but you are willing to let go of the results of your actions.

Equanimity and well-being can be cultivated in a variety of ways. Some people have a natural equanimity and tend to react to life's events with balance and even-mindedness. Others can be a bit more (or a lot more) overreactive. Yet, with gentle reminders, anyone can learn to have more balance. You can remind yourself that a difficult situation is only temporary. Or that getting overly upset about a situation will not change its outcome. You can ask yourself whether a difficult situation you are facing will last forever. These cognitive approaches can strengthen your equanimity.

Additionally, mindfulness meditation can be a training ground for equanimity. As you sit in meditation, mindful of whatever is arising, you may experience physical pain, emotional difficulties, surprising bliss, loud disturbing noises from the outside, or anything else. Yet your task is to stay mindful, curious, and accepting of whatever comes up. For example, you don't jump up and yell at the person making loud noises, but instead notice your reactivity: *Wow, I'm really annoyed.* With mindfulness, you attend to the sounds, noticing them coming and going, and recognize that they are merely sounds. You can also allow annoyance to be present exactly as it is, accepting of the fact of the moment (that you are annoyed). In this practice, equanimity is being developed. Over time, it grows and strengthens through the simple acts of repetition and practice.

Finally, equanimity can be developed through deliberate cultivation practices. To cultivate equanimity, you can repeat a series of phrases that bring to attention the feeling and attitude of equanimity: "Things are as they are." "May I accept things just as they are." By repeating these phrases, directing them toward particular situations, and noticing their impact over time, you can cultivate equanimity.

Loving-Kindness

In the science section, we mentioned "loving-kindness" as an important quality of mind connected to happiness that can be cultivated through practice, and the remainder of this chapter focuses on it. Loving-kindness is "the quality of tenderness and love and goodwill that naturally awakens in us in response to seeing goodness."[48] It is a genuine wish for happiness directed at ourselves or another. People often mistake loving-kindness for some kind of saccharine or fake-nice feeling. True loving-kindness could not be further from fake sentimentality. Loving-kindness is authentic and in no way overly sweet.

The attitude you cultivate in mindfulness practice—one of acceptance and openness—feels similar to loving-kindness. In mindful acceptance, a quality of kindness is present; you are kind to yourself and to your experience of the moment. And loving-kindness can also be cultivated as a separate practice. It is an excellent complement to mindfulness.

If you have awareness but are disconnected from your heart, your wisdom is skewed—somewhat dry and uncompassionate. Yet being overly loving, with no wisdom behind it, can lead to burnout, being overwhelmed, and an unrealistic view of the world. Thus, the two practices make perfect companions.

Unworthiness and Self-Judgment

One of the most disturbing aspects of contemporary U.S. culture is the degree to which self-hatred runs rampant. Nearly everyone I encounter expresses some amount of personal dissatisfaction and harbors a ruthless critic within who compares them to others and judges everyone they meet. I even once read an interview with Meryl Streep in which she confessed to believing she couldn't act![49] Unfortunately, most people have been conditioned by cultural norms, family, media, and a host of other influences to feel inadequate and unworthy.

Keep in mind that sometimes your thoughts tell you important and useful information about yourself. For instance, you might think, *Hmmm, I really should get out and exercise.* That kind of voice is not the problem. Usually, however, there are other, negative voices attaching a huge amount of judgment to such thoughts—*I'm lazy, I'm ugly, I'm bad*, and so on. Learning to be less susceptible to these negative voices and cultivating loving-kindness for yourself does not mean ignoring the wisdom that comes from seeing yourself clearly.

The opposite of self-criticism is self-compassion. As we saw in the science section, self-compassion combines mindfulness, loving-kindness, and a sense of shared humanity. Cultivating loving-kindness provides an antidote to these voices of self-criticism. Your mindfulness practice, together with the loving-kindness you cultivate, can help to create more self-compassion. These practices are a healing balm for the contemporary epidemic of self-hatred. In my view, loving-kindness has the capacity to change the very ground of who you are—from doubtful and self-hating to kind and accepting of yourself.

A Natural Quality of the Heart

Loving-kindness is truly not that hard to experience. Contrary to what you might think, it is not a mystical quality reserved for sages and saints. Loving-kindness spontaneously arises in many of us quite frequently throughout our lives.

Right now, bring to mind someone you love—someone with whom you don't have a very complicated relationship. (Your ex-partner is not the best choice for this exercise.) If you cannot think of someone, think of your favorite pet—a dog, cat, or other animal. Babies also work well for this exercise. As you imagine, sense, or feel this being in front of you, check into your body and notice what you are feeling. When I offer this exercise in our MAPs classes, people tend to report a warm feeling in their chests, a smile on their lips, some relaxation, and perhaps an expansive quality in the body. What are you feeling?

The feeling that arises doing this exercise is exactly what I have been referring to as loving-kindness: the natural wish for another to be happy. The feeling may be accompanied by thoughts and a set of bodily sensations. But when you feel it, you recognize it. Further, you can cultivate, deepen, and expand this lovely quality that arises in your mind.

So first learn to acknowledge the goodness that is already present. Second, learn to deliberately cultivate it more and more, so that it can increase within your heart and mind. Third, let it become who you are (even if that's still down the road a bit).

Stage One: Recognizing Loving-Kindness

Once you become conscious of loving-kindness, you can recognize when it is present in your life, which may be more frequently than you would expect. I have noticed how often people tend to not notice their generous or kind feelings. For instance, when you walk down the street and encounter a homeless person, the wave of compassion that arises almost automatically in you may feel like it is no big deal, and you may even begin to criticize yourself for not doing more to help the homeless, rather than seeing the value in the empathy itself. I believe it is important to take a moment to acknowledge when we have kind thoughts, say kind words, or engage in kind actions. As the elder told his grandson, what we cultivate will grow. So it is valuable to see that you already have feelings of loving-kindness and to appreciate yourself for your innate capacity to love and experience compassion. The more you recognize this capacity, the more it will grow and eventually become a state of mind to which you return.

Those who tend toward depression or self-criticism are especially likely to ignore or miss their own kind, loving, and generous moments. The more you are able to acknowledge their daily occurrence, the more evidence you accumulate that your innate loving-kindness is the antidote to the part of you that feels sad, hopeless, or inadequate. Perhaps for a day, just count the number of times you feel compassion, empathy, love, or kindness for another being, whether that being is a plant, an animal, a human, or yourself, regardless of whether or not you act on such feelings. Cheri, a forty-one-year-old mother, tried this exercise:

> I've been struggling with depression for about three years since the loss of my husband. Sometimes it feels as though I'm walking around in a black cloud, like I'm always sad, every moment. I was asked to notice if this were really the case. Were there actually moments of pleasure or well-being in my life somehow sprinkled throughout the day and missed by me? I began to observe. It took a lot of effort, but soon I saw that the story about myself that I never experienced joy was wrong; the truth was, sometimes I did but I usually ignored it. Those moments didn't fit with my story that "I'm depressed." Last week I was at the park with my son, and the sun was setting, and I felt a kind of peace and love for my son, and then instead of denying my experience, I said, "Look, see, you do have joy." The whole thing made me smile.*

---

*Please keep in mind that after a loss you may not believe that it is appropriate for you to be happy. It is important to know that even in the midst of pain or sorrow it is still possible and okay to be happy. These feelings are not wrong.

Stage Two: Cultivating Loving-Kindness

The end of the chapter offers a guided meditation on loving-kindness, but first we will explain the principles. The Buddhist tradition has developed a wonderful practice for cultivating states of kindness and compassion, although we can see similar practices in many other traditions as well, such as Christian, Jewish, Islamic, and Native American prayer and rituals, to mention a few. These practices may come down to us from ancient traditions, but in truth, they are common sense, based on the notion that what you cultivate you will become—as we saw in the story of the two wolves.

We do this practice by bringing people to mind and then imagining that we are sending them kindness. Usually we use words to invoke the feeling of kindness. You can say phrases that invite loving or kind feelings toward the people you have in mind. Indeed, certain words—what we call "well-wishes"—are often used in loving-kindness meditations across Buddhist and other traditions:

> *May you be safe and protected from danger*
> *May you be happy and peaceful*
> *May you be healthy and strong*
> *May you have ease and well-being*
> *May you be free of stress and anxiety*
> *May you accept yourself just as you are*
> *May you be full of joy*
> *May you be well*

These words may or may not work for you. The point is to find phrases that you connect with and that elicit for you these feelings of loving-kindness. You can also try using these well-wishes and also making up your own that feel meaningful and relevant in the moment.

If you have a visual mind—that is, if you tend to think in images—using images may be a very helpful way to develop loving-kindness. When you imagine a person, see what kind of images naturally arise as you think of sending them loving-kindness. Some people have reported seeing light, colors, or images of holding the person or being held. They see themselves or another as a young child. You can be as creative as you wish as you discover how to generate and sustain these warm wishes.

Sometimes it is neither words nor images that come to you, but simply a sense of holding the person in your heart with loving-kindness. This feeling is harder to describe, but when it is there, you know it. People often describe the sensation as their heart feeling open or expansive. In all of these methods for generating loving-kindness, the most important point is to be creative and connected to yourself to evaluate how your attempts are working.

Loving-Kindness for Yourself

Especially as an antidote for self-criticism, some people practice sending loving-kindness to themselves. To do so, you might imagine loving-kindness suffusing your whole body, or imagine yourself sitting in front of you. If sending loving-kindness to yourself feels too hard to do (and for many people it is), imagine yourself at a different time in your life, such as when you were a young child.

This practice is not easy. Give yourself plenty of space and gentleness as you approach it, since sending loving-kindness to yourself can feel threatening, difficult, sad, frustrating, boring, or scary. You may not feel anything at all at first (see next section). My experience has been that with steady loving-kindness practice, we can actually change deep and challenging patterns. You may feel the need to do this practice over many months, until you begin to create a new way of being, one in which you no longer think of yourself as unworthy but hold yourself in a loving, compassionate, accepting embrace.

What If I'm Not Feeling It?

Sometimes when you try this practice you immediately feel connected to the feeling of loving-kindness. It may not last, or it may come and go, but you have a sense that loving-kindness is being developed and is present for you.

At other times, however, not only may it be difficult to feel loving-kindness, but you may even feel something altogether different from what you intended, such as sadness, numbness, regret, or even anger.

If this happens as you practice loving-kindness meditation, do not be alarmed. This response is actually a normal and expected part of the practice. Not feeling loving-kindness actually means that the practice is working! As you attempt to cultivate loving-kindness, you begin to see what gets in the way of having loving-kindness. And for most of us there is a lot in the way, whether it is our own self-hatred and regrets or complex and unresolved feelings and resentments from the relationships themselves.

When you experience these other kinds of feelings, you can then bring your mindfulness practice into the foreground. What is it you are feeling? Can you notice it with a kind attention? Can you feel it in your body? (Use RAIN to help you here.) You might even say, "May I hold this in loving-kindness." Or you may be drawn to sending loving-kindness to yourself in the moment of feeling these other feelings, inviting yourself to be happy and at ease, holding yourself in the great heart of compassion.

Many people report that when they try this practice, it feels like nothing is happening—their experience feels dry and sterile. Again, this is not a problem. If this happens to you, remember that cultivation practices are like planting a seed. You plant the seed with no idea when the plant will sprout, but you trust that at some point you will see the results. Last year I planted some seeds in our garden and was disappointed when the surrounding plants grew and mine did not. My husband, who is an excellent gardener, had planted the beds near mine, and his grew fast and hardy. I was sure that I had done something wrong and that, because gardening is not my forte, I had failed at seed planting.

Well, ultimately the seeds grew. Not on my schedule, and not in the same way my husband's grew, but sure enough, with time and patience on my part, my seeds grew.

So it is with meditation and the cultivation of loving-kindness, as Suhail, a twenty-seven-year-old graduate student, experienced:

I was very skeptical about loving-kindness practice. I tried it because several of my friends said they got a lot out of it. Whenever I practiced it, it felt dry, boring, like I was just mouthing the words. "May I be happy," blah blah blah. After about a month of practicing it daily, I had pretty much given up. Then last week I noticed the strangest thing. Normally when I'm working on my dissertation I'm always judging myself. But last week I was saying to myself, *Your writing is terrible, you'll never complete this*, when this other voice I've never heard inside myself before said, *Of course you will, it's going to be fine*. I was utterly shocked, but I guess I'll chalk it up to the loving-kindness.

Expansion

As we practice loving-kindness, we can begin with the easy ones—people we love, pets, dear friends, family members we get along with, and so on. Starting where it is easy is a good way to allow the feeling of loving-kindness to grow and develop and will give you a sense of the many dimensions of loving-kindness.

Then you may find that you want to expand the loving-kindness to other individuals. You can move on to more neutral people next—acquaintances or people you don't have strong feelings about—and then go on to include difficult people. This could be someone you are having a hard time with, or perhaps someone you don't know personally but have difficulty with, such as a political figure. It is unusual to send loving-kindness to people with whom we have difficulty. Often it can be very challenging, but students report real transformation in their relationships to these difficult people. This story is from Suzanne, who is thirty-nine and in sales:

> I started sending loving-kindness to my boss on a regular basis. It felt radical to do it, because she's so difficult, but I realized, she treats me and others so badly, she must be unhappy. So I began to wish her well, whenever I remembered. When she was particularly mean to someone, I wished it even harder. What I found was the more I practiced loving-kindness, the softer my heart grew towards her. Shockingly, the other day she invited me for coffee. Was it because of the meditation? I don't know.

A common way to practice is to begin by using the "I" pronoun in your well-wishes (*may I be well, may I be happy, may I be free from suffering, may I be full of joy,* and so on), changing the pronoun to "you" for a second round of well-wishes, and then, for the final round, changing the pronoun to "all." It is a powerful practice to send the kindness to all beings around the planet, especially those who are suffering from the effects of war, sickness, poverty, or other challenges.

Can Others Feel It?

I am often asked whether other people feel the loving-kindness we send to them. This is a good question. Why spend all this time sending loving-kindness if the recipient is not even going to notice?

The answer is twofold. First, experientially we can verify that other people's moods and ways of being have an impact on us. For instance, when you encounter a truly loving person, you can feel it—that is, you find that you want to be in the presence of that person. Being around a loving person is enjoyable, soothing, perhaps uplifting. Conversely, a person in a grouchy or complaining mood can put a damper on your own mood. Not that we are promoting false cheeriness, but everyone knows from their own experience that moods seem to be contagious. It is more than possible that someone senses when you are sending kind thoughts their way. In fact, we saw in the science section that new research is documenting exactly that!

Second, this practice is a cultivation practice for *you*. When you are sending kindness to someone in your life, regardless of how it is received, you are changing your own brain, developing your own best qualities, and connecting with feelings that are important and meaningful to you. Whether or not you have an impact on another person, you know for sure that you're having an impact on yourself! Again, science is beginning to unveil the mechanisms by which our bodies and brains can change our feelings and attitudes.

Using Loving-Kindness in Your Life

Loving-kindness can be a wonderful practice to use at any time of the day: while walking down the street, waiting in line at the supermarket, visiting a sick friend, or reading the newspaper. I like to do it in elevators, particularly the ones at my workplace, which are extremely slow and crowded and seem programmed to stop at every floor. I can spend my time fostering irritation, or I can shift my mind to send kindness to my elevator-mates. This practice certainly changes my own attitude. One friend of mine sends loving-kindness whenever she hears the sound of an emergency vehicle, wishing well the person in trouble and their family. Another person I know uses her cell phone: While she waits until the second or third ring to pick up, she uses the first one or two rings to send loving-kindness to whoever is calling. Another friend sends loving-kindness to the recipient of every e-mail he writes.

Stage Three: Embodying Loving-Kindness

Ultimately, as we practice over time, loving-kindness becomes more and more who we are, as we saw in the wolf story. You will find yourself naturally being kinder, more forgiving, and less judgmental to others as well as to yourself. You might notice words or feelings of loving-kindness spontaneously appearing in your mind. You might notice yourself reacting with kindness in situations where previously you would have reacted with fear or contempt. When this shift happens—over a period of time that differs from person to person—it is startling. When you begin to touch it, however, you know you are touching your deepest capacity for love, present within you all the time.

THE PRACTICE:
LOVING-KINDNESS MEDITATION

To begin this practice, let yourself be in a relaxed and comfortable position. Bring to mind someone who makes you feel happy the moment you think of them—a relative, a close friend, someone with whom you don't have too complicated a relationship. You can pick a child, or you can always choose a pet, a dog or a cat or any creature that is fairly easy to feel love for. Let this person (or animal) come to mind—if you can, have a sense of this person being in front of you, to be felt, or sensed, or seen. And as you imagine this, notice how you are feeling inside. Maybe you feel bodily warmth, some heat in your face, or a smile, or a sense of expansiveness. This is loving-kindness, a natural feeling that is accessible to anyone at any moment.

While imagining your loved one in front of you, begin to wish this person well: *May you be safe and protected from danger. May you be happy and peaceful. May you be healthy and strong. May you have ease and well-being. . . .* You can use my words or your own words to say what feels meaningful to you. As you say these words, have a sense of letting this loving-kindness come from you and begin to touch your loved one. You might think in images, you might have a sense of color or light, you might just have a feeling. The words may continue to bring on more of this feeling, and I encourage you to say whatever feels meaningful to you. . . . *May you be free from stress and anxiety. May you be free from all fear.*

As you are sending out these words and these feelings of loving-kindness, also check into yourself and see how you're feeling inside. Now imagine that your loved one turns around and begins to send loving-kindness back to you. Try to receive this loving-kindness as your loved one wishes you well and says:

May you be happy. May you be peaceful and at ease. May you be safe and protected from all danger. May you have joy and well-being. Let yourself take it in.

If you felt nothing earlier in the meditation and are still not feeling anything at this point, that is not a problem. This is a practice that plants seeds. And if you are feeling something other than loving-kindness, just check into that. What is it you are feeling? There may be something to learn here. You can say, *May I hold this too* (whatever you're feeling) *with loving-kindness.*

Now try to send loving-kindness to yourself. You can imagine it radiating throughout your body from your heart. Or you can just have a sense of it: *May I be safe and protected from danger. May I be healthy and strong. May I be happy and peaceful. May I accept myself just as I am.* You can ask yourself: What do I need to be happy? See what arises and offer that to yourself. *May I have meaningful work. May I have a joyful life. May I have close friends and family.* . . . Now check into yourself and notice what you feel as you do this.

Let yourself bring to mind one person or a group of people to whom you wish to send loving-kindness. Imagine them in front of you—sense them, see them, feel them. . . . *May you be happy and peaceful. May you be free from all stress and anxiety, fear, worry, or grief. May you have joy and happiness, well-being.* Let this loving-kindness expand, spreading out and touching anyone you want to touch right now. Let it go in all directions, toward people you know, toward people you don't know, toward people you have difficulty with, toward people you love. Imagine expansive and pervasive loving-kindness, touching and changing every person and every animal. . . . *So may everyone everywhere be happy and peaceful and at ease. May we all experience great joy.*

You can do this practice daily, weekly, or as you feel so inclined. You may wish to do it for several weeks or on an ongoing basis. You can also do loving-kindness practice in combination with your mindfulness practice, either beginning or ending the sittings with loving-kindness. In that case, just do loving-kindness for a few minutes. The full meditation could take up to ten minutes.

8

PAY ATTENTION, BUT HOW?

The moment one gives close attention to anything, even a blade of grass, it becomes a mysterious, awesome, indescribably magnificent world in itself.

—HENRY MILLER

Attention is our most precious commodity. We make others feel important or unimportant by either attending to them or ignoring them. We have all felt the weight of being ignored or being the focus of praise or ridicule, experiencing everything from no attention to too much attention throughout our lives. We shape our worlds by it. If you are not sure how much this cognitive process influences your world, consider what happens when you buy a new car—suddenly the same car is everywhere you look. Or if you have been pregnant or are trying to get pregnant, pregnant women and baby things are everywhere you turn. And if you happen to be remodeling a house, fixtures, sinks, and door handles seem to pop out from houses, restaurants, and stores to capture your focus, as if you are a gifted architect.

We are blindsided by attention or lack thereof at times. Have you ever had the experience of something happening right before your eyes but you didn't notice it? This is the trick of the magician's trade: The magician directs our eyes so that what we *think* we see mystifies us. There are many examples of this that can be seen outside of a magician's act. In a classic attention experiment developed by Daniel J. Simons, a professor at the University of Illinois, a video is shown of several people passing a basketball back and forth among them. Half the people are wearing white T-shirts, and half are wearing black ones. The instruction to the viewer is to count the number of times the ball is passed among people wearing white shirts. As the viewer focuses solely on the people in white shirts, counting methodically the number of ball passes, something quite unusual happens.[1] The experiment demonstrates how powerful attention is and how easy it is to ignore information not relevant to the task at hand. This chapter is about our cognitive process of attention, how we can regulate it, how it can shape our lives, and how mindfulness can alter it.

THE SCIENCE

For most of us, attention is a single thing: We either pay attention or we don't, although we all pay attention to varying degrees. (Compare your attention when listening to a monotone speaker versus your hyperfocus in the final minutes of an NBA playoff game.) Attention has been a subject of psychology and neuroscience for over one hundred years, having first been spotlighted as important by William James, the godfather of psychology. Before James raised interest in attention in the midnineteenth century, most philosophers and psychologists believed that experience was all that mattered.[2] James made the case that experience is inextricably connected to attention—that is, if you change your attention, you change your experience. He wrote, "Millions of items of the outward order are present to my senses which never properly enter into my experience. Why? Because they have no *interest* for me. *My experience is what I agree to attend to.*"[3]

Many Kinds of Attention

Michael Posner has spent his academic career figuring out the biology of attention. He describes three types of attention: alerting, orienting, and conflict. Each of these has distinct brain circuits involving different brain regions.[4] Alerting attention is pretty much what it sounds like: It is attentional readiness, or how alert or ready we are to take action or attend to a particular object, thought, or stimulus. We all fluctuate in alertness from morning to evening, and we know that many things can change it, such as coffee, alcohol, or fear. Environmental context also influences alertness. You are probably more alert when you are lost in a forest than while sitting on a couch in your living room. Alerting does not require voluntary effort (an "I" directing it) and as a consequence is sometimes referred to as a "bottom-up" type of attention.

In contrast to alerting, Posner's group identified two "top-down" processes of *voluntary* attention: orienting (also called selective) and conflict (also called executive attention). Orienting refers to the kind of attention you use when you *direct* your attention to something, someone, or some object (a car sound, a cloud, a song on the radio, a thought, a feeling, an internal state such as leg pain). You orient or turn your attention to that thing—right now we hope your attention is oriented on this book.

Orienting is considered voluntary, although you need not be conscious of it; for example, you might turn your head toward an oncoming car while talking to someone on the phone and not even notice that you've done so. We orient our attention all the time depending on what interests us (as James suggested), unconsciously and consciously. The other type of voluntary attention, conflict attention, reflects your ability to continue to attend to something in the face of intruding or distracting information. With this type of attention, you must inhibit a conflicting response to maintain your attention—for example, to continue to read this book despite phone, television, or friend interruptions is to use conflict attention. You use this kind of attention all the time to focus and get things done.

In mindfulness, when you observe your breath and distracting thoughts or feelings or bodily sensations compete for your attention, you use conflict attention to inhibit the intrusions and stay focused on your breath. A common way to measure this type of attention in the laboratory is by a task called the ANT (Attentional Network Task).[5] In the ANT, a subject is asked to focus on the center of a computer screen and to hit a button, either left or right, depending on the direction an arrow is pointing (left or right). An arrow is flashed on the screen either alone or flanked by arrows pointing in the same direction or in the opposite direction. The length of time it takes for a subject to press the button is influenced by the arrows flanking the center arrow. Usually it takes longer to press the button when the flanking arrows point in the opposite direction because you have to "inhibit" the conflicting information to get the answer right. The extra time taken for the mixed-arrow trials compared with the trials in which the arrows point in the same direction is a measure of conflict attention.

A similar test is one in which names of colors, like "red" or "blue," are presented in different colors of ink (say, green) and you have to name the color while inhibiting the response to read the word. It is pretty hard to inhibit reading the word to attend to its color once you know how to read automatically (by about eight years of age for most people). Conflict attention is measured by how much harder it is for you to do this task (meaning how much longer it takes you) when you have to inhibit an automatic response to accomplish it.

You use conflict attention all the time to override intrusive information and stay attentive to the task at hand, whether it is hitting a tennis ball, reading a book, or making dinner. If you cannot regulate your attention, it is as if you are lost at sea in an ocean of sensory experience. And conflict attention is key to self-regulation—the ability to monitor and change behavior to meet goals or adapt as necessary.[6] To self-regulate you need to attend to certain bodily sensations, thoughts, and feelings while overriding others. Real-world examples of self-regulation would be staying calm in the face of someone angrily shouting at you (self-regulation of emotion), ignoring a phone call while in the middle of a conversation (self-regulation of attention), or breathing slowly in the midst of a rigorous workout (self-regulation of body).

These three attentional systems begin in infancy; alerting and orienting attention reach adult levels in childhood, while conflict attention continues to strengthen until young adulthood. The continuing emergence of conflict attention corresponds to the development of greater and greater self-control or self-regulation with age.[7] And conflict attention is strongly influenced by the prefrontal cortex (see Figures 2 and 3), a key brain region for self-regulation, decision-making, and reasoning that you will hear more about in Chapter 9.

We all differ in our attentional capacities. Some of us are hyper-alert— always ready to respond—while some of us are hypo-alert, or difficult to rouse. Some of us get stuck on a topic, unable to shift our attention, while others find that it is virtually impossible to stay on task for more than a few seconds. For some of us, the tiniest distraction sweeps us away from what we are doing; for others, only catastrophic events have this effect. Again, our DNA plays a role in shaping these differences, but experience can modify them as well. (Remember, "genetic" does not mean "fixed.") Many genes are thought to play a role in attention, and those involved in dopamine regulation seem to play a critical role.

Dopamine is a neurotransmitter (a chemical involved in cell communication in the brain) that is regulated by a vast array of genes, including ones that move it between cells (transporter genes), ones that provide a means for its binding to cells (receptor genes), and ones involved in its production and degradation (packaging, producing, and recycling genes). Scientists can take a gene involved in dopamine regulation and remove it ("knock it out") from an animal like a mouse or rat and then study what changes in the animal, physically and behaviorally, compared to the same genetic strain with the gene intact. Such knock-out models have greatly increased our understanding of the function of genes, including those involved in dopamine regulation. In a knock-out mouse strain with the dopamine receptor gene (called DRD4) removed, mice show poor attention along with increased hyperactivity and impulsivity. This same gene has been associated with attention deficit hyperactivity disorder (ADHD), conflict attention, and novelty-seeking behavior.[8] It is one gene of many involved in attention, but one that is known to explain a little bit (maybe 2 to 5 percent) of the differences we see among us in our attentional differences.

ADHD: A Highly Heritable Disorder of Attention

In thinking about differences in attention among people, ADHD soon comes to mind. ADHD is a disorder defined by poor attention and sometimes also by increased hyperactivity-impulsivity; the disorder causes significant problems at work, home, and school. When it was first described in the early 1900s, it was called "minimal brain dysfunction" and was thought to affect some 1 percent of children. By 1983 the name had changed to "attention deficit disorder" and it was seen by then to affect some 3 percent of children. Today what is now called attention deficit hyperactivity disorder (ADHD) affects as many as one in ten youth worldwide and one in twenty adults.[9] The diagnoses of ADHD became broader with time, capturing more people under its label. Yet our DNA makeup did not change. It is likely that part of the increase is due to the increasing demands on our attention; those who two generations ago would have had no difficulties may meet the criteria for ADHD in today's information age.[10]

Jeffrey's daughter was diagnosed with ADHD. When he sat down to do a Google search on the symptoms of ADHD, he noticed that two common ones are forgetting things and losing things. That reminded him of how often he lost his keys, forgot about a meeting, or failed to remember important appointments. He Googled "memory loss" and began reading about Alzheimer's disease. That reminded him of his mother, whose health was failing, and their current discussions about the use of the herb gingko biloba. The word "biloba" reminded Jeffrey of the beautiful city of Bilbao, Spain, which he and his wife had visited the previous year. As he searched on Bilbao, he remembered the Guggenheim museum there that had reminded him of billowing clouds; that made him think of the wind and kite flying. He found himself on a website about "making a kite" when he realized that an hour had gone by and he couldn't quite remember why he was searching anything on the computer at all. Then he remembered—his daughter and ADHD.

Whether Jeffrey had ADHD or not, he clearly had a difficult time holding the goal (reading about ADHD) in mind; his attention wandered from topic to topic fairly unconstrained. This free-range flow of attention can be extremely useful in creative endeavors, but it poses problems when you have to get something done. This problem alone is not enough to warrant an ADHD diagnosis, which, according to the *Diagnostic and Statistical Manual of Mental Disorders*, requires a clustering of multiple symptoms (like forgetting, losing things, failing to finish tasks, and difficulty paying attention) or signs of hyperactivity-impulsivity (fidgeting, failing to stay seated, interrupting) with impairment and childhood onset. Jeffrey may have ADHD (as do about 20 to 30 percent of mothers and fathers of ADHD children), or he may fall short of meeting all the criteria but still have some characteristic symptoms, since much of the predisposition to ADHD (about 76 percent) is encoded in our genes.

We use the word "trait" to describe this predisposition, which varies in people just as height, weight, and IQ vary. At the extreme on this continuum (analogous to being very tall or very short) is an increased risk for impairment, and that is where ADHD is diagnosed. The continuum probably reflects several processes of brain structure and function, hemisphere utilization, personality, emotion, and cognition. Although the trait is complex, *impairment*—the key to the "disorder"—arises from the interaction of the trait with the environment. If a child with poor conflict attention faces an environment that places heavy demands on him (such as sitting in a classroom for long stretches of time), he will tend to squirm, jump out of his seat, fail to pay attention, and so on. At the same time, the child may be constantly exploring new things (novelty-seeking personality), and his prefrontal cortex, which regulates the emotional centers of the brain, may be less well developed (so that emotional highs are higher and lows are lower and movement between the two is more rapid). Put these elements together, and the child soon reaps criticism from those around him—teachers, pupils, and parents—just at a time when self-mastery and small successes are most needed. Instead, failure becomes the norm for this child, and impairment (problems, problems, problems) ensues.[11]

Can Mindfulness Training Help ADHD?

We found that, among parents of ADHD children, those with ADHD described themselves as less "mindful" than did their non-ADHD counterparts.[12] Although those with ADHD had difficulties with aspects of mindfulness such as "describing emotions" and "accepting things without judgment," only those mindfulness items *related to attention* truly differentiated the groups once other factors were considered. In a pilot study at UCLA, the psychiatrist Lidia Zylowska and I examined the role of mindfulness as a complementary program in treating ADHD. We found that adults and teens with ADHD liked the program, stuck with it (78 percent completed it), and showed improvements in conflict attention. Since it was a feasibility study, there was no control group to determine the magnitude of the effect of mindfulness on ADHD.[13] In a separate uncontrolled study of ADHD children and their families conducted by researchers in Australia, a six-week meditation program reduced ADHD symptoms and improved family-child relationships.[14] The studies to date are small and designed in ways that make interpretation of the value of meditation for ADHD challenging; however, they are promising enough to suggest that meditation may be a useful complementary practice for ADHD and other attentional difficulties and that further research is needed.

Attention and Mindfulness

Mindfulness is a particular way of attending to experience, one that is open and curious. The open-awareness practice of meditation has been called "open monitoring" in contrast to other forms of meditation that are focused on a single object of attention (like a mantra or the breath), which are called "focused attention" practices.[15] As noted by Buddhist scholars, however, mindfulness meditation actually includes both: An open monitoring is realized fully when attention is stable and focused.[16] We see emerging from the science evidence that mindfulness meditation training increases attention and that focused attention training increases mindfulness. For example, in a study of the focused-attention practice Transcendental Meditation (TM) conducted at American University in Washington, DC, mindfulness, as measured by a self-report questionnaire, significantly increased for students taught TM compared to controls.[17]

A positive relationship of mindfulness practice to attention suggests that it may affect the neural circuits involved in attention. The cognitive psychologist Amishi Jha at the University of Pennsylvania compared experienced mindfulness meditators to nonmeditators on the computerized ANT described previously.[18] Experienced meditators with an average of about ten years of meditation practice were much more capable than nonmeditators in both conflict attention and a "readiness" to pay attention. The readiness difference emerged only after an intensive three-month meditation retreat, while their differences in conflict attention were present before the retreat period. When nonmeditators were taught to meditate, they also showed improvements in both conflict and orienting attention, but only their orienting attention was significantly different from that of controls.

In a study of college students taught mindfulness meditation in a program called Integrative Body-Mind Training (IBMT), researchers at the University of Oregon found that their conflict attention (but not their orienting or alerting attention) improved significantly *in just twenty minutes of meditation practice a day for five days* compared to students not given the practice.[19] Two other studies support the Oregon team's finding that conflict attention seems to change more quickly than other forms of attention in relatively short periods of meditation training.[20] Taken together, these studies demonstrate that mindfulness meditation improves conflict attention quite readily and that changes in orienting and alerting attention may require more practice. Since conflict attention is key to self-regulation, a little bit of meditation might go a long way toward improving your capacity to regulate your body, thoughts, and emotions.

Teaching the Brain to Attend More Effortlessly

The brain uses about 20 percent of the body's energy but makes up only 2 percent of its size.[21] In the mid-1950s, scientists discovered that this 20 percent usage is pretty constant regardless of whether the brain is solving a crossword puzzle, resting, performing at Carnegie Hall, or swimming at the Olympics. The overall net use, while constant, shifts from various parts of the brain depending on what you are doing or not doing (resting). It was not until 2001 that a scientist, Marcus Raichle,[22] described the so-called default brain state—a specific brain pattern that is active when the brain is not doing anything specific, that is, when it is just "being." Meditation practice seems to affect not only different aspects of attention (the brain "doing") but also this default brain state (the brain "being").

Helen Slagter, a researcher the University of Wisconsin, used a task called the "attentional blink" task to investigate how meditation affects attention and energy use in the brain. Energy utilization in the brain can be examined by using imaging techniques such as fMRI or by taking measures on the surface of the scalp of specific signals generated from electrical activity, called evoked related potentials (ERPs). When a brain region is actively utilizing brain resources (involving oxygen utilization, chemical activity, and electrical firing of neurons), there is a particular scalp surface electrical signal (an ERP) that reflects it. Researchers measured this signal while meditators and nonmeditators did an "attentional blink task."[23] In an attentional blink task, stimuli are presented rapidly in succession on a computer, and the subject must respond to the various stimuli presented. For example, a series of letters is presented sequentially, and the subject is asked to respond when a number pops up among the vast series of letters. If the number 3 occurs, followed by T, X, N, R, S, and then the number 9 occurs, the 3 is the first target and the 9 is the second target. People differ in how many letters (time) are needed before they can detect the second target following the first. The process requires attending to the first target, disengaging from it, and then getting ready to detect the next number. Longtime meditators were much faster at disengaging compared to nonmeditators, they were ready more quickly, and *they needed less brain energy to perform the task* than their nonmeditating counterparts.[24]

How much practice is needed to achieve such heightened readiness and reduced energy expenditure? An intriguing study by Julie Brefczynski-Lewis and Richard Davidson's group suggests that the amount of practice is far from trivial.[25] Meditators with an average of 19,000 hours of practice consistently showed a pattern in which the brain needed *more* energy directed at the attentional task to perform better than nonmeditators, but meditators with an average of 44,000 hours of practice looked different. In that group, much less brain energy was needed to carry out the attentional task. Like other skills that become automatic with time and require *less energy* to perform (for example, playing piano at the concert pianist level), attentional regulation may become automatic through meditation, requiring less mental effort.

But if you can't imagine getting anywhere close to these extreme numbers of hours of meditation, don't worry. As described earlier, attentional changes can begin to happen after just twenty minutes of meditation training a day for five days.[26] These findings about the virtuosos of meditation will give you an idea of the power of practice, but in just a short time you can learn to meditate well enough to reap some benefit, just as you can play a song after only a little piano practice.

Is such a finding a result of meditation or a reflection of the kind of people who meditate? Do longtime meditators—many of them monks—have a different sort of brain altogether? Exactly what kind of brain chooses to become a monk? Studies by Davidson's group on Tibetan Buddhist monks suggest that their brains (or specific brain functions) are quite different from an average person's brain. Is that because of their extensive amount of meditation practice, or was the difference inherent in their brains long before they began to practice? We do not yet have studies of brain changes among so-called naive meditators before and after extensive practice (thousands of hours) to determine the degree of change possible. Longitudinal research may hold the key to answering the extent to which brain differences are a consequence of meditation or part and parcel of the brains of people who dedicate their lives to it. Studies showing a positive correlation of brain changes with hours of practice suggest that it is, at least in part, a function of the practice itself and not merely inherent differences.

Alan Wallace of the Santa Barbara Institute for Consciousness Studies, in collaboration with scientists at UC Davis, is conducting a study that may just provide a more definitive answer. Wallace recruited seventy meditators to participate in a three-month meditation study in which they meditated approximately eight hours each day. (What kind of person [and brain] chooses to participate in such a study is another question.) Researchers are studying the changes in their brains over time, both structurally and functionally, to see the effects of these hours of meditation practice. It will be fascinating to see the extent to which everyday Joes (or Joanns) can improve their attentional capacities and the brain functions underlying them with intensive meditation.

THE ART

Alicia, who is eight, has always had trouble focusing in school. One day in class when her teacher calls on her, she is startled because she has been daydreaming as usual. Her mind was off on an imaginative fantasy about a story she wanted to write where she takes a trip to the moon and visits a fairy who helps her understand why countries fight wars . . . but wait, the teacher is calling her name, asking her to solve a math equation. Alicia's eyes sting with tears. *If only I could pay attention,* she thinks, *but I just can't. Why is my mind all over the place?*

From our earliest years, we are told to pay attention. How many times as a child were you instructed by your parents and teachers to pay attention? Probably the most common refrain in any classroom is "Pay attention, class!" Yet children are given very little training or practice in regulating their attention; they just do it or they don't, and they suffer when it is the latter. As we saw in the science section, mindfulness may be a cutting-edge tool to help people with attention issues by teaching them both to concentrate and to respond appropriately in the midst of multiple demands competing for their attention.

As you begin to understand the roles of concentration and mindfulness in your meditation practice—how they can be cultivated and how they differ—you can put them into practice in your life to help regulate your attention. This practice can be beneficial whether or not you struggle with attentional disorders like ADHD or are simply seeking peace amid a busy, hectic, modern life.

Concentration Meditation

There are hundreds of kinds of meditations, and they appear in almost all spiritual traditions. The two kinds most relevant to our discussion of attention are practices that cultivate concentration and those that develop mindfulness. As we saw in the science section, "focused attention" and "open monitoring" are the two types of attention that correspond with these two types of meditation.

Concentration meditation practices cultivate focused attention, but as explained in the science section, mindfulness can also be affected. As we saw already, mindfulness combines both: It develops focused attention as well as open monitoring of present-time experiences. To start, we examine concentration practices.

Focused attention or concentration meditation practices are varied, but they have a similar method. Generally, you place your attention on a single focus, such as a candle, a repeating word, an image, or your breath. The goal is to train your distracted mind—the mind that has been metaphorically running around all over the place—to stay put in one place. As your mind stays put, your attention gathers and begins to unify and collect.

A magnifying glass is a good metaphor for the concentrated mind. When your mind is scattered, it's like sun rays landing anywhere. But when these rays are focused through a magnifying glass, they unify and develop an increased power. Suddenly, diffuse rays of light are strong enough to light a piece of paper on fire. (Remember doing this as a child?) Similarly, when your mind is scattered, it has no power. But through the practice of concentrating your mind—that is, by unifying, collecting, and gathering your scattered attention—you develop an increased ability to regulate it.

Over the long term, when meditators practice concentrating attention, they find that their minds become more pliable and flexible and that their ability to stay present with a meditation object increases. Their minds, rather than wandering everywhere, lost in thought, tend to stay firmly fixed on an object, such as their breath, unless they *choose* to move it. Ultimately, most long-term concentration meditators report the states of bliss and joy that come with sustained practice.

Often this kind of blissful state happens in secluded meditation retreats, over a period of time, because the environment is set up to heighten the likelihood of the experience. Living in seclusion may not be too practical for anyone living a busy life, and that is one of the reasons we advocate mindfulness, since it can be done anywhere at any time. Transcendental Meditation, which was first brought to the United States in the 1970s, is a concentration practice in which you repeat a word, or "mantra," to develop deep states of concentration and inner restful alertness. Although the goals of TM may differ from those of mindfulness, the two forms of meditation influence some shared effects. For example, we saw from the science section that the concentrated practice of TM can increase self-reports of mindfulness and that mindfulness practices can increase aspects of concentration. Both are thought to increase the relaxation response as well.

Mindfulness Versus Concentration

Although we value the benefits that come from exclusively practicing types of concentration meditation, mindfulness meditation may be better tailored to some people, and it may offer alternative benefits. One important reason why we see mindfulness meditation as particularly useful is that it teaches you to be present with whatever life brings you. You are not trying to attain a particular state of mind, although experiences of "self-transcendence" may arise. The ability to find peace and ease within yourself, no matter what the conditions, may be the greatest gift you can give yourself. Second, practiced formally, mindfulness meditation reaps the benefits of concentration meditation too, since mindfulness incorporates concentration, as you will see. Finally, mindfulness can be practiced at any time of the day, which makes it a powerful tool to address anxiety and stress in the moment you are facing it. Richard, a forty-eight-year-old engineer, told us:

> I don't know how I'd face job stress without mindfulness. Last week at 4:00 PM on a Friday, my boss handed me a pile of data to analyze. I couldn't believe it. I was insanely irritated. So I just began to breathe mindfully and notice my body state: My heart was beating fast, my stomach was clenched. I felt my feet on the floor and noticed my angry thoughts, and after a little while I had calmed down and not reacted to her in some way I would later regret.

Concentration in Your Life

As we saw in the science section discussion of conflict attention, depending on genetics and other factors, people have varying degrees of ability to concentrate. Everyone has to concentrate in order to function in life. You would not be able to read or drive or carry on a conversation without some level of concentration. Those people who seem to have more concentrative ability from the start than others can be viewed as having a talent for concentration, like athletic talent or musical ability. I recently visited with a woman who knew me well as a child. She told me that one of the striking things she remembers about me is that I had strong powers of concentration even at a young age. She would hand me a puzzle or toy and even at three years of age I would sit for hours working intently on the puzzle. It is interesting that I went on to become a meditation teacher!

On the other hand, there are many meditation teachers who, by their own admission, have had difficulties with concentration or who have an attentional disorder such as ADHD. Whether or not concentration comes easily to you or you have some difficulty with it, what you practice you will enhance. As with any talent, if you develop it, it will grow—and if you don't, it will remain dormant. The research clearly shows that attention can be changed with practice. Through persistent and regular practice in holding your attention to a single object, you will nurture your concentration.

The Mindfulness Spectrum

Concentration is a significant feature of mindfulness meditation, although it is only one aspect of it. Generally you develop enough concentration to stabilize your attention so that you can begin to see the present moment more clearly. You can think of a spectrum of mindfulness: On one end, mindfulness is similar to a concentration practice in which you develop focused attention. You focus your attention on a single object in the present moment (such as the breath) and repeatedly bring your attention back to this object. This is the foundational practice of mindfulness. Since many people have fairly wild and distracted minds, the first exercise in the practice section, counting the breath, is one that develops concentration. Whether you spend some time being aware of the breath in just one sitting session or practice concentration over an extended period of weeks or months, this exercise can help tame the busyness you may have in your mind.

At the other end of the spectrum is the cultivation of a different type of attention—"open monitoring" is a wide-open, spacious attention focused not on a single object but on many objects. With open monitoring, you are aware of the thoughts, emotions, sensations, and sounds around you. You focus on these objects—floating from one to the next—depending on what grabs your attention. Or you might have a more general awareness of multiple experiences happening simultaneously. This kind of attention is taught in second exercise in the practice section, the hearing meditation.

To experience open monitoring briefly, when you finish reading this, stop for a moment, relax back into your chair, and let your gaze be soft. Take a few breaths and observe whether that calms and relaxes you a little bit. Then, if this is possible, observe what your mind notices: What just pops into your awareness? Don't try to pay attention only to one thing, but notice all that you can in your current experience. You might perceive sights in the room, you might feel your body against the chair, or you might notice a fleeting thought or even a scent. Let your mind observe whatever it is drawn to. Be mindful of each present-moment experience. Stop after a few minutes. If the experience feels overwhelming, just relax and don't try too hard.

Open monitoring can develop a powerful state of awareness in which you are present exactly with life unfolding, seeing things change from moment to moment. You can use open monitoring during your formal practice or at any moment throughout the day—while driving, walking down the street, or sitting in a meeting. Rather than directing your attention to one object, such as the breath, open your attention to the array of experiences without getting lost in the content. Simply be aware of each experience—whether a sight, sound, image, thought, emotion, or sensation—as it enters your consciousness. Twenty-nine-year-old Tamara, a mother, described her experience with open monitoring:

> I was at the park with my daughter, who was playing on the swing set. You know how noisy parks are. There were about twenty kids with moms and dads and dogs and the freeway not too far away. I wondered if it might be possible to meditate here while watching Sara. So I just relaxed on the bench and became aware of everything. Not in an overwhelming way—I just let my attention go to whatever it was drawn to and saw if I could be mindful of it without getting too caught up in my ideas and stories about the experience. I simply noticed what was present, this vast array of sounds and sights and smells, and as I did it I felt so relaxed and present and even more connected to my daughter, who was at least ten feet away. My mind seemed settled somehow.

Regulating Attention

Let's return to Alicia in her classroom. She is struggling because she doesn't know what kind of attention is appropriate, how to access it, and when to do so. In class a child needs to be able to regulate her attention. Nothing is wrong with writing a story in her head or daydreaming, but she needs to know when to do these things, especially when there are expectations placed on her. During class a student needs a single-minded focus (focused attention) on the blackboard and the teacher's words. But in acts of creativity, having a wide-open, spacious mindfulness (open monitoring) is very appropriate. The ability to recognize these various states of attention and move between them at will, depending on the context and need, is the key to successful regulation of attention. Certainly meditation is not the only tool to regulate attention, but as we saw in the science section, it clearly has an impact on attention; however, in some cases, medication or other interventions may be necessary, depending on the individual.

A camera provides an example of movement between focused attention and open monitoring. Sometimes you take a photo with a telephoto lens so that you can look very closely at the subject of your photograph. At other times you use a wide-angle or panoramic lens, which opens up the picture, broadening the view. Neither is better than the other; they simply serve different purposes.

Similarly, you learn to adjust your attention to situations through mindfulness. If you are practicing mindfulness while driving, you do not want to be so focused on a single object, such as the road in front of you, that you miss taking in input from your peripheral vision, from sound, and from your own gut and best intelligence. Mindful driving does not use a "telephoto lens"—except perhaps on a dangerous, windy road where you really have to concentrate—but instead benefits from a panoramic view.

If, after taking a mindful walk in the woods when you focused solely on sensations in your feet and legs, you leave the woods feeling unsatisfied—as though you might as well have been in the gym considering that you took in none of the surrounding nature—perhaps you realize that you would have benefited from a more panoramic-style mindfulness than the narrow focused attention you brought to the experience. Over time you will learn which kind of mindfulness to apply when. You will experiment and see what works, and you will learn a lot from your mistakes. After a while applying the appropriate kind of attention becomes second nature.

This is why we recommend that you use both styles of mindfulness in a daily formal mindfulness practice. That way, you become familiar with both ways of being mindful. You want to respond flexibly to your experience. Mindfulness instruction usually begins with an exercise to stabilize the mind; you concentrate on breathing to bring forth some unification of your mind. But over time you learn that there are many other phenomena to be aware of. You can be aware of sounds outside yourself, bodily sensations, emotions, and thoughts when they become predominant. When they no longer hold your attention or have stopped, you return to your breathing.

One type of attention is not better or more advanced than the other. Each type is called for at different times. Sometimes you may find that your mind naturally wants to open up to multiple experiences. At other times your mind seems naturally more focused. It is important to follow your intuition either way. Sometimes the two practices seem to combine—for example, when your attention is mostly wide open, you may still return from time to time to your breathing to create more stability and focus. Again, the instruction is to follow this impulse.

Discriminating Awareness

As we have seen, mindfulness can be single-focused or multi-focused. But what helps you decide how to regulate or place your focus? With mindfulness, a more "discriminating" awareness often emerges and brings wisdom to your practice. This kind of mindfulness might help you to see a situation clearly and then have an appropriate response. For example, while meditating, your mind gets caught in a host of concerns and worries—obsessing about your finances, for instance. With discriminating awareness, you might see that you are obsessing, label this focus of your attention as a worried thought, and redirect your attention to a more neutral object. If Alicia had been practicing mindfulness and had cultivated discriminating awareness, in class when she notices her mind wandering she might recognize that it probably is not a good time to be lost in reverie, or to get mad at herself for wandering, and then gently and firmly return her attention to her teacher's voice.

Now we can see how the camera analogy relates to this spectrum of mindfulness. Discriminating awareness is like adjusting the camera— regulating the focus, finding the right frame, and so on. Wisdom kicks in when you are taking a photo. *I need to back away . . . I need to correct the light meter . . . I should find better lighting. . . .* With discriminating awareness, you apply your own best wisdom in whatever situation you are in. Sometimes it tells you to focus your mind, and at other times it tells you to relax and create more openness in your attention.

When you sit down to meditate and notice your mind wandering all over the place, your discriminating mind is activated and suggests that it might be helpful to stay with your breath for the duration of the sitting. Another time you may feel well rested and energetic in your meditation and are pleasantly aware of your breath, but suddenly an emotion is quite strong and present, so you turn your attention to the emotion. The discriminating awareness reminds you that this emotion will not stay forever. Feeling a sense of relief, you watch the flow of energy as your body contracts with the emotion. During another meditation session, you may notice that your mind feels tight, everything irritates you, and you are not relaxed at all. With discrimination, you might decide to open your attention to the sounds in the room in order to relax yourself.

Even if you think you don't have that much wisdom, through practice you will develop it. Through trial and error, you will learn the appropriate ways to regulate your attention.

Discriminating awareness, cultivated through mindfulness, is the seat of wisdom. You may not have much discriminating awareness when you begin, but as you practice mindfulness this part of the spectrum strengthens. You begin to see more clearly which kinds of thoughts and emotions lead to difficulties and which bring in more relaxation and well-being. You then begin to apply this discriminating awareness to your actions. You learn to discern when your actions are hurtful and when they are beneficial. By stilling your mind through concentration, opening your awareness to whatever is present, and letting wisdom emerge, you can learn to live a joyful and skillful life—one that keeps stress to a minimum and promotes internal and external peace. Janelle, a fifty-six-year-old who works in advertising, made this discovery:

> I started meditating because of the chaos in my life. I lost things constantly, couldn't focus, my house was a mess! And certainly now I'm

much better at being concentrated, although it's still not easy. I just kept remembering to bring myself back to the present moment in my meditation and throughout my day. I got better at it. (Believe me, it was challenging!) Ultimately I noticed all those voices telling me what a failure I was. Whenever I became mindful of them, I told myself to relax and breathe. And I did. I became more confident, more relaxed, not so scattered. And I began to trust myself a lot more. This helped how I related to my family and friends and colleagues. People say I'm different. I chalk it up to mindfulness.

THE PRACTICES

In this section, we offer two practices. The first exercise emphasizes concentrating your mind (focused attention). The second helps you to widely open your awareness to take in multiple experiences (open monitoring).

Exercise 1: Counting Your Breath to Deepen Your Concentration

Let yourself get comfortable in a sitting posture. Find your breathing at the area in your body you prefer (abdomen, chest, or nostrils). As you have been practicing, feel one breath and then the next. To develop more concentration, count each breath, with a full rising and falling or in and out as 1, moving up to 10. Say the number softly in your mind. When you arrive at 10, start over again at 1: 1, 2, 3, 4, 5, 6, 7, 8, 9, 10, 1, 2, 3. . . . If you find yourself lost in thought, label that experience "thinking" or "wandering" and then return your attention to your breathing. Start over at 1, no matter where you were when you lost track. If you find this exercise helpful, practice it for five to ten minutes a day for a few weeks. After that, return to it on days when you feel particularly scattered.

Exercise 2: Open Your Awareness with a Hearing Meditation

Get comfortable in your meditation posture. Take a few deep breaths to help yourself relax a little bit. Now simply listen to the sounds around you. There may be sounds in your room, outside the room, or even inside your body. Try to listen with openness and curiosity. If you pay attention, you will notice that many sounds come and go, while others seem constant. Can you notice the sounds passing through your awareness? Can you also notice the silence in between the sounds?

Try to avoid making up a story about the sounds; just listen to them exactly as they are. It is natural for your mind to say, for instance, *That's a car*, or, *There's a person talking in the next room.* That ordinary recognition of a sound is not a problem. But try to avoid thinking in more detail about the sound: *Hmmm, what kind of car was that? Is it my neighbor's? I think it really needs to go to the mechanic, I can hear a bad clunking sound. . . .* This is what we call "making up stories." It takes you out of the direct experience of the moment and puts you on the conceptual level. Try to stay with simply hearing the sound and avoid making up stories. When your mind wanders off, return your attention to the hearing. Try this practice for five minutes or for as long as you feel drawn.

9

STRESSFUL THINKING

*I am an old man and have known a great many troubles,
most of which have never happened.*

—Mark Twain

John Steinbeck wrote in *Cannery Row*:

> Casting about in Hazel's mind was like wandering alone in a deserted
> museum. Hazel's mind was choked with uncatalogued exhibits. He
> never forgot anything but he never bothered to arrange his memories.
> Everything was thrown together like fishing tackle in the bottom of a
> rowboat, hooks and sinkers and line and lures and gaffs all snarled up.[1]

Our thoughts can be like Hazel's—tangled, disorganized, and snarled up—
or they can be clear, orderly, and aligned, but one thing is for sure: We all
think, and our thinking changes over time. Thoughts rise into consciousness
and disappear. Thoughts can be jumbled, bizarre, rapid, slow, methodical,
wandering, disassociated from reality, self-centered, altruistic, compassionate,
violent, peaceful, loving, angry, simple, complex, futuristic, fatalistic, or joyous.

To think and reason may be one of the most important evolutionary
changes that humans made from our nonhuman ancestors—as reflected by
our scientific name, *Homo sapiens sapiens* ("rational rational man"). Being able
to think, however, is not always a good thing: Sometimes thoughts create confusion and worry that makes us feel distressed. Mindfulness of thought can

help clear away the tangle. With practice, you can learn to disidentify from your thoughts, just as with your feelings, so that a kind of space appears between yourself and your thoughts and your subsequent actions. With mindfulness, you can hone the skill of neutral examination of your thoughts as they come and go; then you will begin to discriminate among them more skillfully and, ultimately, act accordingly.

In the previous chapter, we saw that mindfulness can improve attention, particularly conflict attention, an important component of planning, organizing, and carrying out goals (the so-called executive function of the prefrontal cortex). Here we review the biology of thought, its relationship to our perception of self, the role of the prefrontal cortex, and how mindfulness modifies the types of thinking that cause distress: decision-making, worry (obsessive thoughts or rumination), and multi-tasking. We then offer practices that will help you cope with such distress through disidentification of thought and other mindfulness techniques.

The Science

When symbolic language arose some 77,000 years ago and the frontal region of the brain expanded, our capacity to know that we know, to think about thinking, and to share ideas across space and time began to unfold. The prefrontal cortex is the reasoning center of the brain and the most recently developed structure in human evolution. This part of the brain is proportionally larger than expected for our body and brain size compared with other species.[2] For instance, in cats the prefrontal cortex makes up 3.5 percent of the brain, while in humans it is ten times that size.[3]

The Intimate Relationship Between
Thought and Self-Consciousness

When you think, ideas come into your consciousness and you ponder, monitor, modify, and make decisions. But much of the time decisions go by unnoticed, out of the realm of consciousness. How many times have you driven from home to work completely unaware of how you stopped and started along the way, avoided cars and pedestrians, and made hundreds of little decisions, all outside the realm of consciousness? We do a lot of things unconsciously. In fact, our brains automate things whenever possible so that energy can revert back to the default, resting brain state or be directed toward other activities.[4] A vast array of our actions happen without our conscious awareness, and it is this lack of a one-to-one correspondence between our behavior and our consciousness that makes it so hard to determine who or what is conscious—an ant, a cat, a dog, a dolphin, a monkey?

Humans have subjective experiences and experience a "self," a temporal and spatial agent "I." It is this self-consciousness that allows us to think about a future or past (to place the "I" in different points in time) or to perceive the world from the perspectives of others (to place the "I" in different vantage points in space). Without an awareness of self, there is only present experience.[5] Einstein captured this dependency between the "I" experience and time when he explained relativity as follows: "An hour sitting with a pretty girl on a park bench passes like a minute, but a minute sitting on a hot stove seems like an hour."[6]

Humans are not alone in the capacity to be self-aware. In the 1970s, researchers used a simple task, the "mirror recognition test," to discover that a variety of animals, such as chimpanzees, dolphins, and elephants, are capable of self-recognition. The test involves simply putting a mark (odorless dye) on the animal's forehead or body and seeing whether it touches or examines its image more often than without the mark.[7] In 1996 the neuroscientist Giacomo Rizzolatti and his team at the University of Parma discovered brain cells, called mirror neurons, in the frontal and parietal lobes that probably play a role in self-awareness.[8] These neurons appear to be crucial to our ability to imitate and understand the intentions and feelings of other people.[9] In an experiment conducted by Lucina Uddin at UCLA, fMRI scans showed that the parts of the brain in which mirror neurons are found become active when a subject looks at an image of herself (versus an image of a best friend). Using an apparatus called "transcranial magnetic stimulation," the same regions of brain could be temporarily disrupted, and when they were, subjects had a loss in self-recognition. Taken together, the studies support the role of mirror neurons (based on their known locations in the brain) in self-recognition and possibly self-awareness.[10]

But our sense of self changes over time. We only begin to detect our self at about eighteen months of age, when symbolic language, memory, and the prefrontal cortex are developed sufficiently.[11] (Younger children don't pass the mirror recognition task.) Marco Iacoboni, a neuroscientist at UCLA, argues that the mother-child interaction (baby smiles, mother smiles back) is crucial for shaping mirror neurons in development.[12] Soon after that, we learn to project our self through space and time—a function formed about age four. We can then move our self into the future (imagine), into the past (remember), and into another's perspective (empathize), and we can view an object from a different vantage point (project self into a different location).[13]

Thoughts of Self-Projection in Space and Time

When I was five years old, I thought I could fly. I remember sitting at the top of my linoleum stairwell in our house in Indiana and projecting my self to the bottom of the stairs without moving. I would project my self into other people—a little girl in an adjacent car at a traffic light, for instance—and experience their view, their feelings, their world. Yet flying did not fit with the reason-based world in which I was immersed, so my thoughts of flight withered away.

These experiences probably signaled an important stage of my unfolding self-consciousness: the emergence of an agent of self that could be projected across space and time. The ability to "self-project" is proving to involve brain circuitry that uncannily matches that of the default brain state (discussed in Chapter 8).[14] Remember, the default state is what your brain does when you are not *doing* but are in a state of *being*. It is quite feasible that the default brain state is important in the development and fine-tuning of self-awareness.[15]

The Biology of Executive Function

When we are *doing*, using thought and reason, we leave the default brain state and activate the prefrontal cortex and its connections to other brain regions. The prefrontal cortex coordinates or orchestrates action, like the CEO (chief executive officer) of a company or the conductor of an orchestra (see Figures 2 and 3). I like the analogy of the prefrontal cortex as a sort of master architect. Our goals or intentions are like the buildings an architect creates, and the tools used to construct these "buildings" are called the "executive functions" of the prefrontal cortex—functions such as shifting attention, inhibiting distractions, accessing information from working memory, and monitoring and adjusting thoughts and actions. The architect of the brain may not know how to do a specific task (language), but it can find and coordinate the parts of brain that do so, from start to finish. Depending on how good the architect is—like the CEO of any corporation—the final product may be a dream house or an unfinished disaster.

We come with a kind of blueprint—our DNA code—that lays out a plan for how our individual brains will develop, structurally and functionally, including our individual "architect." Experience then shapes and molds the architect, who shapes and molds the experiences—our successes and failures, our intentions, goals, and actions along the way. Sometimes we build from scratch, and sometimes we remodel. A good architect has a clear picture of a building (goal) in mind and knows whom to hire, how to coordinate the work through time, where to purchase the right materials, and how to integrate it all into a whole, finished product. Selecting materials, contractors, and subcontractors and monitoring and modifying the project along the way are under the guidance of the architect. Sometimes the architect attends to micro details—the shape and size of doorknobs, for instance—and other times she attends to the macro "big picture," stepping back to look at the emerging structure and check it against the imagined outcome. To get things done, to accomplish, to produce, to make things happen, our prefrontal cortex shifts from micro to macro activity all the time.

As with architects, our individual prefrontal cortices differ in how well they execute. Some expert architects require little training; others need many years of apprenticeship. Some architects constantly create new structures, while others repetitively build the same house over and over again. Some architects plaster cosmetic features on structures, ignoring rotting wood or maligned electrical wiring, while others strip a house to studs. These differences reflect our DNA blueprints and the experiences that have shaped their expression patterns, which we reshape through our experiences and actions. Most of us don't need a blood test* to know where we fall on the "architect" spectrum (the functions of the prefrontal cortex). Do you start a lot of projects and then let them all fall by the wayside, or do you set realistic goals and achieve them with small methodical steps? Or are you somewhere in between?

_____

*There is no blood test to determine executive functioning abilities as of this date.

Mindfulness Training and Thought

A friend once asked me, "Does mindfulness keep you from running through the series of steps to do something? Will I just be present and not think about things in the future?" She was planning a trip from London to Los Angeles and had a huge to-do list, including packing, feeding her cats, getting her tickets, getting to the airport, changing planes in New York, remembering to bring her U.S. cell phone, and so on. Would mindfulness, she wondered, put her securely in the present but not help her prepare to get to L.A.?

Mindfulness doesn't change the need to prepare, to follow a sequence of steps to get something done, and to use the tools you have to do that (remember them, write them down, make lists, and so on). That is the function of the prefrontal cortex: to plan, organize, and carry out steps toward your goals—getting to Los Angeles in my friend's case. Mindfulness does not make it any less necessary to carry out these functions, but it can help you distinguish the necessary steps from all the *unnecessary* ones (like worrying all night long that she would miss her alarm or miss her connection or fail to feed her cats) and then apply them.

Using Mindfulness to See Conceptual Frameworks

We have emphasized throughout this book that mindfulness is a means of seeing the conceptual frameworks by which you live—how your thoughts shape your worldview. We repeat this point because it is so hard to remember when we get stuck in one way of thinking; we forget that this way of thinking was created to a large extent by our own thoughts.

Remember your worldview when you were five years of age? When you were fifteen? Or twenty-five? Or fifty? The body of knowledge you accumulate, your thoughts, your interactions, memories, and experiences, all shape and reshape your worldview, which is the lens through which you filter your experience. Mindfulness is a means of investigating such frameworks—your belief systems, your biases, your blind spots.

To see how mindfulness affects conceptual frameworks, Daniel Brown of Harvard studied the impact of meditation on interpretation of Rorschach blots.[16] Rorschach blots are those black-and-white inkblot images that psychologists use to examine personality and emotional differences based on what patients "see" in the figures. Using Rorschach blots, Brown elicited responses from thirty meditators before and after they went on a three-month intensive mindfulness retreat. Prior to the retreat, responses to the Rorschach blots were basically the same across all subjects—there was a variety of responses, but no real differences between groups who varied in meditation experience. At the end of the retreat, subjects were classified into high- and low-concentration groups based on their teacher's rating and a self-report questionnaire assessing depth of concentration. Rorschach response in the post-retreat period looked very different. The group considered high in concentration rarely produced content or images in response to the inkblots, but rather described the shapes of the ink, the color, the shading, the swirling movement, to a much greater extent than did the low-concentration group. The data support the idea that meditation training lessens our tendency to attach stories to our sensory experiences and heightens our capacity to detect experiences "as they are," with "bare attention."

Even with a minimal amount of information, our brains can identify experiences based on our conceptual frameworks. For example, scientists recently discovered that we can detect an image (like an apple or a tree or a vase) with merely 20 percent of the image present (measured, for instance, by the pixels of a picture).[17] Your mind "sees" an image with just a sketchy imprint of it by tapping into the memory centers of previous experiences. Your brain quickly forms meaning from even the smallest quantity of information, and mindfulness is a means to investigate the automatic patterns you have built up over your lifetime. Using mindfulness meditation to investigate the conceptual frameworks you take for granted, you can bring bare attention to your experience as a matter of choice.

Bear in mind that we could not function as individuals or as a society if we did not share conceptual models of the world and how it works. In certain brain disorders, like schizophrenia, conceptual templates break down, causing disorganized thought and hallucinations; without a framework of the world, experiences are no doubt bizarre and at times frightening. Researchers in quantum physics, the study of the behavior of very small objects, are beginning to study the precise relationship between concepts and physical reality. They are looking at how consciousness influences the behavior of very small objects, and some scientists are extrapolating these findings to see how consciousness may shape the world as a whole.[18] As science moves us closer to understanding consciousness and its role in shaping reality, the nature of reality will become clearer. Mindfulness does not tackle these issues using science per se (remember, mindfulness is a first-person experience), but it can help us uncover our own specific belief systems, biases, and thought patterns and show us how they affect our day-to-day lives and our view of the world and our place in it.

Some of us are so stuck in well-worn, automatic thought patterns, created before we had the capacity to think, that they are hard to see. Finding these patterns may require the help of someone else, but bringing them into consciousness is part of mindfulness. Sometimes in a flash of insight, but more often over an extended period of time, you can recognize such thought patterns. After years of habitual thinking that may have begun in childhood, perhaps you have thought patterns that are no longer useful—or that are even harmful to yourself or others—but you find it difficult to let them go because they are familiar and you are so comfortable with them, like an old worn-out couch you refuse to throw out.

Thoughts Shape Your Reality

Brain imaging studies show that the thought of an object activates the same brain regions as the real experience, although with less intensity.[19] If you think of a shiny red apple, your brain responds in much the same way it would if you were actually holding or seeing a red shiny apple; the response is just an order of magnitude less. This reduction is probably important because if the experience were no greater than the thought, we would probably never get up and do anything. Our thoughts seem real because they trigger brain activity similar to what happens in our brains with the real thing. It is not surprising then that "false thoughts" lead us to perceive reality incorrectly. This is in fact why science is a methodology based on third-person observation: First-person experiences are notoriously subject to error. Because we experience through a lens constructed by our attention and past experiences, the filters through which we interpret the world may differ from reality. Mindfulness is a method to clean the lens of our experience. It helps us move closer and closer to paying "bare attention" to experience, without the filtering.

If how we think shapes how we experience the world, does how we think correspond to how we act in the world? The neuroscientist Marcel Just uses fMRI to "read the minds" of research participants by examining brain patterns as they think about different concepts. His research shows that we can fairly accurately detect what people are thinking about (for example, a hammer, a screwdriver, or a building) by the pattern revealed in their brains.[20] It is only a matter of time before a computer connected to such a scanner can "read" more complex thoughts and intentions; the application of such neurotechnology is already of interest to marketing companies and law enforcement agencies.

The ethical question raised by "neurodetection" is one asked at the level of behavior: How does a thought relate to action? If you think of buying a bottle of Jack Daniels, do you always buy it? If you think of stealing a candy bar, do you do it? Intention and action are not always the same thing, and science is just beginning to reveal their relationship. Mindfulness is a tool for investigating the difference and to begin to discern the space in between. For example, if you are angry and intend to hurl an insult at the driver who just cut you off, do you do it all the time, some of the time, or never? With mindfulness, you increase your level of discernment—that is, your capacity to detect a thought before it becomes an action—and in this discernment *you create a greater capacity to pause and choose among alternative actions.* Because many actions arise outside conscious awareness, mindfulness is a means to broaden the field of awareness.

The Stress of Decision-Making

In *Walden*, Henry David Thoreau gives this advice for better enjoying life: "Simplify, simplify, simplify."[21] We are faced with thousands of decisions every day. Do I have to get up? Should I have tea or coffee? Shower or bath? What day is it? What do I wear? Who is waking up the kids? What's for breakfast? Should I walk the dog? Should I work out?

All before 7:00 AM.

In *all* decision-making there is conflict and stress, albeit of varying intensity. The stress of deciding between coffee and tea is much less than the stress of deciding whether to move to a new city, quit a job, marry, or divorce. Not all decisions are the same. Some are unambiguous and have single correct answers (*What is 150 + 275? What day is it?*), while others are ambiguous and have no correct answer (*Should I wear a coat or a sweater?*). Elkhonen Goldberg notes that we learn how to answer unambiguous questions in our schools—as math, history, physics, chemistry, and so, are taught—yet the real world tends to be largely ambiguous.[22] We prepare our children well to handle decisions that we rarely face in life. Ambiguous decision-making is what we do day in and day out, and how we solve ambiguous problems differs as a function of our genes, our gender, and our environments.

Goldberg and other scientists who study ambiguous decision-making have shown that we naturally "disambiguate the situation" to make ambiguous decisions less stressful. For example, if you ask yourself, "Am I wearing a coat or sweater today?" you can disambiguate the situation by rephrasing the question: "Which of my clothes best match the weather?"[23] If you know that it is a cold rainy day, your answer to the new question is easier (less ambiguous): You will probably wear a coat. Even "big" questions can be disambiguated. For example, deciding whether to quit a job might be less ambiguous (and therefore less stressful) if you reduce the decision to one of finances alone and one job pays more.

Laws provide a useful way to disambiguate situations by providing a qualification that makes the decision easier (*I need money. Should I rob a bank and risk jail or go to work to pay the rent?*). Personal ethics and a code of conduct can help you disambiguate the situations underlying your decisions, as can social rules circumscribed by religion and laws. Mindfulness helps disambiguate situations by clarifying your personal ethic and code of conduct, and thus your subsequent questions. For example, mindfulness led me to feel a strong sense of interconnection with other living beings, and as a consequence I became vegetarian. The previously ambiguous choice between steak and veggies was simplified immensely; the only acceptable decision for me now is one aligned with vegetarianism. But please keep in mind that many people who practice mindfulness are not vegetarians and make different ethical choices.

Multi-Tasking and Its Effects on Learning

In addition to the stress of ambiguous decision-making, constant interruptions from cell phones, Blackberries, Facebook, Twitter, and so on, are creating another source of stressful thinking: multi-tasking. Today multi-tasking is the norm rather than the exception, and science is showing that it can hurt our ability to learn. Russell Poldrack, a psychologist at the University of Texas in Austin, studied subjects' ability to learn a simple task (categorizing cards by shape and size) in an uninterrupted situation and then also while being asked to count the number of high-tone beeps from a beeping noise.[24] Subjects' performance on the task did not differ between the two situations, but under the distracting condition they could not recall the cards or very much information about the task itself. Under both conditions, the brains of the subjects were examined using fMRI. The part of the brain that is important in learning and memory, the hippocampus, was active only during the uninterrupted condition, while another part of the brain—the striatum—became active during the interrupted case.

The study suggests that when we multi-task a different part of the brain is involved in carrying out any one task, and it is not a part of the brain that is very efficient for memory and learning. This study by Poldrack and his colleagues does not demonstrate that, for instance, listening to music or exercising when learning is unhelpful, but rather that interruptions *that disrupt focused attention* may impair learning. Focused attention appears to be vital for maximizing our learning potential, and as we saw in the previous chapter, mindfulness may be an important way to enhance focused attention in the midst of a multi-tasking environment.

Mindfulness and Obsessive Thoughts

Meta-cognitive awareness is known to reduce the stress associated with obsessive or repetitive thinking. The psychiatrist Jeffrey Schwartz showed that this stance can help individuals with obsessive-compulsive disorder (OCD), which is characterized by "distressing, intrusive and unwanted thoughts (obsessions) that trigger intense urges to perform ritualistic behaviors (compulsions)."[25] His four-step program includes a meta-cognitive awareness stance that significantly reduces the obsessions and compulsions of OCD patients. In fact, patients who have undergone the four-step program show brain changes (as assessed by PET* scans) comparable to those found among patients given traditional pharmacological treatment for the condition.

---

*PET scans use a radioactively labeled sugar dye to trace sugar (glucose) uptake in the brain using a positron emission spectrum machine that reveals the varying activity in the brain.

Is mindfulness effective in rewiring our thoughts because it calms us down, or does it do more? Researchers at the University of San Diego compared pure relaxation exercises to mindfulness meditation and found that obsessive thoughts (or ruminations) were reduced more with mindfulness than with relaxation alone.[26] Mindfulness meditation affects how you relate to your thoughts, changing your participation in them from "entangled" to "unentangled," similar to how we saw it enable you to disidentify from positive and negative emotions. In the disidentification, a sense of space between you and your thoughts grows, allowing you to evaluate, release, and let go of destructive thought patterns and ultimately revalue constructive ones. (This last step is of crucial importance in Schwartz's four-step program and highlights not only the importance of mindfulness but the value of evaluation and reevaluation.) Psychotherapy, narrative therapy, and other psychoanalytic approaches may be useful in such efforts, either alone or in tandem with your mindfulness practice.

Change Your Thoughts and Change Your Brain

Meditation, including mindfulness, may affect how we think and the brain structures and functions underlying our thinking. We saw in Chapter 5 that longtime meditators have thicker brain regions than nonmeditators.[27] While *overall* brain thickness was the same in the two groups, certain brain regions were thicker in meditators, particularly the right insula cortex, a region of the brain important for integrating sensory, cognitive, and emotional information. A thicker cortex is thought to represent more gray matter and more neurons communicating.

Your brain cortex changes in thickness throughout your life. When you are young, your brain fills up with neurons (thickness), followed by a period of thinning (called pruning) during which extraneous cells and connections are removed. These processes correspond with an increase in the ability to organize, remember, attend, inhibit, and carry out complex cognitive tasks. But as you move through adulthood, your brain thins again, this time through the gradual loss of neurons and their branching, a process that accompanies mental decline with age. Nevertheless, older meditators did not show the same loss of cortical thickness that nonmeditators of the same age showed in certain brain regions, suggesting that meditation may prevent the normal thinning of the brain with age.[28]

Not only does the structure of the brains of longtime meditators and nonmeditators appear different, but brain *function*—revealed through EEG, fMRI, or PET imaging—changes as well. In the study of OCD patients, PET scans revealed a clear reduction in activation of the neural circuit known to be involved in obsessive-compulsive disorder in patients given a ten-week mindfulness-based practice, a finding similar to that seen in patients given medication treatment for the condition.[29]

EEG studies also demonstrate that meditation changes brain function. With meditation, theta waves increase in the frontal cortex, consistent with the idea that the front part of the brain is becoming calm.[30] Another finding from EEG studies is that there is a change in the activity of the right versus left frontal hemispheres: More alpha wave activity occurs on the right before meditation compared to more alpha wave activity on the left during or after meditation. EEG alpha wave change does not give a straightforward accounting of what is happening inside the brain—some scientists argue that an increase in alpha means the brain is *more* active, while other scientists think it reflects less activity—and the relationship may be even more complex, that is, it may mean different things depending on where in the brain it is observed. Interpretation of some EEG changes is still a topic of debate because without looking at activity inside the brain (using fMRI, for example) simultaneously, interpretation can be difficult. Despite questions regarding interpretation at the level of brain function, these EEG changes during meditation correlate with behavior and body changes. Davidson's group found that more alpha wave activity in the left hemisphere corresponds to a feeling of happiness and a boost in the immune response.[31]

EEG patterns also reveal that not all meditation practices are alike with respect to how they may affect the brain. Mindfulness meditation shows EEG patterns that are different from those of concentrative meditation or deep relaxation. In one study comparing the three, mindfulness meditation showed patterns consistent with both concentration and relaxation, while the other two methods showed only one or the other.[32] Lastly, EEG patterns reveal increased coherence, suggesting that meditation creates synchronization of various brain regions, from front to back and between the left to right hemispheres.[33]

THE ART

For most of us, a day barely goes by when we don't find ourselves mired in our thoughts. I woke up this morning with a slight backache. As I felt the pain, my mind immediately took off like a rocket: *Wow, this mattress is really too soft, I've got to call the mattress store, maybe I can exchange it for a harder one. This is the fifth time I've gotten a backache, I wonder if something is seriously wrong. What if it doesn't go away? I better call a chiropractor. . . .* And so on and so on.

Sound familiar?

Of course it does; most of us are not unique in how we think. Something sparks a thought—a memory, an internal or external stimulus—and our minds run with it. Much of the time our thinking is simply functional or neutral and not particularly positive or negative. We plan our day, figure out what we need to get at the grocery store, choose our clothes, wonder where the cat is, and so on. Sometimes our thoughts are pleasant, creative, loving, or compassionate—we notice a homeless person on the street and think *I want to help him out*, or we create a poem in our head, or we invent a new way to recycle waste water. But some thoughts can be repetitive, painful, obsessive, or hurtful and can lead to suffering, either our own or another person's. Mindfulness helps us work with these difficult and stressful thoughts.

The Top Ten

As we learned in the science section, thoughts arise from electrical and chemical brain processes, and the prefrontal cortex plays an important role in their modulation. Many thoughts are emotionally neutral, and some are pleasant; it is the unpleasant ones that tend to pose the greatest problems for us. We all have our "top ten" problematic thoughts: those kinds of thoughts that recur frequently and are especially challenging. For one person, it's worried thoughts (*What if my child gets sick?*) For another, it's grief-based thinking (*I'll never get through this day*). For some, angry thoughts are the ones that recur too frequently (*He left the dishes in the sink again; I'm going to explode!*) And for still others, desirous thoughts are the problem (*He has to fall in love with me, it's the only thing that will make me happy*). Some people may have trouble with the flow of thought itself—too many, too often, too distracting.

A thought category that tends to cause people a lot of suffering is one we might call "self-hating" thoughts. You think you are not good enough, not pretty enough, or not successful enough, and you judge your looks, your capacities, your skills, or how your life has turned out. You think you are not tall enough, not attractive enough, or not smart enough; you are sure that you are going to fail at your job, your relationship, your (you name it). These are thoughts in which you compare yourself to others or to some standard you have for yourself.

Any of these thoughts can be difficult because they cause pain. When you have them, you can feel twisted up inside, overwhelmed, or fearful. These thoughts can make you anxious, angry, deeply sad, regretful, ashamed, or remorseful. In the previous chapter, you learned some tools for working with difficult emotions; here you will learn how to work with the thinking that leads to and reinforces the difficult emotions.

Psychologists have long used certain tools to change the content of thoughts, the most common practice being cognitive therapy (CT), described in Chapter 6. The major difference between CT and mindfulness practice is that in the former you attempt to change the content of your thought, while in the latter you change your relationship to thought. When you change your relationship to thought, it may even be easier to then change the content of your thought. Mindfulness is a tool to change how you relate to your thoughts.

Begin by identifying your top ten troublesome thoughts. What kinds of thoughts drive you crazy? The answer may be immediately obvious to you (worry, for example), or it may take a little self-observation. If you are not sure, during the course of the coming week try to notice the recurring thoughts you have that cause you discomfort or pain. The next time you are feeling bad (anxious, upset, angry), try to identify the thoughts that brought you to this state of mind.

Coping with Difficult Thinking

If you, like most people, have spent a lifetime with challenging thoughts, you have probably learned ways to cope with them—some of which are helpful, and some of which are not. When thoughts overwhelm you, maybe you go out for a run or call a friend. You may choose to have a cocktail or to calm your thoughts by eating. Many people distract themselves with excessive Internet use and television- or movie-watching, which, in the extreme, can become addictive.

One of the main ways people deal with difficult thinking is through thinking itself. You can use thoughts to soothe other thoughts and feelings. For example, if you are anxious because you are caught in traffic and late to an appointment, you may start talking to yourself: *It's okay, I don't have control over the traffic, I'll get there when I get there. . . .* This is quite a skillful response to the situation. Called "positive self-talk," or self-soothing, it's a kind of thinking you use to counteract other kinds of thinking in order to soothe yourself, regulate your emotions, or generally bring some wisdom to the part of your mind that may seem out of control because you are scared, angry, or sad. For instance, if you are angry and having all sorts of rage-filled thoughts about the jerk who just cut you off on the freeway, positive self-talk is another kind of thinking that may kick in, intervening in your mind and saying, *Relax, it's not a big deal, he didn't mean it.*

There are additional ways of using thought to counteract difficult thinking. Thought replacement, for example, is taking a negative thought and replacing it with a positive thought: *I'm definitely going to get fired* becomes *I am doing a good job at my work.* Another technique is using affirmations: telling yourself something positive in the expectation that through repetition you will begin to believe it (*My financial situation can improve day by day, I have nothing to be afraid of.*)

The Mindful Approach—Don't Get on the Train

All of the tools to reduce stressful thinking described here are useful. Mindfulness is another very helpful approach that you can add to your tool kit—one that may even go above and beyond certain other techniques. How might you be mindful of your thoughts?

Stop for a moment and reexamine how your thoughts may cause you pain. Generally, thinking cascades: One thought leads to another, then to another, and meanwhile some of these thoughts are evoking emotions that lead to more thoughts, and so on. You can learn, in the midst of your thinking, to be mindful of thinking without getting caught up in the thought. You can learn to merely see the thought as a thought and then let it go.

Here is an analogy that may be helpful. You are standing on a train platform. A train is leaving the station, and it symbolizes your thoughts. The
train builds up momentum, starting small but soon beginning to race, speed-
ing down the track. Most of us will jump on that train (get caught in our
thoughts) and then find ourselves twenty miles down the road before we realize how lost in thought we have been. If you are mindful of your thoughts instead, you remain standing at the train platform as the train takes off rather
than jumping on board the "thought train." The difficult thought happens,
but you do not get caught in it, nor do you let it speed up, grow, and prolif-
erate. You understand that you do not have to get on that train.

What might this look like in practice? Begin by returning to the disidentification process. You can be aware of your thoughts rising and departing
without being caught up in them—you can have "unentangled participa-
tioin" in them. You might feel as though you have some space from your
thoughts. You can notice your thoughts—*Here's a fearful thought, there goes
an angry thought*, and so on—without being identified with them. In other
words, you can watch the angry "thought train" leave the station without getting on it—that is, without getting identified with the thought. You can perceive the thought as "just a thought" passing through your mind. You are
aware of it, even curious about it, but you are not hooked by it, and therefore
it does not cause you suffering.

Alan Wallace, a Buddhist scholar, uses an interesting example to illustrate
this point. Make a hook with each of your index fingers and then hook them
together. This is what two thoughts catching one another is like—what
jumping on the train looks like, if you will. Straighten just one finger and the
other finger (the thought) cannot stay hooked on to it. Straightening your
finger is not jumping on the train but letting go.

Don't Believe Everything You Think

I once saw a bumper sticker that could sum up this chapter: DON'T BELIEVE
EVERYTHING YOU THINK. Most of the time we believe our thoughts. They
hook us, so much so that we become them; we lose touch with the fact that
they are merely thoughts flowing through our minds. Mindfulness is a
means to separate yourself from your thoughts and be able to participate in
them but be disentangled from them. That is, you can create them, but you

do not need to become them. Think about the way a camera works. It "sees" everything that happens within the frame of the picture, but it is not affected by anything it focuses on. The camera can take any image and simply frame it—just as you can learn to do with your thoughts.

Let me give you an example. Lena is at work when she receives an e-mail from her boss. Before she opens it, her thoughts immediately start racing: *Uh-oh, this is it, I screwed up big-time on the last project, and they know it, I don't know what I'm going to do. . . .* She feels her hands starting to sweat, her face heating up, her stomach churning. Lena is identified with her thought—she has gotten aboard that train. Alternatively, when Lena sees the e-mail she could take a breath, step back, and notice the thoughts coming: *Wow, I'm having a lot of anxious thoughts.* She could label the thoughts: *Worry, fear, anxiety.* She could feel the emotions and sensations inside her body (tense stomach, shortness of breath). Once she recognizes the thoughts, she could use some positive self-talk: *Okay, relax, I really have no idea what this e-mail contains.* The mindfulness stance makes space between Lena and her thoughts, creating a different sort of relationship. Using mindfulness, Lena can prevent her thoughts from spiraling out of control and let them leave the station while she stays on the platform. With mindfulness, Lena is able to *disidentify* by not believing her thoughts so thoroughly, thus creating more peace of mind rather than agitation.

How Do We Disidentify?

One main tool for disidentifying in the midst of difficult thinking is to label your thoughts, just as you label your emotions. When a thought arises that clearly is going to lead to suffering, you can say, *Worried thoughts . . . fearful thoughts . . . angry thoughts. . . .* Labeling thoughts functions in much the same way as labeling emotions in that it regulates the emotional circuitry in the brain that creates an overall calming effect, helping you get a little separation from all-compelling thoughts.

You can also pay attention inside your body when you have a repetitive thought. Often repetitive thoughts are fueled by underlying emotions, and if you can become aware of the emotion, particularly as it manifests in your body, you can notice the thought is accompanied by a collection of sensations: churning in your gut, vibration in your chest, and heat in your face, for example. As you take your attention off the content of the thoughts (*He's such a jerk, I can't believe he did that to me, oh no, I'm going to get sick!*) and place it instead on any bodily sensations you might have (*My stomach is very tight*), you can avoid getting on the train leaving the station. You become mindful of the sensations associated with the thoughts and thereby start to witness your experience rather than be caught in it.

By placing your attention on bodily sensations rather than on the story you are telling yourself, you can relax a bit, and the thinking may even stop on its own—trailing off or completing itself. It is no longer fueled by underlying bodily sensations.

A PRACTICE: NOTICING YOUR BODY AMID DIFFICULT THOUGHTS

The next time you find yourself caught in a difficult or obsessive thought, bring your attention directly into your body and feel what is happening inside. Discover whether the thought seems to have an underlying bodily sensation or emotion. In the beginning it may be difficult to identify any bodily sensations, but give it a try.

To start, take a few mindful breaths to bring some focus to yourself. If it helps you relax a bit, try breathing a little bit longer. Then sense your body—what do you notice? First check your stomach area. Notice whether there are any sensations in your gut. Is it clenched or relaxed? If you find a particular sensation, stay aware of it for several seconds and notice what happens to it as you become aware of it.

Next check your chest area. Notice any particular sensations such as tightness, constriction, vibration, or heaviness. Again, if you notice some sensation, keep your awareness in the area to observe what happens to the sensation. It may intensify, decrease, or stop; it may change into another sensation in the same or another part of your body. It may stay the same. Try to have no agenda for it, but observe and feel with curiosity and openness.

Then bring your awareness to your throat area. Any sensations there? Tightness, constriction, heaving? Pay attention in the same way you did with your stomach and chest.

Finally, notice your face. What sensations are present there? You may feel heat or tightness or vibrations or something else I have not mentioned.

If the sensations start to feel overwhelming, you can always return to your breathing. And of course, do this only as long as it feels helpful. This practice may last one minute or much longer, depending on your sense of what is needed. ■

You can also disidentify from your thoughts by counting your thoughts, a technique that helps make apparent the habitual nature of thinking. Try this: Each time you have a judgmental thought (criticizing yourself or others), count it. For example, you wake up in the morning feeling immediately critical of yourself: *Ugh, I slept through my alarm, I'm such a jerk.* That's 1. You walk into the bathroom: *Oh no, I forgot to buy toothpaste, I'm so forgetful.* That's 2. And so on.

If you reach judgmental thought number 82 and it's only 10:00 AM, you may begin to see something about the habitual nature of your mind. Your mind thinks; that is what it does. Just as your heart pumps blood and your lungs take in air, your mind produces thoughts. Much of your thinking is habitual, conditioned by family, media, and so on, and you have internalized this kind of thinking. You have been thinking these thoughts for most of your life and take them to be accurate and unchangeable.

By counting difficult thoughts, you can bring a little humor into the situation: *These are just my thoughts, but there certainly are a lot of them, and are they ever critical!* You can find some space and a quality of disidentification that allows you to recognize that whatever is causing so much inner disturbance is just another thought arising in your mind; it is not you, it is not personal. Jeanette, a thirty-nine-year-old business owner, described this experience:

I am waiting for my plane to leave. It is 10:53 PM. It is delayed by over four hours. I don't like flying. It makes me anxious, so I am using this as an opportunity to practice working with thoughts: *The plane is delayed . . . that's a sign that there is something wrong.* Fearful thought 1. *Image of plane falling from sky.* Scary image 1. *We're all gonna die.* Fear 2. *It was crazy of me to take this trip to Chicago when I'm already so busy! That's what happens when you make bad choices.* Self-judging thought 1 . . . and on and on and on. . . . I can feel my anxiety mitigating. I feel more relaxed as I disidentify myself from these thoughts and images.

Down the Road

You may ask, does stressful thinking ever go away? If you are mindful enough, will you be able to stop the thoughts that have tormented you for so long? The answer is yes and no. Difficult thinking does lessen over time, but since thinking is a core part of the human experience, there will probably always be more to come. One friend of mine refers to herself as a "recovered fretter": Her anxious thoughts, which ruled her for most of her life, are not nearly as strong as they used to be, but she still has to work with them to a certain extent since fretting is a tendency of her mind. Regardless, learning to relate differently to your thoughts can be a life-saver, as Anne, a forty-three-year-old researcher, relates:

> Before meditation, I was constantly struggling with self-sabotage. You wouldn't believe the kind of things my mind would tell me—that I'd never be able to hold a job, that my boss hated me. Then it would say I was too good for the job anyway, and what did I care. So I'd have an attitude and then get fired, and I'd say, "Big deal," but inside I was devastated. After some years of practicing mindfulness, I've had much more success with working with my thoughts. I worked really hard to be aware of the self-sabotaging thoughts, to see them as just thoughts. I was very vigilant for years, it seemed. Therapy helped too. And then the strangest thing happened. They stopped coming so much. Or they'd only come when I was really stressed out. I have been in my current job for the last three years, and I love it, and my boss loves me. It's kind of unbelievable considering my job history.

By using mindfulness with continued vigilance and combining it with the cultivation of positive emotions, you are likely to see these thoughts arising less frequently. Even if they still arise, they will hardly have the same impact on you that they used to; you might say to yourself: *Oh, that's just an anxious thought, I know you, not a big deal.*

You can still have anxious, sad, angry thoughts, but you see them for what they are—anxious, sad, or angry *thoughts*—and you can choose to identify with them or not. Over time they may still arise, but if you learn to notice them with compassion and mindfulness, you can let them be and not be so affected by them. David, a fifty-year-old producer, reported this change:

> For most of my life I was very judgmental. When people would do something I thought was wrong, wow, my mind would go off. I'd have a million judgments about how stupid this person was, how I could do it better. Truthfully, I had a lot of moral superiority, and it hurt me. I felt so different than them. Worse, I would feel embarrassed that I had these thoughts all the time. Couldn't I just be kinder? So I really worked with these thoughts using mindfulness. It's been a number of years now, and what I notice is that I can still get judgmental, but instead of getting mad at myself for it, I say, *There's another judgment!* I sort of laugh about it and see it as my habit of mind. It's so much less of a problem. Honestly, it's a big relief!

THE PRACTICES

Read through these practices a few times to get a firm idea of them and then try them on your own.

Exercise 1: Thoughts Laboratory

Begin your meditation with five minutes of breath awareness. Notice your breath rising and falling in your abdomen or chest, or moving in and out of your nostrils. When your mind wanders, simply bring your attention back to your breathing.

Once your mind feels steady, try an experiment. Imagine you are a scientist observing the "laboratory" of your mind to learn how thoughts work inside a mind. What do you notice about your thoughts? Do they come quickly or slowly? Use labeling to help you recognize the different thoughts. When you notice a planning thought, label it *planning*, label a worried thought *worrying*, label a memory *remembering*. See if it is possible to be mindful of your thinking. If this feels complicated, return to your breath and notice a few breaths until your mind regains a feeling of stability, then try again. If you have repetitive difficult thoughts, you can check in with your body and see if something is happening inside. Check for any physical sensations of emotions. Notice whether you are getting on the train or staying on the platform. Enjoy being a scientist of your mind.

Exercise 2: Adding Thoughts to Your Daily Mindfulness Meditation

The general principle of mindfulness meditation is to keep your mind focused on your anchor—which for most people is the breath. When something else enters your awareness more strongly than the breath, such as sounds, bodily sensations, emotions, or thoughts, you turn your attention to this new focus. You notice what happens to this new focus, and how it changes. When it has stopped or no longer holds your attention, you return to the breath, your anchor.

At this point in the book, you have received many ideas about objects to be aware of in your meditation. You have your breath as your anchor, you notice sounds, bodily sensations, and emotions, and now you can also be aware of thoughts. As with earlier instructions, keep your attention primarily on your breath during this exercise. Thoughts may be in the background; if so, just let them pass through. However, if a thought becomes repetitive, obsessive, or predominant, then you can let go of your breathing, bring your attention to the thought, and give it a label (*planning, remembering, worrying,* and so on). Notice what happens to thoughts as you become aware of them. Do they dissolve? If so, return to your breath or whatever is predominant. If not, you may notice an underlying emotion or strong sensation behind the thought. Check into your body. Make sure to breathe. Try to have some space in the midst of the thought. Once the thought no longer captivates you, return to your breathing.

Exercise 3: The Clouds and the Sky

In this exercise, you let go of your anchor to explore how open monitoring (described in Chapter 8) works with thoughts. Try this exercise when you have been sitting and meditating for a while and your mind feels fairly present and aware. If you start to get too spacey or to feel lost, go back to your anchor. Don't dwell too much in the analogy; just use it as one approach to meditating.

Let yourself bring to mind the following analogy: Imagine that your mind is like the sky; it is vast, open, spacious. Bring to mind a clear blue sky and try to sense that your mind is like that sky: open, expansive, vast. Now know that everything that moves through your mind is like clouds passing across the sky. Each thought that comes and goes is like a cloud flying through your sky. Can you sense your thoughts as clouds in the sky of your mind?

You might notice sensations, emotions, and sounds flying by as well. There might be wispy clouds or stormy clouds, maybe some beautiful birds or rainbows. The sky is not disturbed by a stormy turbulent day, nor does it get overly excited by rainbows; it is merely present, the backdrop through which the clouds pass.

Try this practice for five or ten minutes, or as long as you feel drawn to it. If it feels too difficult, you can always return to awareness of your breathing.

10

WHAT GETS IN THE WAY?

Life's challenges are not supposed to paralyze you, they're supposed to help you discover who you are.

—BERNICE JOHNSON REAGAN,
AMERICAN HISTORIAN AND MUSICIAN

We may have the best intentions, but things get in the way of practicing mindfulness *all the time*. You may feel like you are mindful one minute and mindless the next. Or just when you think you are most mindful, *boom!* You realize that you have completely missed the boat. That is human nature, and the reason why you need a good sense of humor to develop a mindfulness practice and attempt to live more mindfully. What gets in the way? A simple three-letter word: YOU. This chapter will teach you how to work with yourself.

THE SCIENCE

Perhaps it seems circular to argue that *you* begin a mindfulness practice and then *you* get in its way. What do we mean by that? From the science perspective, it means that you are human—you are a biological organism responding, reacting, and learning in life.

We humans may have a level of self-consciousness unmatched by other species, but we are still living, breathing biological organisms who share large quantities of DNA with other species and with one another. And as humans, we eat, drink, breathe, and reproduce to survive from birth to death and across time. Our survival may take a somewhat different form than it does for other species on the planet, what with our Blackberries, computers, and flat-screen televisions, but in many ways we are also very much the same as other species: We compete over resources, whether for food, water, shelter, or jobs, and we cooperate for survival through mother-child attachment, group living, and sexual reproduction. We are both the same as each other (shared DNA and shared experiences) and different from one another (unique DNA and unique experiences), and we are both the same as and different from other organisms by degree.

When you practice mindfulness, you may have every intention of attending to the present-moment experience, yet encoded in your biology is a full spectrum of response patterns (physical, mental, and emotional) with millions of years of development behind them, as well as memories of past experiences, both individual memories from your lifetime and the ancestral memories we all receive through culture. You are likely to be swayed by the magnitude of these influences and lose your attention to present-moment experience, *repeatedly*, despite your intentions. Individual biology and past history may even shape the specific obstacles by which you are distracted away from the present, but the sense of being swept away from the present—whether the sensation is small or large, frequent or infrequent—is part of being human.

Understanding more about your own biology, such as personality and cognition, may help you prepare for the specific type of difficulty you are likely to face in mindfulness meditation, but bumping into obstacles is something we all experience. Obstacles never disappear completely, but with practice you can learn to lower the height of the barriers they pose. Knowing that obstacles are part of the process may make their arrival less threatening or frightening, and maybe it will give you an opportunity to laugh at the shared and repetitive nature of it all.

The Genetics of You

We have talked about genetics and how it influences the way you think and feel, along with the environmental experiences you have had, but what can we learn about the likeliest obstacles to mindfulness practice based on genetic blueprints? Let's start with the well-known heritable response patterns of temperament. Remember that temperament describes our individual differences in how we respond to experience and our regulatory behavior, as characterized along three or four dimensions. The Cloninger model includes four scales of temperament: approach to novel stimuli (novelty-seeking), avoidance of negative stimuli (harm-avoidance), dependency on reward (reward-dependence), and persistence.[1]

Understanding temperamental differences is one way to think about how you deal with different obstacles to your mindfulness practice. Certainly any obstacle can come your way, but temperamental differences may explain why certain obstacles are more common for you, while different obstacles plague other people. It is pretty easy to assess yourself for temperament using a wide number of self-report questionnaires.[2] As we will discuss more fully in the art section, there are seven common obstacles to mindfulness practice: sleepiness, restlessness, doubt, craving, aversion, boredom, and fear. Because mindfulness is a relatively new area of scientific investigation, there are no studies yet available that examine how to counter these obstacles or that suggest why they might arise. But from the 2,500-year history of mindfulness practice—largely within Buddhist communities—specific strategies to deal with these obstacles are available, and we discuss them in the art section. Right now, we draw on a large body of science of temperament to consider the obstacles you might be most likely to encounter.

Temperament is evident in infancy, relatively stable throughout the life span, and about 50 to 60 percent due to genes. If you are a highly novelty-seeking individual, just the thought of sitting quietly in meditation probably scares you away from even buying this book. On the other hand, novelty-seekers tend to be extremely curious, so you might be drawn to the book out of curiosity and be open to reading it (a little). Statements that reflect a novelty-seeking temperament are ones like: "I often try new things just for fun or thrills, even if most people think it is a waste of time"; "I like it when people can do whatever they want without strict rules and regulations"; and "I often do things based on how I feel at the moment without thinking about how they were done in the past."[3] If you are highly novelty-seeking, you are likely to feel restless much of the time and may be easily bored. Perhaps you have tried lots of different meditation practices, but once the novelty of the experience wears off, you get restless and bored. Restlessness and boredom are therefore likely to be two key obstacles to your mindfulness practice.

If you are harm-avoidant by temperament, you do not like painful situations. You react strongly when a tiny pain arises in meditation, and you may regularly avoid the meditation cushion or chair (or even the room they are in) to keep away from a mindfulness practice. A harm-avoidant temperament is measured by statements like: "I often feel tense and worried in unfamiliar situations"; "When I have to meet a group of strangers, I am shyer than most people are"; or "Usually, I am more worried than most people that something might go wrong in the future."[4] Someone who is highly harm-avoidant often worries and is anxious, doubtful, and fearful in day-to-day life. In meditation, the obstacles of doubt, fear, and aversion are likely to affect the harm-avoidant individual more than others.

Individuals who are very reward-dependent are sentimental, sociable, warm, and sympathetic compared to low-reward-dependent people, who are more critical, aloof, detached, and independent. Statements that measure reward-dependence include: "I like to please other people as much as I can"; and "I am more likely to cry at a sad movie than most people."[5] If you are a low-reward-dependent type, you are likely to be highly critical of your practice—you talk yourself out of practicing for numerous reasons, you may not tell others that you practice, and you often feel too independent to do something other people are touting as useful. Doubt and boredom are probably your most common obstacles to practice.

Persistence measures how well you can stick with something. People who score high on persistence are eager, determined, ambitious, and perfectionist. Those who score low on persistence are apathetic, spoiled, underachieving, and pragmatist. Statements that reflect persistence include: "I usually push myself harder than most people do because I want to do as well as I possibly can"; "I am usually so determined that I continue to work long after other people have given up"; and "I am more hardworking than most people are."[6] After the initial newness of mindfulness wears off, those with low persistence are likely to meet the obstacles of craving (desiring something else) and aversion (giving up and staying away from the practice). Were you one of the first to buy a treadmill and enthusiastically begin a daily running regimen, but within a week lost your motivation and turned the treadmill into just another place to hang your clothes? That may be a sign of a low-persistence temperament. Boredom and restlessness may prove to be obstacles for the low-persistent individual, while doubt and avoidance may emerge for the highly persistent, perfectionist individual who "can't seem to meditate just right."

Sleepiness is another common obstacle, one that arises not only from physical fatigue or lack of sleep but also from some of the temperament features described here. For example, you may get sleepy when boredom sets in or as a way to avoid the obstacle of aversion.

As far as we know, no studies have investigated individual differences in temperament and the types of obstacles that people face with a mindfulness practice, but we think it could be a valuable line of research. We offer these possible associations based on the obstacles to mindfulness noted in the Buddhist tradition and the dimensions of temperament from psychology that predict how we will respond to experiences in general, mindfulness included. Learning more about your own temperament may help you anticipate potential barriers to developing and continuing a practice. Most importantly, recognizing your tendencies may help you accept the inevitable challenges and enable you to observe them with a sense of humor and kindness. Just knowing that you may be prone to one type of obstacle more than another because of your temperament may help you counter obstacles as they arise. That self-awareness will also enable you to use the methods for countering obstacles described in the next section more effectively.

THE ART

As we saw in the science section, most of us have the best of intentions to be mindful of our breath and body when we meditate. We sit down to meditate with renewed commitment and vigor, but inevitably something begins to disturb even our best-laid plans. We drift off, get lost in fantasies, worry about a project coming up at work or school, or grow concerned over issues in our family. We become anxious, sleepy, moody, frustrated, doubtful, and on and on. Generally, when this happens, we think we are doing something wrong, but that may not be the case at all.

Obstacles arise in meditation practice because obstacles are a part of life. No matter what we do, we sometimes encounter difficulties. Say I want to climb a mountain, and my intention is to reach the pinnacle in four days. Well, as we all know, anything can derail that intention. External obstacles are certainly a possibility: I might encounter inclement weather that delays me, or I might get lost, take the wrong turn, or fall and hurt myself. Internal obstacles are another potential hazard: I might get scared, anxious, confused about directions, doubtful that I can make it to the top, exhausted, and so on. The idea of a backpacking trip going off without a hitch is wishful thinking!

With mindfulness practice, you can also encounter obstacles, both inner and outer, as you meditate. The outer obstacles might be your children or pets coming into the room to interrupt you, an important phone call ringing in the middle of a meditation, or a life event so difficult and time-consuming that you don't take the time to meditate for weeks. Inner obstacles include everything just mentioned that could go wrong on a backpacking trip—fear, anxiety, confusion, exhaustion—and more. You have to take the outer obstacles as they come—adjusting your schedule when you can, setting limits if it's appropriate to do that, and closing doors to keep pets out. Inner obstacles are another matter, and handling them is the focus of this section.

The good news is that the more conscious you are of your obstacles, and the more tools you have to work with them, the less you struggle with them. When you encounter doubt or restlessness, for example, you will have a useful set of tools to address them in the moment. Certain obstacles will also become familiar to you. The more easily you can recognize them, the less personally you will take them. Many meditators encounter a particular obstacle during meditation and then blame themselves for failing at meditation. When they learn that what they have encountered is an obstacle that everybody grapples with, they can relax and stop taking the experience so personally, as if it were their own fault.

With vigilance and mindfulness, obstacles can be transformed. You can bring your mindfulness to the obstacle itself and learn more about yourself in the process. In this way the obstacle stops being an obstacle and becomes merely another step on the path of self-discovery.

Sleepiness

One of the most frequent experiences that beginning students report is sleepiness. "I felt close to falling asleep," they say, or, "I was dreamy, kind of groggy, half asleep." I have even heard people say, "What a pleasant meditation! I was sound asleep."

Sleepiness in meditation is extremely common, for a variety of reasons. Most of the students in our MAPs classes, as well as my friends and family, report not getting enough sleep. Our lives are so busy that we simply don't have enough time for everything, and so sleep is the first thing to go. It is no wonder that when people come to a peaceful meditation class or begin meditating on their own, they close their eyes, their minds make an association with sleep, and the next thing they know they are snoring.

I often suggest to these students that they need this sleep, since many people who join our classes have sleep issues, including chronic insomnia. It is not the worst thing, in my view, for a student to get a little sleep during meditation. My eighty-five-year-old aunt has been taking MAPs classes for about a year, and she says that she gets the best sleep of the week in our classes. However, it can certainly be frustrating to feel as though you are not getting anywhere with your meditation because you're asleep for most of it.

The time of day you choose to practice is relevant here. As you experiment with establishing a daily practice, remember that it is important to practice at a time of day when you will be most alert. For some people this is morning, and for others it is afternoon or evening. Of course, depending on your lifestyle, you will struggle to some extent with sleepiness at various times in your meditation practice, in spite of the time of day. Also, a mind that is concentrated can veer off into a dreamy, sleepy state. So even if you are not generally tired but instead a well-rested and energetic person, you may find that sleepiness still arises now and then in your meditations.

If you find yourself feeling drowsy—groggy, heavy, dreamy, or actually falling asleep during meditation—you can try a few strategies to awaken some energy. Open your eyes. Take a few deeper breaths. Stand up. Stop sitting and do some brisk walking meditation instead.

You can also learn to bring your mindfulness to sleepiness itself. This technique may be the most helpful in the long run because it's a way of learning how to be mindful in the midst of whatever life brings you, whether or not the experience is a desirable one. The ability to use mindfulness in the midst of whatever you encounter in life makes your mindfulness more flexible and adaptable.

How can you be mindful in the midst of sleepiness? Well, you can notice what sleepiness feels like in your body in the present moment. It might be a sluggish, heavy feeling. It might be a kind of woozy feeling; you may feel your body swaying or your mind fogging up. It may feel vaguely unpleasant. Noting these sensations is mindfulness of sleepiness—bringing your attention to exactly what the present moment brings. As you do this, sleepiness becomes less of an obstacle to your meditation practice and more of a passing event—one that comes into your consciousness but eventually shifts, and one that you can use to learn to be mindful in the midst of whatever life brings.

Restlessness and Wandering Thoughts

Many people encounter restlessness right away in meditation. You may sit down intending to be peaceful and instead your mind is a rush of thoughts and uncomfortable bodily sensations. You feel like you want to jump up and stop meditating immediately; it is just too uncomfortable.

Again, restlessness is normal, and a common human experience. Most of the time, however, you can avoid it through distraction. When you feel restless, without even being conscious of your restlessness you probably do something to change your state of mind. So, for example, at home when a little bit of restless energy comes over you, you might find yourself checking the refrigerator four times, randomly surfing the Internet, tidying up mindlessly, checking cell phone messages, and leafing through the newspaper. Perhaps you even do all of this at the same time! Sometimes restless energy passes, and sometimes it remains for a long time.

The difference in meditation is that, when you are restless, you have nothing with which to distract yourself. You sit down to meditate and find that your mind is all over the place, restless energy is coursing through your body, and your inner response is to run from the room. The alternative is to learn to meditate *with* this restlessness. You can transform it from an obstacle into just another mental state to become aware of.

Restlessness can manifest itself in the form of lots of thoughts. You want to stay with your breathing, but your mind is replaying memories from your childhood, the entire plot of *The Godfather* (all three installments), and the best of the Beatles. You learned earlier in this book that when your mind wanders, it is helpful to say to yourself, *Thinking*, or, *Wandering*, and then gently return your attention to your breathing. But what happens when thoughts wander to an extreme and lead to a lot of restless feelings?

First, it can be helpful to relax a little bit. A body that is very tense or tight can make restlessness worse. Some people find that when they are restless in meditation, it's time to take a more relaxed meditative approach, such as awareness of sounds (see Chapter 8).

Next, you can learn to be mindful in the midst of restlessness. The principle is the same as with sleepiness. Bring your attention to the restlessness itself. What does restlessness feel like in your body? Generally people feel high energy, perhaps vibration in their chests, notice racing thoughts, and have an antsy feeling throughout, like pins and needles. Sometimes—but not always—the act of bringing your attention to the sensations can even calm them down.

When you learn to meet restlessness with a kind and open attention, you can bring this skill to the rest of your life. You can recognize restlessness when you are at work, during a meeting, while talking on the phone, when you're driving, and so on. In your daily life, you can use the same techniques to manage restlessness that you use in meditation.

When Sleepiness and Restlessness Are Masking Something Else

Sometimes you are restless or sleepy for very good reasons—you stayed up late the previous night or had a lot on your plate at work. But other times there is no obvious reason. In this case, sleepiness or restlessness may cover up another emotion you are feeling but may not want to feel. Mary, a forty-eight-year-old mother and editor, told us this story:

> I was fighting with my seventeen-year-old daughter Alyssa again, this time over whether Alyssa could borrow the car. Alyssa ran out of the house shouting, "You are the worst mother ever!" I stood alone in my living room, and the next thing I knew I was leafing mindlessly through a pile of old scrapbooks. That got boring, so I started aggressively scrubbing the kitchen tile and then found myself watching cats on the toilet on YouTube. Suddenly I realized, *Wow, I'm restless.* I stopped, felt the restlessness in my body, and took a breath or two. The restless feeling began to calm down a little, and I noticed some sadness coming into my heart. Then I had a realization: I feel so hurt by what Alyssa said, and so

confused about how I'm supposed to discipline her yet give her indepen-
dence. I felt a wash of tears. I noticed the restless feelings had dissipated,
and all I felt was sadness, yet also relief in understanding myself better
and some forgiveness for myself.

If you are feeling restless—or sleepy—for no apparent reason, you can
ask yourself: *If I weren't restless (sleepy), what would I be feeling?* See what
comes up in your mind. There's no need to judge—just make a lot of room
for whatever is true.

Doubt

Doubt is a common obstacle for many meditators. It can arise in all sorts of
forms, from confusion about the technique (*Should I be aware of my breath at
my belly or my nostrils?*) to larger issues (*Will mindfulness make any difference
in my life whatsoever?*). Some people, finding their minds racked with doubt,
become very discouraged (*I can't do this at all, I'm terrible at meditating!*).

Please keep in mind that having lots of questions is an appropriate response to learning anything new. If you were to start learning to play tennis,
for instance, it is likely that you would have a lot of doubts and questions.
How do I hold the racket? How do I keep score? And so on. You might also feel
frustrated: *I'll never be any good at this, will I?*

Learning something new involves a period of doubt. So it is important
not to get discouraged as you learn meditation, but to recognize doubt for
what it is—just doubt.

Unlike the other obstacles, doubt is not so easy to feel in your body. Nevertheless, it is important to recognize when you are caught in it (*Oh, there's
doubt!*) and remind yourself of your motivation for learning meditation.
That can help put you on the right track. This is the discovery that Jack, a
fifty-seven-year-old attorney, made:

When I feel confused or doubting in my meditation practice, I try to remember why I started meditating. Years ago I wouldn't have been caught
dead meditating, but after a second heart attack (where I *was* almost
caught dead), my doctor recommended it to me. At first I noticed I was
feeling less stressed out all the time. The biggest change was in the way I

approach my anger. I used to explode, almost instantaneously, but now, when I feel anger coming, I just stop and breathe. Of course, it doesn't always work, but I'm convinced it helps with my heart concerns. When I feel doubtful, I just go back in my mind to those early days and think about how much has changed with mindfulness.

Desiring

Often a pleasant image, thought, or memory arises in meditation, and the next thing you know you have spent five minutes thinking about it. It can be quite delightful, reminiscing about your honeymoon or the really amazing pizza with everything on it you enjoyed last week. In fact, the image can be so pleasant that your entire meditation period passes in a very enjoyable manner—except for one thing: You did not really practice mindfulness at all.

Pleasant ruminations can be an obstacle in meditation that does not seem like an obstacle. But if you are using your meditation time to fantasize, then you are not benefiting from the positive effects of meditation. Please don't think that having a pleasurable fantasy is a problem. It is not. But look at the context: You are meditating to reduce stress, relax, find ease, work with difficult emotions, and so on. If you spend time lost in daydreams, you miss your meditation time and lose the opportunity to develop those qualities and skills.

There are other times when you might not be lost in a fantasy while meditating but you are still caught in the obstacle of desire because you are desiring something subtler, such as a "good" meditation experience. For instance, if you had a very peaceful and concentrated meditation on Sunday, you may spend Monday through Thursday wishing you could re-create it. Once again, your mind is not in the present moment but lost in desire for a particular experience that you think will make you happy.

We would encourage you to become aware of when you are lost in pleasant thoughts, fantasies, or desires and to redirect your attention back to your present-moment experience. And as with doubt, you can reconnect with your motivation for practicing by reminding yourself of your reasons for learning mindfulness in the first place.

Learning how to be mindful in the midst of desiring involves bringing your attention into your body. Take a moment right now to imagine something you really crave: a person, an event, an object, an experience (how about that trip to Hawaii?). Get a sense of it and then check into your body. You may discover a lot of bodily sensations like clutching, tightening in your chest, a sense of moving forward, yearning. You may also feel pleasantness inside your body as you think of what you desire. Sometimes just in the act of noticing the pleasant or clutching feelings in your body you can let go of the desire and return to your breathing.

Awareness of when you are lost in a craving for a pleasant experience is a useful life skill. We all run into problems when we are unconscious about our cravings. When we rush madly after something, thinking it is going to solve all our problems and provide us with happiness, we are often ruled by that sensation of clutching that impels us forward to staunch the craving feeling—often with an impulsive purchase.

For instance, imagine going into a bakery and seeing a gigantic and fantastically crispy-looking chocolate chip cookie in the case. Your mouth starts to salivate, and images of devouring it pop up in your mind. The next thing you know your hand is on your wallet, you have bought the cookie, you have shoved it in your mouth, and it is gone. You are left with a vaguely unsettling feeling: *What just happened?* Maybe you are amped up on sugar. Or maybe you want another.

There is no problem per se with wanting or eating a cookie. The problem is wanting or eating a cookie unconsciously. In the bakery scenario, you were ruled by unconscious desires that started with just a pleasantly enticing image or sight or memory, and then you instantly satisfied it, without much thought in between. With mindfulness, you bring your attention to that sense of desire welling up in your throat and chest, the longing feeling, the sense of moving forward. Then you have a little more choice in the matter: You may remember, *Well, I've already had five cookies today, I don't need another*, or you may decide, *Yes, I'm going to get this cookie, but I'll be aware of this choice and will consider it when I'm eating again later today*. When you learn how to be present with desire in your meditation, you can use this skill and insight to achieve more awareness elsewhere in your life.

Aversion: Frustration, Anger, Irritation, Grief, and Hatred

We all recognize the collection of obstacles we might call aversion—displeasure, dislike, irritation, frustration, anger, and so forth. I can confidently say that anyone who meditates will at some point experience some form of aversion. Why? Because all human beings have aversive reactions to things in their lives at one time or another.

You can experience aversion in meditation when your mind remembers or imagines something distasteful (*Oh, I have a big meeting coming up that I am not looking forward to*). Your mind begins to "stew" in the aversion, thinking about all the things you hate about these meetings, from the people who will be there to what a waste of time it will be. As you meditate, you become filled with aversion toward this imaginary scenario or the memory of a previously unpleasant experience. Or you might have aversion to the meditation itself: *This is stupid, why am I even bothering?* Or: *My body feels so uncomfortable I could scream!* Or: *I'm bored to death!*

How can you work with aversion when it arises in your mind? As suggested earlier, the best approach is to bring mindfulness to the aversion itself. Once again, take a moment to imagine something you have difficulty with in your life: a person, an upcoming event, something you may be resistant to (for me that would be eating broccoli). Let the image come to mind and again, check into your body to see if you have any particular physical sensations.

Usually people report a heavy feeling in the chest or a pushing sensation in the abdomen. Some people have a dry-mouthed feeling, a wrinkled nose, or a general heaviness. This is the bodily manifestation of aversion, which can come in many forms, from subtle to gross. If you can begin to identify it, however, you can work with it, recognizing, *Aha, I am in the midst of aversion, it's not personal to me, it's just a passing mental state.*

The chapter on positive emotions offers some exercises to cultivate pleasant mental states. Bringing in positive emotion to counteract the difficult feeling is another way to work with aversion. If you are feeling a lot of displeasure, irritation, or some other aversive feeling, you might try wishing yourself well and bringing some loving-kindness for the part of you that gets irritated.

It is very useful to be aware that these common mental states that you can encounter when meditating can also arise in the rest of your life. Alexandra, a twenty-eight-year-old environmentalist, told us this:

> One evening I got angry with my husband for something he said that I thought was entirely insensitive. My usual approach is to make a rude comment towards him—to, I don't know, in some way hurt him back.

But instead, without really making a conscious effort, I noticed that I was becoming mindful of the aversion. I felt a sense of anger rising up in my body. I thought, *Hmm, I'm really angry.* Because I was conscious of anger rising and knew my usual pattern was to lash out at my husband, instead I decided to relax a little and be a bit kinder. I think it was the first time I had ever watched a difficult emotion come and go without acting on it. I felt like I had more choice in the matter, like I was controlling the emotion rather than the emotion controlling me!

A Special Note on Boredom

Boredom in meditation can be extremely frustrating. You are sitting down, you have good intentions, you are prepared to feel your breathing, and then some thoughts start to creep in—*Wow, this is dull . . . I've got a lot to do and nothing is going on for me . . . hmmm, this is really boring*—and so on, until you are under a full-fledged boredom attack. Boredom is quite common in meditation, and truthfully, it's understandable: There are so many colorful distractions and exciting things to do, people to talk to, websites to peruse, all of which have much more interesting sensory inputs than merely sitting in silence with your eyes closed, observing your breathing.

Once again, however, I would encourage you to remember your motivation for practicing mindfulness and then try to pay closer attention. Boredom comes when we are skimming the surface of an experience. If you can bring your attention in more closely, your interest will perk up; in fact, you will begin to see a lot of things to pay attention to.

The idea here is to increase your level of interest. If you are reading a book you consider dull, such as a history of phytoplankton (I apologize if this is your favorite topic), your mind generally has a hard time staying with it. If you are reading the latest book by your favorite spy novelist, suddenly it is extremely easy to concentrate. In both cases you are reading; the difference is in the level of interest you bring to the experience. José, a sixty-one-year-old contractor, explored this in his meditation:

I was outside doing walking meditation. My mind was spaced out and bored. I decided it was time to stop meditating when I remembered I could pay closer attention—it might help with the boredom. So I stood still and took really slow-motion steps. As I did this, the sensations in my feet came alive. They became fascinating, interesting, bigger than life. Suddenly I realized I was no longer bored!

And, of course, you can always bring your mindfulness to the boredom itself. What does boredom feel like in your body and mind in the moment it arises?

Worry, Fear, and Anxiety

We discussed some of the principles for working with anxiety in its many forms in earlier chapters. Here we offer some specific techniques for dealing with worry and anxiety.

If you are in the midst of a particular worry or anxiety, ask yourself: Is this true? Is it really true? You might remind yourself that the worry is a passing thought, not something to be attached to. If you can remember the present moment, you can be less subject to anxiety. Anxiety needs a future (and is often fueled by the past). Check out the present moment: Do you see that things are pretty much okay right now? The problem is the fear of the future. Ask yourself: *Am I okay NOW?* As always, notice the anxiety itself; how it feels in your body is a great way to work with this emotion.

Also try tuning in to the times you don't feel anxious. When we are anxious or fearful, we often think that those feelings are always going to be present. In truth, anxiety is present only some of the time. Try to notice times of ease in your mind. There may be more of these moments than you would expect.

᷍᷍᷍᷍

When I think back to backpacking trips or other experiences that were fraught with inner and outer obstacles, I realize now that the obstacles were how I learned. If things had gone smoothly, I might have gone on obliviously, but instead I had to face my fears and the external hardships. And of course, the trips with the biggest obstacles make the best stories, precisely for that reason. It is through obstacles that we are stretched and learn something new about ourselves: our fortitude, courage, persistence, and ingenuity, for example. So please know that when you meet obstacles in your meditation practice you are actually learning skills that will make you healthier and stronger in the long run. And as you learn to deal with these mental states in your practice, your facility at facing them in life will grow. Daniel, a forty-year-old analyst, described this experience:

> I went to a party at an acquaintance's house, and the second we walked in the door I felt critical. I didn't like the guests, the food wasn't tasty, and there was no one I wanted to talk to. For a while I just stewed in my feelings, but then ultimately my mindfulness kicked in. I turned to my partner and said, "Can we talk?" Then I expressed my aversion, noticing how I was feeling and that I was really amidst an aversion attack. Just talking about it with awareness shifted everything. I realized I was feeling a little anxious. Then I relaxed and actually ended up having a great time at the party!

THE PRACTICE:
WORKING WITH OBSTACLES

When you encounter an obstacle in your meditation, here are a few steps you can take:

1. Apply an antidote:
    - For *sleepiness*: Open your eyes, stand up, and try walking meditation.
    - For *restlessness*: Try hearing meditation—relaxing and giving yourself a wider field of awareness.
    - For *doubt*: Recognize that you are caught in doubt and remember your motivation for practicing meditation.
    - For *desire*: Ask yourself to come back to the present moment and recognize that fantasizing and so forth may be interesting but won't have the same benefits as meditation. You can also remind yourself of your motivation for practicing.
    - For *aversion*: Practice loving-kindness meditation toward yourself or that part of you that is experiencing aversion.
    - For *boredom*: Pay closer attention to your direct experience, get curious about your meditation, and remember your motivation.

- For *anxiety* or *worry*: Ask yourself: *Is this true?* and *Am I okay now?*

2. Apply mindfulness to the obstacle itself:
   - First label the obstacle (doubt, aversion, and so on).
   - Then notice how this obstacle feels in your body (for example, *I'm having aversion, and I notice my belly is clenched*). Often noticing how your body feels in the presence of the obstacle will allow the obstacle to relax its grip on you. Sometimes it may even go away. Even when it does not, you can find a measure of non-identification with it.

3. Remember: Obstacles are a normal part of meditation practice!

11

MINDFULNESS IN ACTION

Mindfulness must be engaged. Once there is seeing there
must be acting. Otherwise what is the use of seeing?

—THICH NHAT HANH,
AUTHOR AND ZEN MASTER

Mindfulness practice begins inside a single individual. Each of us, working to regulate our attention, reduce our reactivity, and cultivate more
positive emotions, can improve our own health and happiness. With this individual focus, mindfulness may appear to be just a self-improvement technique,
but it is much more than that. Not only is mindfulness a valuable tool for seeing our thoughts, feelings, and habitual patterns more clearly, but it is from this
knowledge, coupled with reflection and kindness, that wisdom and compassion emerge. It is in our actions and our interactions with others and the planet
that the effects of mindfulness, wisdom, and compassion can ripple around the
world. Here we describe our thoughts on how mindfulness might do that. Because of the speculative nature of these thoughts, we have put aside our "art"
and "science" format in this last chapter, but we still offer you practices.

MINDFULNESS, WISDOM,
AND COMPASSION

A metaphor for the potential role of mindfulness in increasing wisdom and
compassion appears in Figure 5.

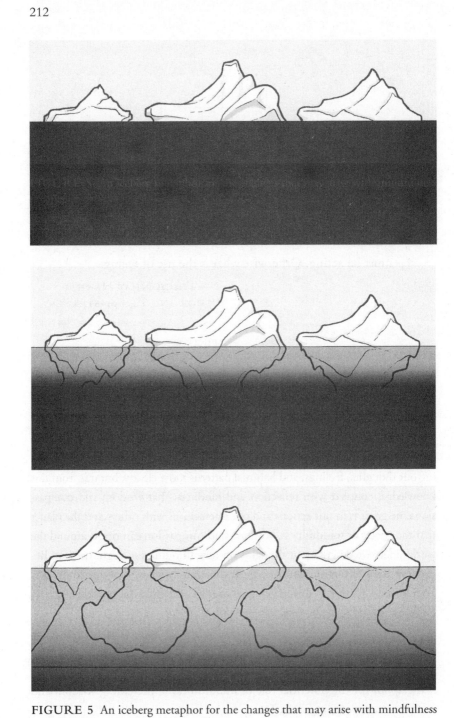

FIGURE 5 An iceberg metaphor for the changes that may arise with mindfulness practice.

At some point in our lives, most of us have had the experience of living on the "tip of the iceberg." This metaphor refers to times when you may have had a limited view of yourself and of the thoughts and emotions underlying your actions (in the iceberg metaphor, actions and conscious thoughts and feelings are above the surface), and maybe you felt alone or isolated. With mindfulness, you may uncover what lies beneath the surface of your individual actions (the middle image) and will act from a greater sense of understanding (and conscious choice). As you continue exploring your life with mindfulness or other meditation practices, you may uncover more and more of the ground from which your individual actions arise, and you may discover that it is a ground shared by everyone (lower panel).

In other words, you may come to an intuitive understanding or experiential sense of our interdependent nature. You may see that humans are interconnected with each other, the planet, and the universe at large (observable through DNA, ecosystems, interpersonal biology, quantum physics, and so on). From this experiential sense of our interdependent or interconnected nature may emerge increasing wisdom and compassion—for how could you intend to hurt a part of yourself?

This increasing wisdom and compassion from *insight* into ourselves can lead to *action*. Once we see ourselves clearly, we might set out to act in nonharming and respectful ways with our families, coworkers, and communities. Or we may form a desire to go beyond simply nonharming, in order to serve or effect positive change in the world. Or we might help develop or change an institution from within so that it embodies wisdom principles. Many meditation students have told us that after practicing meditation for a period of time they experienced the natural emergence of compassionate action in their lives on a greater scale than they could have ever imagined. One student, originally a self-described "selfish" software developer, now travels in Africa helping to provide impoverished villages with links to microfinancing.

EVOLUTION OF THE WISEST

Jonas Salk once wrote that the next phase of human evolution would be less biologic and more "metabiologic"—that is, concerned with transcendence or going beyond the ordinary limits of living matter. Salk described the next phase of human evolution: "The evolutionary need is to increase our *breadth of consciousness* as human beings, to expand our range of choice for the wisest alternatives. . . . The human capacity to *anticipate and select* will be the means whereby the future of human evolution will be determined."[1, 2] In metabiological evolution, *creativity* and *choice* function as the key mechanisms of change, just as mutation and selection do in biological evolution.

As these two processes (biological and metabiological evolution) work in concert, a new kind of human animal may arise, a human embodying what Salk described as "survival of the wisest." "The wisest" are those individuals who comprehend both biologic and metabiologic processes and make choices consistent with that wisdom.[3] We see such wisdom in the shift from a self-centered worldview (top panel of Figure 5) to one in which the self is seen as part of a much larger, interconnected whole (bottom panel of Figure 5).

James Carse wrote about living life from these two perspectives in his metaphor of life as a "game of play" with two types of players, finite and infinite. Game strategies differ for these two types of players. Finite players live life from a short-range perspective, and their objective is to win and end the game. Infinite players live life with a long-range view, and their goal is to keep the game going and to engage as many players as possible.[4] Like "infinite" players, "wise" individuals make choices and take actions that benefit the long term—*the future generations yet to come.*

Although wisdom naturally unfolds with age, with mindfulness, reflection, and kindness practices you can begin to act more wisely at any age of the life span. In this chapter, we discuss two areas in which mindfulness can be brought into action across the life span: mindfulness in our communication (speech and listening) and mindfulness in our institutions (from schools to the workplace). But applications of mindfulness, wisdom, and kindness to other problems of the world—war, social inequities, the climate crisis, poverty, AIDs—have been under taken by many committed citizens throughout the world.[5] There are unlimited ways to take mindfulness, wisdom, and compassion into action. Here are two—with the evidence of their positive impact.

MINDFUL COMMUNICATION

Harmonious relationships stem from a foundation in speaking and listening with mindfulness. Instead of mindlessly spouting whatever pops into our thoughts, we speak mindfully when we use words that reflect our values and a deeper connection to ourselves. Mindful speech is also truthful, thoughtful, and nondivisive. Mindful listeners are those who make you feel heard and understood and who offer a natural presence and kindness just by virtue of their listening skill. Both mindful speech and mindful listening can be taught and practiced, like any other skill (see the practice section). Both involve attending to another person with full attention while being aware of your own "self" (body, thought, and emotion) so as not to react without clear forethought.

Ellen Langer, a professor at Harvard University and an expert on mindful communication and learning, has studied the impact of mindful communication on learning (education), decision-making, and interpersonal relationships. Others have extended her work to investigate the effects of mindful communication on workplace communication, cross-cultural understanding, and media effectiveness.[6]

Studies show that mindful communication affects our decision-making. For example, a study by Jackie Krieger when she was a graduate student at Western Michigan University theorized that mind*less* communication is at the core of poor decision-making in crisis situations. Using volunteer aviation students, she created dyads with a "captain" and a "first officer" to explore how communication contributes to the human error that accounts for 60 to 80 percent of airline crashes. In her fake cockpit crises, dyads that demonstrated mindful communication made the most effective decisions and circumvented failure. Mindful dyads shared several communication traits: They sought *information*, they reasoned from a *positive* perspective, they perceived *multiple* perspectives, they could *describe* thoughts and feelings, they *acknowledged* their partner's communication, they used *participative* language, and they demonstrated *turn-taking*.[7] These are all components of mindful communication.

Decision-making is not the only outcome affected by mindful communication. Judith Burgoon, a professor of communication at the University of Arizona, has demonstrated that mindful communication reduces interpersonal conflict, stereotyping, and cross-cultural misunderstanding.[8] Such findings suggest that if the practice of mindful communication were widespread in the world, people would be less inclined to fall into "better than/less than" thinking.

Science has shown that "better than/less than" thinking, or *perceived inequality*, is the source of most of the violent and so-called evil behavior in the world. Philip Zimbardo's classic social experiment in the 1970s, the Stanford Prison Study, demonstrated this point. In this experiment, college students were assigned to be "guards" or "prisoners" to study the effects of such designations. The guards' behavior rapidly escalated into sadistic and inhumane treatment of their fellow student "prisoners," so much so that the experiment had to be called off.[9] The perception of the guards that they were "better than" the prisoners, in a context that supported that belief, resulted in malevolent behavior on the part of otherwise kind students.

With the practice of mindfulness, we can catch "better than/less than" thoughts *before* they turn into action and thus reduce the possibility that we will engage in harmful actions. And increasing our compassion toward others takes us a step further in the other direction, toward *helpful* actions. We saw many examples throughout this book of practicing to increase positive emotions, particularly loving-kindness and self-compassion. Taking mindfulness into action through mindful communication, coupled with exercises to enhance compassion (see sidebar), could bring about more peaceful and harmonious communities.[10] We might also imagine that mindful speech, when practiced by large groups of people and incorporated into our institutions, could have an impact on the culture at large.

A PRACTICE: MINDFUL SPEAKING AND LISTENING

Enlist a friend for this exercise. You will alternate between speaking and listening. Decide who will speak first. That person then practices mindfulness while speaking without being interrupted for two minutes (set a timer). The speaker can pick a topic of interest to him or her, such as, "What brings me joy?"

The other listens mindfully, practicing the following:

1. Noticing his or her body from time to time
2. Noticing his or her thoughts and reactions from time to time
3. Most importantly, trying hard to offer complete attention to the speaker

The mindful speaker practices the following:

1. Noticing his or her body from time to time
2. Articulating what he or she is aware of from time to time
3. Speaking authentically and from the heart

At the end of two minutes, both of you close your eyes and check into yourselves to see how it felt to do this exercise. Then reverse. At the end of two more minutes, close your eyes again and check in with yourselves. For a third time, have a conversation about the experience of doing the exercise and follow up with any questions or reflections you may have for your partner. ■

A PRACTICE: CULTIVATING COMPASSION FOR THE WORLD

The next time you are caught in a difficult situation, particularly one in which you feel sorry for yourself—such as when you are struggling with physical or emotional pain—try this exercise.

In a comfortable posture, take a few minutes to connect to your breathing. As best you can, allow your mind to settle and to calm down. Then recall or turn your attention to the difficulty you are currently facing. You might have an image, story, or sensations in your body related to this difficulty. Notice how you feel as you recall your particular problem.

As you continue to be aware of your breathing, let yourself bring the "bigger picture" to mind. For instance, try to imagine others who are struggling with the same affliction. Bring to mind either a few people or as many as you can think of. You may see, sense, or feel the presence of others who are suffering in the exact same way. For instance, if you have a toothache, let yourself bring to mind the countless people across the planet who have a toothache in this moment.

As you imagine these others, check into your body and heart to notice how this makes you feel. If you feel a bit overwhelmed, just bring one or two people to mind. If you feel a sense of compassion and connection and have a thought like, *We're all in this together*, keep going with the practice. Imagine yourself breathing out and sending kindness to all these people. Wish them well. Wish for the end of their suffering. ■

MINDFULNESS IN INSTITUTIONS

In a culture based in reason, intuition—a nonrational means of knowing—is generally not valued, yet unfolding in the twenty-first century is a growing interest in it. Best-selling books like *Blink* by Malcolm Gladwell explain the powerful value of intuition and its complement in action, creativity.[11] We see mindfulness and other practices that enhance intuition, such as meditation, yoga, art, nature, music, as a crucial complement to the role of reason (critical thinking) in our institutions.

Bringing mindfulness to institutions—from schools to workplaces—is one means of increasing intuition across the life span while not diminishing the valuable role of reason. Evidence is emerging that doing just that, bringing mindfulness into schools, institutions like hospitals, and businesses, has beneficial effects on health and well-being. We focus here on institutions that have integrated mindfulness into their curricula or business practices to examine the effect. Of course, there are many ways to enhance intuition, and mindfulness is just one (see sidebar for a meditation practice to develop intuition). The examples we provide here are just the beginning. We like to imagine a future in which intuition, kindness, and mindfulness can become more fully utilized and integrated into a range of cultural, social, and political institutions.

Schools

The premise that both rational and intuitive ways of knowing are needed to create healthy children and engaged world citizens is a foundation of the Alice Project, a school in Sarnath, India. An Italian schoolteacher, Valentino Giacomin, founded the school for the poorest and lowest-caste children of this rural village. He decided to use the principles of what he called "universal education," which brings together the best wisdom of all religious traditions, science, and philosophy. The students at this school, who were illiterate when they enrolled, now study the government-mandated curriculum—math,

Hindi, geography, and so forth—but their studies are combined with classes on art and music, meditation, yoga, massage, ecology, philosophy, world religions, and social and emotional learning skills. The children at the Alice Project have far exceeded comparable schools in standardized testing, and psychological testing has shown them to have high levels of self-knowledge and emotional intelligence.[12]

In the United States, a growing number of studies demonstrate that introducing mindfulness into schools, from prekindergarten to college, enhances the health, well-being, and learning skills of students. Lisa Flook, a clinical psychologist now at the University of Wisconsin, carried out a project with Sue and our center investigating mindfulness delivered to children in school-based settings. After a feasibility study, two controlled trials were conducted—one for preschool and kindergarten children and one for second- and third-graders at UCLA campus–affiliated schools. The mindfulness program, developed by Susan Kaiser Greenland, consists of age-appropriate games and exercises designed to enhance mindfulness.[13] Students given the program improved in attention, planning, and organization skills compared to those not given the program; however, the differences were most striking for those children who had the greatest difficulties with these behaviors.[14]

Studies of programs to bring mindfulness to school or after-school curricula for students, from very young children to adolescents to adults (college and postgraduate), are flourishing. Educators at Arizona State University studied mindfulness in a sample of 132 second- and third-graders and found that attention improved and anxiety decreased compared to controls.[15] In New York City a program called Inner Resilience Training (including mindfulness) was delivered to 57 teachers from public schools and evaluated for outcomes among teachers and 857 students in their classes. The program led to significant improvements in wellness for the teachers and third-, fourth-, and fifth-graders in the study.[16] In a study of 291 high school students in the United Kingdom, a stress reduction program (including mindfulness) resulted in one-letter-grade-higher academic performance for students given the program over those who were not given the program, along with improving indices of health and well-being.[17] The benefits of mindfulness practice have also been demonstrated among college students—in terms of reducing stress and improving well-being.[18] These data, taken together, suggest that integration of such practices is possible across educational levels (from pre-kindergarten through college) and that it may enhance well-being and learning at all stages of development.

☙ A PRACTICE: REFLECTION MEDITATION

This practice is useful for accessing your intuitive knowing to balance your rational ways of trying to solve a problem.

Sit comfortably and spend the first part of your meditation finding some calm and ease. You may wish to focus on your breathing to help your mind become more concentrated, letting yourself gently arrive in the present moment as you practice returning to your breath.

When your mind feels calm and stable, bring to mind the question you are struggling with. Drop the question into the stillness in the same way you would drop a pebble into a pond. Then, although your tendency might be to want to think and ruminate about the issue, try not to let that happen. Instead, see what kind of response surfaces on its own. What kind of ripples does the pebble make in the pond? In other words, "listen" rather than try to "figure out." Allow the answer to come from a place deep inside. Keep coming back to your breath if you find yourself getting lost in thoughts about the problem. Once you are calm and relaxed, ask again. ∎

Health-Related Settings

Certainly institutions devoted to physical and mental health—hospitals, veterans' administrations, psychiatric units, rehabilitation centers—may benefit from introducing mindfulness. We have discussed the health benefits of mindfulness throughout this book. But a growing body of research suggests that bringing such practices into the training of the next generation of health professionals is equally important.[19] At our own institute, we introduced mindfulness into the medical student training curriculum so that all third-year students would have some exposure to mindfulness in their coursework on complementary and alternative medicine (CAM). Centers such as the one started by Jon Kabat-Zinn at the University of Massachusetts Medical School have long offered classes to medical students, but now many medical schools across the country are making it part and parcel of training.

Creating space for mindfulness practice is important for such programs to flourish. At UCLA we created a meditation room—called C-Space—for faculty, staff, and students to use for individual meditation or group instruction in yoga, t'ai chi, and mindfulness. The response has been very positive: More than four hundred people a month use the space, which is only somewhat larger than a classroom. The University of Vermont Medical School recently followed suit and created a comparable room for its medical students.

Businesses

A small but growing number of businesses have incorporated mindfulness into the workplace, with promising benefits. One example is Green Mountain Coffee, a small public company of some 1,300 employees located in Burlington, Vermont. Mindfulness is an integral part of Green Mountain Coffee; there is an on-site meditation room, and the company offers mindfulness classes to employees led by an experienced teacher, Shinzen Young, with the support of founder and chairman Robert Stiller. The company regularly appears on the *Forbes* list of the top two hundred most financially successful small to medium-sized companies (number 88 in 2007, number 55 in 2008) and the "great places to work" list. Even in the economic downturn, while the stock market plummeted, Green Mountain Coffee showed a boost in stock prices.[20] The quality of its coffee is certainly key in these numbers, but the company's mindful approach may make a difference too.

FINAL THOUGHTS

Every person has their own degree of awareness and its flip side, ignorance. In the same way that you do not know what you do not know, you cannot force awareness on anyone, not even on yourself. We encourage you to attend to your own awareness with whatever method is best for you—whether the mindfulness practices detailed in this book or other forms of meditation, walks in nature, running, yoga, art, and so on.

Each increase in awareness, however small or large, will require that you let go of past beliefs and habitual and reactive patterns. Changes in awareness and old beliefs and patterns go hand in hand because from each discovery emerges a need to let go of a previous belief or view of yourself in relation to the world prior to the discovery. As you move along your own path of self-investigation and discovery, you might notice that the process of awareness and letting go is never-ending. An intuitive understanding of the infinite nature of awareness and the interconnectedness of all beings may emerge, and with it, wisdom and kindness. A more mindful society is ultimately a kinder society. It is our wish that this book will help this kindness unfold. As Henry James so succinctly put it:

> Three things in human life are important. The first is to be kind. The second is to be kind. And the third is to be kind.

AFTERWORD

If you realize that all things change, there is nothing you will try to hold on to.

—Tao Te Ching

It has been over a decade since we first published *Fully Present* and, like everything else, mindfulness has changed. If there is anything mindfulness helps us notice most, it is this constancy of change. While the *art and practice*—defined by mindfulness tools and techniques—has not transformed in any significant way, one's personal experience with mindfulness certainly evolves over time. It changes as we change, as we discover insights that shift the way we relate to our own thoughts, feelings, bodily sensations, actions, and awareness. The change is subjective—a first-person experience—that requires each of us to make our own evaluation.

As for the *science*, there are about five times the number of scientific studies on mindfulness since our first publication. Investigations into the impact of mindfulness practice on improving health span a broader range of conditions beyond those covered in our book and include autism, schizophrenia, bipolar disorder, multiple sclerosis, Parkinson's disease, cancer survivorship, and Alzheimer's disease. Studies of mindfulness practice in the general population have expanded to include specific groups that suffer from increased trauma or stress, such as members of the military; health care workers, including doctors and nurses; teachers; students; and parents. Finally, basic research into how mindfulness leads to change and who benefits from what types of practices has grown as well. There are many more

223

studies expanding the work described in our book, now with larger samples, more "active" control groups, and meta-analyses (i.e., methods that pool data across studies). These new studies further strengthen the conclusion we drew that mindfulness is beneficial to individual well-being, as well as to societal well-being by virtue of how we treat one another.

As for the *mindfulness field itself*, the last decade has seen unprecedented growth in the spread of mindfulness. Our University of California, Los Angeles' (UCLA) Mindful Awareness Research Center (MARC) has expanded research, teaching, and access to mindfulness practice in the last decade as well. MARC has been conducting research on our Mindful Awareness Practices (MAPs) program with breast cancer survivors, Alzheimer's caregivers, and medical trainees, among others, as well as offering more mindfulness classes to the UCLA campus, UCLA health system, and general public through live and online classes, workshops, and retreats that have a global audience. We pioneered a mindfulness teacher's training program since 2011, offered college credit classes for students, and brought mindfulness to countless organizations through collaboration, advising, and resource sharing. Our free UCLA Mindful App, with meditations in sixteen different languages, has had over 300,000 downloads and was featured in 2021 on the California governor's COVID-19 Response website, CalHOPE.

In subsequent sections, we share new findings on the science of mindfulness and new developments in its delivery and practice, but to contextualize that, we first want to highlight some current topics of concern as mindfulness spreads more globally. In 2017, meditation reportedly became a billion-dollar (and growing) industry due to an upsurge of access to classes, apps, books, and supplies.[1] The intersection of business and mindfulness has raised questions around the integrity or lack of integrity that can accompany the explosive growth of mindfulness into the for-profit sector. A second topic of concern is that mindfulness practices when delivered in secular settings may become divorced from ethical teachings that are integral when taught in a Buddhist setting. Without explicit attention to an ethical framework, could mindfulness result in nonbeneficial outcomes? For example, if used in the military to reduce the impact of stressors on health, might it also improve the ability of a troop member to inflict harm on an enemy that in itself is at odds with the roots of mindfulness? Or in the workplace, could mindfulness be used to improve productivity at an individual level without addressing the systemic issues that may lead to burn out?

Others feel concerned about issues of cultural appropriation. Is Buddhism being given adequate credit for its role in the "research and development" of mindfulness practices or is mindfulness seen as a secular, Western innovation, without adequate reference to the 2,600 years of teachings proceeding it? The practice of mindfulness can be transformational for people of any background or religion, so minimizing the Buddhist reference may have served to bring mindfulness more thoroughly into the mainstream. At a minimum, some acknowledgment of the history of mindfulness is crucial and respectful.

In addition, there are concerns regarding the lack of diversity across the secular mindfulness field. Although we are seeing more mindfulness teaching in historically marginalized communities, as well as new teacher trainings that incorporate indigenous wisdom with mindfulness, such as Braided Wisdom Cross-Cultural Mindfulness Leadership Program, there is still much work to be done in this direction.

Finally, the greater access to secular mindfulness has resulted in a plethora of mindfulness programs directed at beginners. Some are concerned the popular mindfulness field has watered down the full potential of teaching and discovery available to practitioners if there aren't continuing programs of study available. Happily, new directions for deeper practice are developing in the field. These include advanced mindfulness teachings, adaptations of mindfulness teachings for social justice, and opportunities for longer term immersion, such as secular retreats (which were originally taught only in Buddhist contexts).

In a celebration of the original *Fully Present* and in looking forward to the decades ahead, we want to share some key scientific findings and changes in the mindfulness field overall.

THE SCIENCE

Depression and anxiety continue to be on the rise globally, particularly among youth. Social media and digital devices have created an increasing overload of information and continuous digital engagement that are having detrimental effects on physical and mental health.[2,3] In addition, the global pandemic exacerbated depression and anxiety due to greater social isolation, loneliness, fear, and uncertainty. Mindfulness-Based Programs (MBPs) gained more attention and have had an impact in reducing depression and anxiety.[4-7] However, the effect of MBPs on depression and anxiety is small to medium in size and depending on the program (e.g., Mindfulness-Based Cognitive Therapy [MBCT]) *comparable* to other forms of interventions, like cognitive behavioral therapy (CBT), psychotherapy, and medications.[8-11] There are certainly other criteria to be used in the selection of treatment given comparable effect sizes, including access, cost, ease of sticking with treatment, long-term effects, and individual differences in outcome, all of which require more research. In studies looking at *how* MBCT might lead to improved emotional health, several factors have been suggested, including reducing repetitive thinking about the past, increasing self-compassion or self-esteem, and metacognitive awareness.[12,13] At the same time, researchers are seeing that different types of mindfulness practices have different effects on physical, cognitive, and psychological states.[14]

We have also seen new findings around anxiety disorders, including consistent positive improvement of anxiety symptoms with MBPs.[6,10] Among those with *anxiety disorders*, MBPs and CBT work equally well, while among those with *anxious symptoms*, but not a diagnosis, MBPs performed slightly better.[10] Research on MBPs for specific anxiety disorders including posttraumatic stress disorder (PTSD),[15] social anxiety,[16] and generalized anxiety disorder[6,17,18] all look promising.

While MBPs may have different effects based on their specific types of practices, at the same time, people respond differently to the same sort of practice for a variety of reasons. Asking "who responds best to what treatment" aligns with growing interest in precision medicine and precision psychiatry and is likely to reveal optimal interventions for people based on genetic, psychosocial, and environmental influences. For example, among people with anxiety disorders, researchers found that among those with mild to no depressive symptoms, CBT was more effective than MBSR, but among those with moderate to severe depressive symptoms, MBSR was more optimal at three month follow-up.[19] In a separate study, researchers found that heart rate variability among patients with generalized anxiety disorder was a predictor of who would respond best to medication versus an MBP.[20]

In the general population, mood and anxiety measures continue to show improvement with mindfulness practices.[5,7] Studies have found that emotional change through meditation may depend on baseline emotional state and the type of meditation practiced. For example, studies showed that someone in an angry state responded better to a calming practice than a kindness practice, while someone in a distressed/anxious state responded best to an "engaging in the senses" practice.[21,22] This sort of fine-tuning the types of interventions, including MBPs and their specific content, to individual differences, whether baseline emotional state, specific biomarkers, or other factors, is an area of active research.

In trying to understand *how* mindfulness leads to greater health and well-being, a few studies stand out for their impact in the last decade. Wendy Hasenkamp[23] conducted a functional magnetic resonance imaging (fMRI) study of healthy adult meditation practitioners while they were meditating for twenty minutes. The meditators were asked to maintain focused attention on the breath and when they noticed that their mind had "wandered" (which we know happens frequently), they pressed a button and returned to their breath. By asking the person to report when they noticed their own mind-wandering, they could examine the brain changes during four states known to be involved in meditation—focused attention, mind-wandering, noticing, and shifting back to focused attention. As the researchers expected, brain activity shifted from regions thought to underlie focused attention to those known to underlie mind-wandering (i.e., the default mode network) to those involved in "noticing" and in "shifting" attention. It was the fine-tuned measurement of brain changes across time during meditation, and the subjective report by the person in the scanner, that made this project different and provided additional support that cognitive and neurobiological states change during the practice. Mind-wandering is associated more often with negative emotions than attending to the present no matter what one might be doing,[24] so these data suggest that practice alters mind-wandering and focused attentional states and that this may improve well-being.

Sara Lazar's group at Harvard took a deeper dive into how changing brain states with meditation corresponds to heightened states of well-being,

approaching it from personality constructs. In that study, adults who identified as yoga practitioners, meditation practitioners, or neither were given
a personality inventory called the Maturity Assessment Profile (MAP).[25]
The MAP generates a score that assigns people to a stage of maturity, from
very "ego-focused" (who tend to be impulsive and intolerant) to much less
"ego-focused" (who view self, others, and the world in complex ways, tol-
erating greater degrees of ambiguity or uncertainty). Along with getting
scores on the MAP, the participants underwent a magnetic resonance imaging (MRI) scan to correlate brain structure with MAP scores. Meditators
and yogis scored significantly higher than participants with no practice
and despite more average hours of practice in the yogi group, the meditator
group had significantly higher scores overall. Only one brain network—that
default mode network known for its role in mind-wandering *and* narrative
self-referencing[26]—showed strong correlations with the MAP scores. This
research suggests that mindfulness practices may facilitate maturity—
marked by less ego attachment—and that may reflect underlying differences in connectivity of the default mode network. However, more research
is needed on both structural and functional brain changes with meditation.

Mindfulness practice seems to impact many systems of the body, potentially through its role in buffering stress.[27] As a health promotion tool, mindfulness might be considered as important a pillar of health as diet, exercise,
sleep, and social connection. Data from the immune system, inflammatory
systems, and epigenetic markers of health suggest that this may be the case.
Steven Cole at UCLA has studied epigenetic markers of stress for several
decades and has shown that psychosocial factors have a big impact on these
biomarkers.[28] For example, stress and loneliness change gene expression in
a way not conducive to health while well-being and social connection lead
to the opposite effect.[28-30] Mindfulness has been shown to boost well-being
and lead to changes in immune function.[31,32] The body is always interacting
with the environment and some interactions are felt as stressful while others
not; mindfulness practice may lead to altered relationships of self to such
stressors. It is an area where more work is greatly needed.

As we discussed in the preceding chapters, mindfulness may be no *better*
of an intervention than another when looking at a single outcome like high
blood pressure, heart disease, depression, and so on, but it may have ripple
effects across multiple systems that can only be realized if a whole person

approach to health is used. It is also crucial to note that we are inextricably intertwined with our environment, so the health and well-being of a person needs to be considered in the context of family, friends, work, social structures, and other aspects of their life. Mindfulness may impact us in ways that are not yet realized without a broader scope of view in research.

Some of the emerging research in kindness lends support for this broader lens. A group at Northeastern University led by David DeSteno set up psychological experiments where a "subject" participating in the study is invited to the lab. The subject is asked to fill out paperwork and shown to a room where there are two chairs, one already occupied by someone, secretly a "plant" who works for the experimenters but is apparently completing forms too. The subject sits in the empty chair and begins completing their paperwork. When a new person enters the room minutes later wearing a cast on one leg and obviously in pain, the experiment measures how often a subject offers their chair to the person in pain. Without any mindfulness practice, the subject gives up their seat 14% to 16% of the time but if given a mindfulness course (vs. active control program) beforehand, they offer their chair three times as often.[33,34] Other groups, using different approaches, have found the same thing. Michael Irwin, Director of MARC at UCLA, found that giving behavior (i.e., donations) increased 2.6-fold as a function of mindfulness practice over a control condition.[35] The practice of mindfulness leads to kinder actions.[36] At a time when a global pandemic, war, climate change, and political divisiveness have swept across the planet, boosting kindness in human interactions is of utmost importance; mindfulness practice may be a simple tool for doing that.

Currently, there are many more population-based randomized control trials of mindfulness compared to a decade ago with positive results reported across a range of clinical and nonclinical conditions, yet there is a need for more individualized longitudinal designs.[37] As we stay open to new research, including the incoming wave of the use of psychedelics in psychiatry, the arrival of the metaverse, the expansion of Artificial Intelligence (AI), and the use of digital twins, the next decades will surely uncover a host of new discoveries around mindfulness and its impact to each of us individually and to society as a whole. As more scientists practice mindfulness themselves and integrate their first-person approach with the third-person approach of science, a more mindful science may emerge as well.

THE MINDFULNESS FIELD NOW

Over the last decade, we have watched mindfulness move more prominently into the public sphere. Mindfulness as a *secular* approach, distinct from Buddhism yet rooted in Buddhist meditation practice and theory, is now a worldwide phenomenon, spread far from the Asian countries in which Buddhism originated. Accelerated by media and research, many more people worldwide have heard of mindfulness compared to 10 years ago. However, while a comprehensive 2017 U.S.-based survey notes significant growth in numbers of people who reported meditating in the 12 months prior to the survey—from 4.1% in 2012 to 14.2%—only a small portion of the general U.S. population meditates.[38,39]

In the last decade, mindfulness has become more thoroughly integrated into a variety of sectors, and the creative innovations are constantly evolving. Mindfulness is now being more widely offered at hospitals, clinics, and health centers, and integrated into medical school curriculum and as part of continuing education for medical professionals. It is now prominent in the field of psychology, integrated into a variety of clinical treatments, and a generation of mental health professionals is being trained in, at the minimum, the basics of mindfulness.

Businesses have brought in mindfulness to address employee burnout, provide self-management skills, and increase productivity; some businesses have implemented mindfulness courses for their employees, often worldwide. Business coaches are integrating mindfulness with their clients. We can see a growth in the incorporation of mindfulness classes and programs in all sizes and types of companies, from Fortune 500 to small businesses.

Mindfulness programs are more widely integrated into schools than a decade ago. Some programs, like the United Kingdom's ".b" (dot-be), train schoolteachers in a mindfulness curriculum. Others, like Peace in Schools, have a district-wide reach in Portland, Oregon, and offer for-credit high school mindfulness programs, bringing qualified mindfulness teachers into the classroom. The Holistic Life Foundation has provided a comprehensive approach to mindfulness education for underserved Baltimore residents starting with schools and moving beyond into recreation centers, juvenile detention centers, and much more. In addition, we see countless grassroots examples of schoolteachers personally training in mindfulness and then creatively implementing these practices inside their classrooms. Educators recognize mindfulness not as a panacea but as a useful intervention which benefits social emotional learning, attention-building, and decreasing stress and anxiety for students, as well as helping to reduce teacher burnout.

Meanwhile, we have seen the growth of mindfulness in higher education, such as the development of mindfulness centers within colleges and universities. Students are receiving credits for studying mindfulness, including at UCLA where we offer a course in Psychiatry: Mindfulness Practice and Theory. Mindfulness is being brought into law schools, business schools, and beyond in higher education.

The creative innovations in mindfulness are endless. It is being used to help veterans with PTSD, in the military and correctional facilities, and with law enforcement officers to help reduce reactivity and promote compassion. There is mindfulness for pilots, mindfulness for parents, mindfulness for kids of all ages, and so much more. Mindfulness is showing up in creative and artistic venues and settings.

Certainly, the delivery of mindfulness via digital and online learning is one of the biggest changes we have seen in the last decade, particularly increased due to the COVID-19 pandemic. Online courses, digital apps, and businesses now distribute mindfulness tools that afford new forms of instruction, access, and areas of research. Apps such as Headspace or Ten Percent Happier have become household names and offer quality mindfulness instruction. They join a sea of apps of varying quality posing easy access but with new challenges to the consumer trying to wade through the array of choices.

THE FUTURE OF MINDFULNESS

What will the next decade bring? We have come to see mindfulness's ethical counterpart, that is, behavior or how someone conducts themselves in the world, as a crucial piece to its integration. While not explicitly built into many mindfulness programs, we hope over the next decade there might be more research and concrete strategies on the intersection of mindfulness with kindness, altruism, and compassion.

As the field grows, ongoing, rigorous support and training are needed for teachers bringing mindfulness into these diverse sectors and to uphold the integrity of the field as it grows. The International Mindfulness Teachers Association (IMTA; www.imta.org) was established in 2017 to provide accreditation for professional mindfulness teacher training programs and to certify qualified individuals. A decade ago, there were few teacher trainings, now there are hundreds worldwide and the IMTA is a step toward establishing standards, credentialing, and professional training requirements.

We have seen a variety of new trends in how mindfulness is being taught to the next generation of mindfulness teachers. Foremost, we see more trauma-based and trauma-sensitive approaches. In addition, teachers are also being trained to prevent and work with adverse reactions to mindfulness. They are also gaining competency in working with diverse populations, such as how to use accessible, inclusive language for people with all abilities and from a variety of backgrounds. There is also more teacher training connecting social justice issues to mindfulness with an emphasis on how to teach mindfulness in light of current social and political and environmental crises.

For us as the authors, the last decade has impacted our lives and our relationships to mindfulness.

Sue: The last decade has been a whirlwind of new experiences outside UCLA as I moved to an emerita position in 2012. I worked with a global human rights organization focused on women and girls (Equality Now), while also learning about business and investing in companies working to impact mindfulness, mental health, wellness, and social connection. Moving beyond the academic setting has enabled me to see even more deeply the value of mindfulness in all work endeavors and their intersections with individual growth, families, communities, and society at large. I see the importance of bringing mindfulness and kindness together as they are in constant feedback and toward that end I helped create the Bedari Kindness Institute at UCLA, dedicated to the science and impact of kindness on social problems. I have increasing gratitude toward mindfulness for providing never-ending insights.

Diana: Certainly, my teaching has evolved over time, as I am constantly learning and growing as a teacher. What hasn't changed is the basics that I teach people—to pay attention to the present moment with openness, curiosity, and a willingness to be with that experience. All of the techniques, tools, and practices we shared a decade ago are still ones we teach today. Personally, after thirty years of mindfulness practice, I continue to be grateful every day for how my practice informs my perceptions and how I interact in the world. From parenting my now thirteen-year-old daughter, to family and work challenges, to weathering the pandemic, mindfulness remains my touchstone. My meditation practice continues to stay fresh, exciting, relevant, and insightful. As I evolve as a teacher, my biggest change is toward teaching mindfulness not only as stress reduction but also as a method that is deeply needed in this time of calamity. With the intersecting environmental, social, political, and moral crises facing our planet, we need tools that work. Through mindfulness, we can find emotional balance, resiliency, and an oasis of profound well-being to help us weather these challenging times.

Over the last decade, *Fully Present* has impacted countless practitioners—beginners and experienced. It has been taught in college classrooms, given as gifts, translated into several languages, and distributed widely. We have received emails and letters from hundreds of readers who have shared how it transformed their lives, and we continue to be humbled by the reach of this book.

May you benefit from our book.
May mindfulness transform all our lives and move out in widening circles to positively impact our families, relationships, communities, institutions, and the earth itself.

—Sue Smalley and Diana Winston
Los Angeles, California, July 2022

We wish to thank Winnie S. Liang, PhD, for her mindful and rigorous review of the scientific literature and assistance with the Afterword.

GLOSSARY

amygdala An almond-shaped region of the brain located in the temporal lobe that is important in the processing of emotion, particularly fear.

anchor The focal point in meditation; what the meditator always returns to, such as our breath, a repeating word (see *mantra*), or an image.

anchor spot A more specific site connected to the anchor. If breath is the anchor, the anchor spot may be the abdomen, chest, or nostrils.

chi gong A slow, energy-based movement practice to improve health and well-being. There are over ten thousand styles of chi gong, which originated in China.

cognitive behavioral therapy A therapeutic approach that is similar to *cognitive therapy* in its goal of reframing thoughts or reattribution of thoughts, but that also includes changing behaviors to further support or invoke cognitive change.

cognitive therapy A therapeutic approach that uses reframing of thoughts or reattribution of thoughts to improve cognitive and emotional states.

coherence (1) A measure of the degree of dynamic connectivity between different scalp regions, as measured by the degree of correlation of pairs of EEG signals recorded simultaneously from those locations; (2) in Cloninger's personality model, the integration of three character traits and temperament.

discriminating awareness Awareness coupled with discrimination brings wisdom.

disidentification See *non-identification.*

dopamine An important neurotransmitter in the brain involved in a wide range of functions, including emotion, movement, attention, and reward.

epigenetic Changes in gene expression due to the environment or experience but not due to changes in DNA itself; epigenetic changes may be transmitted across generations.

equanimity A state of even-mindedness or balance.

genome The total genetic content of an organism.

homeostasis The ability of the body to regulate internal states in response to changes in the environment in order to maintain a condition of stability or equilibrium.

insula Located in the base of the lateral sulcus, this region of the brain is important in pain, sensory integration, and self-awareness.

interoception The physiological condition of the body and the ability of information about that condition to reach awareness.

loving-kindness A feeling of kindness, love, or connectedness toward oneself or another. Can be cultivated through practice and specific meditations.

mantra A repeating word used to sustain the mind in one spot during meditation (for example, "om").

metacognitive awareness A de-centered relationship of self to thoughts and feelings; the idea that you can be a neutral observer of your own experiences (see *disidentification, non-identification*).

Mindful Awareness Practice (MAP) A name given to the general group of exercises or practices that increase mindfulness or mindful awareness. The classes we teach at MARC are called MAPs.

mindfulness A receptive attention to present-moment experience or attention to present-moment experience with a stance of open curiosity; also called mindful awareness.

mirror neurons Cells found in the prefrontal cortex and temporal lobe of the brain that are probably involved in imitation, empathy, and self-awareness.

neuroplasticity The brain's ability to reorganize itself by forming new neural connections in response to the environment or experience.

nonconceptuality Being aware without being caught in a story about the object of awareness. For instance, feeling the sensations in your hand rather than thinking about how you use your hand, what you like about your hand, and so on.

non-identification When you have a sense of "space" or relief from the things you usually take to be "you." For example, when you are not identified with an emotion you are feeling, you have a sense that it is *the* emotion rather than *your* emotion (also called *disidentification*).

placebo A substance that has no pharmacological effect but is given as a control in testing the clinical efficacy of a medicine.

placebo effect   The improvement that occurs in individuals under the placebo condition in an experimental trial.

pranayama   A Sanskrit word meaning "restraint of the breath" (*prana*). Generally used for the breath practices taught in conjunction with yoga that control the breath.

self-awareness   Awareness of self, including thoughts, feelings, and actions; self-consciousness.

self-regulation   Monitoring and modifying of behavior to achieve a goal or adapt to an environmental context.

t'ai chi   A Chinese martial art practiced worldwide for health reasons. Its slow, often dancelike movements work with energy in the body.

Transcendental Meditation (TM)   A form of mantra meditation introduced worldwide by Maharishi Mahesh Yogi.

NOTES

NOTES TO CHAPTER 1

1. V. S. Ramachandran, *A Brief Tour of Human Consciousness: From Imposter Poodles to Purple Numbers* (New York: Pi Press, 2004).

2. Henepola B. Gunaratana, *Mindfulness in Plain English* (Somerville, MA: Wisdom Publications, 2002), 138.

3. K. W. Brown, R. M. Ryan, and J. D. Creswell, "Mindfulness: Theoretical Foundations and Evidence for Its Salutary Effects," *Psychological Inquiry* (2007): 211–237.

4. S. Bishop, M. Lau, S. Shapiro, L. Carlson, N. D. Anderson, et al., "Mindfulness: A Proposed Operational Definition," *Clinical Psychology: Science, and Practice* (2004): 230–241; J. Kabat-Zinn, *Full Catastrophe Living* (New York: Dell, 1990); J. Kabat-Zinn, *Coming to Our Senses: Healing Ourselves and the World Through Mindfulness* (New York: Hyperion, 2005); E. J. Langer and M. Moldoveanu, "The Construct of Mindfulness," *Journal of Social Issues* (2000): 1–9; J. Schwartz and S. Begley, *The Mind and the Brain: Neuroplasticity and the Power of Mental Force* (New York: Regan Books, 2002).

5. R. J. Sternberg, "Images of Mindfulness," *Journal of Social Issues* (2000): 11–26.

6. R. A. Baer, G. T. Smith, and K. B. Allen, "Assessment of Mindfulness by Self-Report: The Kentucky Inventory of Mindfulness Skills," *Assessment* (2004): 191–206.

7. K. W. Brown and R. M. Ryan, "The Benefits of Being Present: Mindfulness and Its Role in Psychological Well-being," *Journal of Personality and Social Psychology* (2003): 822–848.

8. R. A. Baer, G. T. Smith, E. Lykins, D. Button, J. Krietemeyer, S. Sauer, et al., "Construct Validity of the Five-Facet Mindfulness Questionnaire in Meditating and Nonmeditating Samples," *Assessment* (2008): 329–342.

9. Brown et al., "Mindfulness: Theoretical Foundations and Evidence for Its Salutary Effects."

10. J. D. Creswell, B. M. Way, N. I. Eisenberger, and M. D. Lieberman, "Neural Correlates of Dispositional Mindfulness During Affect Labeling," *Psychosomatic Medicine* (2007): 560–565.

11. A. P. Jha, J. Krompinger, and M. J. Baime, "Mindfulness Training Modifies Subsystems of Attention," *Cognitive, Affective, and Behavioral Neuroscience* (2007): 109–119; S. L. Smalley, S. K. Loo, T. S. Hale, A. Shrestha, J. McGough, L. Flook, et al., "Mindfulness and Attention Deficit Hyperactivity Disorder," *Journal of Clinical Psychology* (2009): 1087–1098; Y. Y. Tang, Y. Ma, J. Wang, Y. Fan, S. Feng, Q. Lu, et al., "Short-Term Meditation Training Improves Attention and Self-Regulation," *Proceedings of the National Academy of Sciences* (2007): 17152–17156; L. Zylowska, D. L. Ackerman, M. H. Yang, J. L. Futrell, N. L. Horton, T. S. Hale, et al., "Mindfulness Meditation Training in Adults and Adolescents with ADHD: A Feasibility Study," *Journal of Attention Disorders* (2008): 737–746.

12. A. Berger, O. Kofman, U. Livneh, and A. Henik, "Multidisciplinary Perspectives on Attention and the Development of Self-Regulation," *Progress in Neurobiology* (2007): 256–286.

13. Ibid., 256–286.

14. G. Berlucchi and H. A. Buchtel, "Neuronal Plasticity: Historical Roots and Evolution of Meaning," *Experimental Brain Research* (2009): 307–319.

15. C. Pantev, B. Ross, T. Fujioka, L. J. Trainor, M. Schulte, and M. Schulz, "Music and Learning-Induced Cortical Plasticity," *Annals of the New York Academy of Science* (2003): 438–450.

16. S. Begley, *Train Your Mind, Change Your Brain: How a New Science Reveals Our Extraordinary Potential to Transform Ourselves* (New York: Ballantine Books, 2007); J. L. Rapoport and N. Gogtay, "Brain Neuroplasticity in Healthy, Hyperactive, and Psychotic Children: Insights from Neuroimaging," *Neuropsychopharmacology* (2008): 181–197.

17. C. Pantev, A. Engelien, V. Candia, and T. Elbert, "Representational Cortex in Musicians: Plastic Alterations in Response to Musical Practice," *Annals of the New York Academy of Science* (2001): 300–314.

18. Langer and Moldoveanu, "The Construct of Mindfulness"; Brown and Ryan, "The Benefits of Being Present"; Sternberg, "Images of Mindfulness."

19. A. Huxley, *The Doors of Perception and Heaven and Hell* (New York: Harper Perennial, 2004), 20–21.

20. J. Bolte-Taylor, *My Stroke of Insight: A Brain Scientist's Personal Journey* (New York: Plume, first printing 2009).

NOTES TO CHAPTER 2

1. D. A. Allport, B. Antonis, and P. Reynolds, "On the Division of Attention: A Disproof of the Single Channel Hypothesis," *Quarterly Journal of Experimental Psychology* (1971): 225–235; S. L. Beilock, T. H. Carr, C. MacMahon, and J. L. Starkes, "When Paying Attention Becomes Counterproductive: Impact of Divided Versus Skill-Focused Attention on Novice and Experienced Performance of Sensorimotor Skills," *Journal of Experimental Psychology* (2002): 6–16.

2. S. Michie, "Changing Behavior: Theoretical Development Needs Protocol Adherence," *Health Psychology* (2005): 439.

3. S. D. Levitt and S. J. Dubner, *Freakonomics: A Rogue Economist Explores the Hidden Side of Everything* (New York: William Morrow, 2005).

4. Michie, "Changing Behavior"; J. M. Strayhorn Jr., "Self-Control: Toward Systematic Training Programs," *Journal of the American Academy of Child and Adolescent Psychiatry* (2002): 17–27.

5. Michie, "Changing Behavior."

6. D. Heber and S. Bowerman, *The L.A. Shape Diet: The Fourteen-Day Total Weight Loss Plan* (New York: Regan Books, 2004).

7. Ibid., 136.

8. Michie, "Changing Behavior."

9. Heber and Bowerman, *The L.A. Shape Diet*, 141.

10. Michie, "Changing Behavior."

11. Strayhorn, "Self-Control."

12. Y. Y. Tang, Y. Ma, J. Wang, Y. Fan, S. Feng, Q. Lu, et al., "Short-Term Meditation Training Improves Attention and Self-Regulation," *Proceedings of the National Academy of Sciences* (2007): 17152–17156.

13. J. A. Brefczynski-Lewis, A. Lutz, H. S. Schaefer, D. B. Levinson, and R. J. Davidson, "Neural Correlates of Attentional Expertise in Long-Term Meditation Practitioners," *Proceedings of the National Academy of Sciences* (2007): 11483–11488.

14. A. Watts, *The Book: On the Taboo Against Knowing Who You Are* (New York: Pantheon Books, 1966).

15. For example, www.dharmacrafts.com or www.zafu.net.

NOTES TO CHAPTER 3

1. P. Rainville, A. Bechara, N. Naqvi, and A. R. Damasio, "Basic Emotions Are Associated with Distinct Patterns of Cardiorespiratory Activity," *International Journal of Psychophysiology* (2006): 5–18.

2. Y. Masaoka and I. Homma, "Respiration and Odor: Their Link in the Human Brain," *No To Shinkei* (2005): 631–638.

3. D. K. Osborn, "Greek Medicine Net," available at: www.greekmedicine .net/b_p/Vital_Faculty.html (accessed February 24, 2010).

4. J. D. Fowler, *An Introduction to the Philosophy and Religion of Taoism: Pathways to Immortality* (Portland, OR: Sussex Academic Press, 2005).

5. N. Ramanantsoa, V. Vaubourg, B. Matrot, G. Vardon, S. Dauger, and J. Gallego, "Effects of Temperature on Ventilatory Response to Hypercapnia in Newborn Mice Heterozygous for Transcription Factor Phox2b," *American Journal of Physiology—Regulatory, Integrative, and Comparative Physiology* (2007): R2027–R2035.

6. Nicholas Institute of Sports Medicine and Athletic Trauma, "NISMAT Exercise Physiology Corner: Maximum Oxygen Consumption Primer," 2007, available at: http://www.nismat.org/physcor/max_o2.html (accessed June 13, 2009).

7. D. J. Gottlieb, J. B. Wilk, M. Harmon, J. C. Evans, O. Joost, D. Levy, et al., "Heritability of Longitudinal Change in Lung Function: The Framingham Study," *American Journal of Respiratory and Critical Care Medicine* (2001): 1655–1659.

8. Ibid.

9. J. A. Dusek, H. H. Otu, A. L. Wohlhueter, M. Bhasin, L. F. Zerbini, M. G. Joseph, et al., "Genomic Counter-Stress Changes Induced by the Relaxation Response," *PLoS ONE* (2008): e2576.

10. I. Homma and Y. Masaoka, "Breathing Rhythms and Emotions," *Experimental Physiology* (2008): 1011–1021; J. Orem and A. Netick, "Behavioral Control of Breathing in the Cat," *Brain Research* (1986): 238–253.

11. B. Ditto, M. Eclache, and N. Goldman, "Short-Term Autonomic and Cardiovascular Effects of Mindfulness Body Scan Meditation," *Annals of Behavioral Medicine* (2006): 227–234.

12. D. Edelman, E. Z. Oddone, R. S. Liebowitz, W. S. Yancy Jr., M. K. Olsen, A. S. Jeffreys, et al., "A Multidimensional Integrative Medicine Intervention to Improve Cardiovascular Risk," *Journal of General Internal Medicine* (2006): 728–734.

13. V. Singh, A. Wisniewski, J. Britton, and A. Tattersfield, "Effect of Yoga Breathing Exercises (Pranayama) on Airway Reactivity in Subjects with Asthma," *Lancet* (1990): 1381–1383.

14. M. B. Ospina, K. Bond, M. Karkhaneh, L. Tjosvold, B. Vandermeer, Y. Liang, et al., "Meditation Practices for Health: State of the Research," in *Evidence Report: Technology Assessment (Full Report)* (2007): 1–263.

15. O. T. Raitakari, M. Juonala, M. Kahonen, L. Taittonen, T. Laitinen, N. Maki-Torkko, et al., "Cardiovascular Risk Factors in Childhood and Carotid Artery Intima-media Thickness in Adulthood: The Cardiovascular Risk in Young Finns Study," *Journal of the American Medical Association* (2003): 2277–2283.

16. V. A. Barnes, H. C. Davis, J. B. Murzynowski, and F. A. Treiber, "Impact of Meditation on Resting and Ambulatory Blood Pressure and Heart Rate in Youth," *Psychosomatic Medicine* (2004): 909–914.

17. C. Glenday, *Guinness: World Records 2009* (Stamford, CT: Guinness Media, 2008).

18. F. A. Boiten, N. H. Frijda, and C. J. Wientjes, "Emotions and Respiratory Patterns: Review and Critical Analysis," *International Journal of Psychophysiology* (1994): 103–128.

19. Homma and Masaoka, "Breathing Rhythms and Emotions."

20. A. D. Craig, "How Do You Feel? Interoception: The Sense of the Physiological Condition of the Body," *Nature Review Neuroscience* (2002): 655–666.

21. "Warm Drink—Warm Thoughts," *Science*, October 24, 2008.

22. C. S. Soon, M. Brass, H. J. Heinze, and J. D. Haynes, "Unconscious Determinants of Free Decisions in the Human Brain," *Nature Neuroscience* (2008): 543–545.

NOTES TO CHAPTER 4

1. A. Miller, *The Body Never Lies: The Lingering Effects of Hurtful Parenting* (New York: Norton, 2005).

2. M. D. Gershon, *The Second Brain: A Groundbreaking New Understanding of Nervous Disorders of the Stomach and Intestine* (New York: HarperCollins, 1998).

3. L. Carroll and W. West, *Alice in Wonderland* (Racine, WI: Whitman Publishing, 1934), 21–23.

4. S. E. Cassin and K. M. von Ranson, "Personality and Eating Disorders: A Decade in Review," *Clinical Psychology Review* (2005): 895–916; J. de Groot and G. Rodin, "Coming Alive: The Psychotherapeutic Treatment of Patients with Eating Disorders," *Canadian Journal of Psychiatry* (1998): 359–360; T. F. Heatherton and R. F. Baumeister, "Binge Eating as Escape from Self-Awareness," *Psychological Bulletin* (1991): 86–108; E. Schupak-Neuberg and C. J. Nemeroff,

"Disturbances in Identity and Self-Regulation in Bulimia Nervosa: Implications for a Metaphorical Perspective of 'Body as Self,'" *International Journal of Eating Disorders* (1993): 335–347.

5. K. A. Phillips, "Body Dysmorphic Disorder: Recognizing and Treating Imagined Ugliness," *World Psychiatry* (2004): 12–17; K. A. Phillips and W. Menard, "Suicidality in Body Dysmorphic Disorder: A Prospective Study," *American Journal of Psychiatry* (2006): 1280–1282.

6. L. Saad, "America's Weight Issues Not Going Away," Gallup, November 26, 2008, available at: http://www.gallup.com/poll/112426/Americans-Weight-Issues-Going-Away.aspx.

7. C. L. Ogden, M. D. Carroll, L. R. Curtin, M. A. McDowell, C. J. Tabak, and K. M. Flegal, "Prevalence of Overweight and Obesity in the United States, 1999–2004," *Journal of the American Medical Association* (2006): 1549–1555.

8. S. C. Hayes, K. Strosahl, and K. G. Wilson, *Acceptance and Commitment Therapy: An Experiential Approach to Behavior Change* (New York: Guilford Press, 1999).

9. K. Tapper, C. Shaw, J. Ilsley, A. J. Hill, F. W. Bond, and L. Moore, "Exploratory Randomised Controlled Trial of a Mindfulness-Based Weight Loss Intervention for Women," *Appetite* 52 (2, 2009): 396–404.

10. For a review, see F. Didonna, *Clinical Handbook of Mindfulness* (New York: Springer, 2009).

11. R. A. Baer, "Mindfulness-Based Cognitive Therapy Applied to Binge-Eating: A Case Study," *Cognitive and Behavioral Practice* (2005): 351–358; R. A. Baer, S. Fischer, and D. B. Huss, "Mindfulness and Acceptance in the Treatment of Disordered Eating," *Journal of Rational-Emotive and Cognitive Behavior Therapy* (2005): 281–300; C. F. Telch, W. S. Agras, and M. M. Linehan, "Dialectical Behavior Therapy for Binge Eating Disorder," *Journal of Consulting and Clinical Psychology* (2001): 1061–1065.

12. J. L. Kristeller and C. B. Hallett, "An Exploratory Study of a Meditation-Based Intervention for Binge Eating Disorder," *Journal of Health Psychology* (1999): 357–363.

13. M. B. Ospina, K. Bond, M. Karkhaneh, L. Tjosvold, B. Vandermeer, Y. Liang, et al., "Meditation Practices for Health: State of the Research," *Evidence Report: Technology Assessment (Full Report)* (2007): 1–263.

14. S. Bowen, N. Chawla, S. E. Collins, K. Witkiewitz, S. Hsu, J. Grow, S. Clifasefi, M. Garner, A. Douglass, M. Lariner, and A. Marlatt, "Mindfulness-Based Relapse Prevention for Substance Use Disorders: A Pilot Efficacy Trial," *Substance Abuse* (2009): 295–305.

15. S. Bowen and A. Marlatt, "Surfing the Urge: Brief Mindfulness-Based Intervention for College Student Smokers," *Psychology of Addictive Behaviors* (2009): 666–671.

16. S. Bowen, K. Witkiewitz, T. M. Dillworth, N. Chawla, T. L. Simpson, B. D. Ostafin, et al., "Mindfulness Meditation and Substance Use in an Incarcerated Population," *Psychology of Addictive Behavior* (2006): 343–347.

17. Bowen, Chawla, et al., "Mindfulness-Based Relapse Prevention."

18. E. Rassin, P. Muris, H. Schmidt, and H. Merckelbach, "Relationships Between Thought-Action Fusion, Thought Suppression, and Obsessive-Compulsive Symptoms: A Structural Equation Modeling Approach," *Behavior Research and Therapy* (2000): 889–897.

19. S. Bowen, K. Witkiewitz, T. M. Dillworth, and G. A. Marlatt, "The Role of Thought Suppression in the Relationship Between Mindfulness Meditation and Alcohol Use," *Addictive Behaviors* (2007): 2324–2328.

20. J. Kabat-Zinn, E. Wheeler, T. Light, A. Skillings, M. J. Scharf, T. G. Cropley, et al., "Influence of a Mindfulness Meditation-Based Stress Reduction Intervention on Rates of Skin Clearing in Patients with Moderate to Severe Psoriasis Undergoing Phototherapy (UVB) and Photochemotherapy (PUVA)," *Psychosomatic Medicine* (1998): 625–632.

21. R. J. Davidson, J. Kabat-Zinn, J. Schumacher, M. Rosenkranz, D. Muller, S. F. Santorelli, et al., "Alterations in Brain and Immune Function Produced by Mindfulness Meditation," *Psychosomatic Medicine* (2003): 564–570.

22. J. D. Creswell, H. F. Myers, S. W. Cole, and M. R. Irwin, "Mindfulness Meditation Training Effects on CD4+ T Lymphocytes in HIV-1 Infected Adults: A Small Randomized Controlled Trial," *Brain, Behavior, and Immunity* (2009): 184–188.

23. L. Witek-Janusek, K. Albuquerque, K. R. Chroniak, C. Chroniak, R. Durazo-Arvizu, and H. L. Mathews, "Effect of Mindfulness-Based Stress Reduction on Immune Function, Quality of Life, and Coping in Women Newly Diagnosed with Early Stage Breast Cancer," *Brain, Behavior, and Immunity* (2008): 969–981.

24. M. Irwin, J. Pike, and M. Oxman, "Shingles Immunity and Health Functioning in the Elderly: Tai Chi Chih as a Behavioral Treatment," *Evidence-Based Complementary Alternative Medicine* (2004): 223–232.

25. M. Csikszentmihalyi and J. LeFevre, "Optimal Experience in Work and Leisure," *Journal of Personality and Social Psychology* (1989): 815–822; S. A. Jackson, "Toward a Conceptual Understanding of the Flow Experience in Elite Athletes," *Research Quarterly for Exercise Sport* (1996): 76–90; T. Sugiyama

K. Inomata, "Qualitative Examination of Flow Experience Among Top Japanese Athletes," *Perceptual and Motor Skills* (2005): 969–982.

26. A. Dietrich, "Neurocognitive Mechanisms Underlying the Experience of Flow," *Consciousness and Cognition* (2004): 746–761.

27. M. R. Leary, C. E. Adams, and E. B. Tate, "Hypo-egoic Self-Regulation: Exercising Self-Control by Diminishing the Influence of the Self," *Journal of Personality and Social Psychology* (2006): 1803–1831.

28. Y. H. Kee and C. K. J. Wang, "Relationships Between Mindfulness, Flow Dispositions, and Mental Skills Adoption: A Cluster Analytic Approach," *Psychology of Sport and Exercise* (2008): 393–411.

29. D. P. Brown, "Mastery of the Mind East and West: Excellence in Being and Doing and Everyday Happiness," *Annals of the New York Academy of Science* (2009): 231–251.

30. F. L. Gardner and Z. E. Moore, "A Mindfulness-Acceptance-Commitment-Based Approach to Athletic Performance Enhancement: Theoretical Considerations," *Behavior Therapy* (2004): 707–723.

31. R. W. van Boven, R. H. Hamilton, T. Kauffman, J. P. Keenan, and A. Pascual-Leone, "Tactile Spatial Resolution in Blind Braille Readers," *Neurology* (2000): 2230–2236.

32. P. Ragert, A. Schmidt, E. Altenmuller, and H. R. Dinse, "Superior Tactile Performance and Learning in Professional Pianists: Evidence for Meta-Plasticity in Musicians," *European Journal of Neuroscience* (2004): 473–478.

33. D. Brown, M. Forte, and M. Dysart, "Visual Sensitivity and Mindfulness Meditation," *Perceptual and Motor Skills* (1984): 775–784.

34. C. E. Kerr, J. R. Shaw, R. H. Wasserman, V. W. Chen, A. Kanojia, T. Bayer, et al., "Tactile Acuity in Experienced Tai Chi Practitioners: Evidence for Use Dependent Plasticity as an Effect of Sensory-Attentional Training," *Experimental Brain Research* (2008): 317–322.

35. Ibid.

36. B. K. Holzel, U. Ott, T. Gard, H. Hempel, M. Weygandt, and K. Morgen, "Investigation of Mindfulness Meditation Practitioners with Voxel-Based Morphomentry," *Social Cognitive and Affective Neuroscience Advances* (2007): 1–7; S. W. Lazar, C. E. Kerr, R. H. Wasserman, J. R. Gray, D. N. Greve, M. T. Treadway, et al., "Meditation Experience Is Associated with Increased Cortical Thickness," *NeuroReport* (2005): 1893–1897.

37. D. Goleman, "The Lama in the Lab," *Shambhala Sun* (March 2003).

38. S. S. Khalsa, D. Rudrauf, A. R. Damasio, R. J. Davidson, A. Lutz, and D. Tranel, "Interoceptive Awareness in Experienced Meditators," *Psychophysiology* (2008): 671–677.

NOTES TO CHAPTER 5

1. Stanford University Medical Center, "Physical Pain Aggravates Majority of Americans, According to Poll," *Science Daily*, May 9, 2005, available at: http://www.sciencedaily.com/releases/2005/05/050509171112.htm (accessed July 28, 2009).

2. "Worldwide Pain Management Market to Reach 43.2 Billion Dollars by 2010," *Medical News Today*, March 12, 2008.

3. M. J. Millan, "The Induction of Pain: An Integrative Review," *Progress in Neurobiology* (1999): 1–164.

4. Ibid.

5. J. Kabat-Zinn, "An Outpatient Program in Behavioral Medicine for Chronic Pain Patients Based on the Practice of Mindfulness Meditation: Theoretical Considerations and Preliminary Results," *General Hospital Psychiatry* (1982): 33–47.

6. A. D. Craig, "How Do You Feel? Interoception: The Sense of the Physiological Condition of the Body," *Nature Review Neuroscience* (2002): 655–666.

7. Ibid.

8. P. Yogananda, *Autobiography of a Yogi* (New York: Crystal Clarity Publishers, 1946).

9. R. Kakigi, H. Nakata, K. Inui, N. Hiroe, O. Nagata, M. Honda, et al., "Intracerebral Pain Processing in a Yoga Master Who Claims Not to Feel Pain During Meditation," *European Journal of Pain* (2005): 581–589.

10. B. K. Holzel, U. Ott, T. Gard, H. Hempel, M. Weygandt, K. Morgen, and D. Vaitl, "Investigation of Mindfulness Meditation Practitioners with Voxel-Based Morphomentry," *Social Cognitive and Affective Neuroscience Advances* (2007): 1–7; S. W. Lazar, C. E. Kerr, R. H. Wasserman, J. R. Gray, D. N. Greve, M. T. Treadway, et al., "Meditation Experience Is Associated with Increased Cortical Thickness," *NeuroReport* (2005): 1893–1897.

11. J. K. Zubieta, J. A. Bueller, L. R. Jackson, D. J. Scott, Y. Xu, R. A. Koeppe, et al., "Placebo Effects Mediated by Endogenous Opioid Activity on Mu-opioid Receptors," *Journal of Neuroscience* (2005): 7754–7762.

12. J. Lorenz, M. Hauck, R. C. Paur, Y. Nakamura, R. Zimmermann, B. Bromm, et al., "Cortical Correlates of False Expectations During Pain Intensity Judgments—A Possible Manifestation of Placebo/Nocebo Cognitions," *Brain, Behavior, and Immunity* (2005): 283–295.

13. S. J. Bantick, R. G. Wise, A. Ploghaus, S. Clare, S. M. Smith, and I. Tracey, "Imaging How Attention Modulates Pain in Humans Using Functional MRI," *Brain* (2002): 310–319.

14. T. F. Sun, C. C. Kuo, and N. M. Chiu, "Mindfulness Meditation in the Control of Severe Headache," *Chang Gung Medical Journal* (2002): 538–541.

15. J. Kabat-Zinn, "An Outpatient Program in Behavioral Medicine for Chronic Pain Patients Based on the Practice of Mindfulness Meditation: Theoretical Considerations and Preliminary Results," *General Hospital Psychiatry* (1982): 33–47.

16. J. A. Grant and P. Rainville, "Pain Sensitivity and Analgesic Effects of Mindful States in Zen Meditators: A Cross-Sectional Study," *Psychosomatic Medicine* (2009): 106–114.

17. Kabat-Zinn, "An Outpatient Program in Behavioral Medicine."

18. J. Kabat-Zinn, L. Lipworth, and R. Burney, "The Clinical Use of Mindfulness Meditation for the Self-Regulation of Chronic Pain," *Journal of Behavioral Medicine* (1985): 163–190.

19. A. J. Zautra, M. C. Davis, J. W. Reich, P. Nicassio, H. Tennen, P. Finan, et al., "Comparison of Cognitive Behavioral and Mindfulness Meditation Interventions on Adaptation to Rheumatoid Arthritis for Patients with and Without History of Recurrent Depression," *Journal of Consulting and Clinical Psychology* (2008): 408–421.

20. L. M. McCracken, J. Gauntlett-Gilbert, and K. E. Vowles, "The Role of Mindfulness in a Contextual Cognitive-Behavioral Analysis of Chronic Pain-Related Suffering and Disability," *Pain* (2007): 63–69.

NOTES TO CHAPTER 6

1. World Health Organization, Department of Mental Health and Substance Abuse, "Prevention of Mental Health Disorders," 2004, available at: http://74.125.47.132/search?q=cache:Ouk4Af8MXDMJ:www.who.int/mental _health/evidence/en/prevention_of_mental_disorders_sr.pdf+world+health+org, 1+in+5+children+with+psychiatric+disorder&hl=en&ct=clnk&cd=1&gl=us& client=firefox-a.

2. A. Caspi, K. Sugden, T. E. Moffitt, A. Taylor, I. W. Craig, H. Harrington, et al., "Influence of Life Stress on Depression: Moderation by a Polymorphism in the 5-HTT Gene," *Science* (2003): 386–389; J. Kaufman, B. Z. Yang, H. Douglas-Palumberi, S. Houshyar, D. Lipschitz, J. H. Krystal, et al., "Social Supports and Serotonin Transporter Gene Moderate Depression in Maltreated Children," *Proceedings of the National Academy of Sciences* (2004): 17316–17321.

3. J. A. Dusek, H. H. Otu, A. L. Wohlhueter, M. Bhasin, L. F. Zerbini, M. G. Joseph, et al., "Genomic Counter-Stress Changes Induced by the Relaxation

Response," *PLoS ONE* (2008): e2576; D. Ornish, M. J. Magbanua, G. Weidner, V. Weinberg, C. Kemp, C. Green, et al., "Changes in Prostate Gene Expression in Men Undergoing an Intensive Nutrition and Lifestyle Intervention," *Proceedings of the National Academy of Sciences* (2008): 8369–8374.

4. J. LeDoux, *The Emotional Brain: The Mysterious Underpinnings of Emotional Life* (New York: Simon & Schuster, 1996).

5. Lao-Tzu, *Tao Te Ching*, trans. D. C. Lau (New York: Everyman's Library, 1994), 29.

6. H. S. Seo, M. Hirano, J. Shibato, R. Rakwal, I. K. Hwang, and Y. Masuo, "Effects of Coffee Bean Aroma on the Rat Brain Stressed by Sleep Deprivation: A Selected Transcript and 2D Gel-Based Proteome Analysis," *Journal of Agricultural and Food Chemistry* (2008): 4665–4673.

7. LeDoux, *The Emotional Brain*.

8. C. E. Izard, *The Face of Emotion* (New York: Appleton-Century-Crofts, 1971); J. Panksepp, *Affective Neuroscience: The Foundations of Human and Animal Emotions* (New York: Oxford University Press, 1998); R. Plutchik, "The Nature of Emotions," *American Scientist* (2001): 344–350.

9. National Institute of Mental Health, "The Numbers Count: Mental Disorders in America," 2008, available at: http://www.nimh.nih.gov/health/publications/the-numbers-count-mental-disorders-in-america/index.shtml.

10. J. R. T. Davidson and H. Dreher, *The Anxiety Book: Developing Strength in the Face of Fear* (New York: Riverhead Books, 2003).

11. American Psychological Association, "Stress in America," October 24, 2007.

12. V. Lobue and J. S. DeLoache, "Detecting the Snake in the Grass: Attention to Fear-Relevant Stimuli by Adults and Young Children," *Psychological Science* (2008): 284–289.

13. LeDoux, *The Emotional Brain*.

14. R. Bor and L. van Gerwen, *Psychological Perspectives on Fear of Flying* (Burlington, VT: Ashgate Publishing, 2003).

15. J. Kabat-Zinn, *Coming to Our Senses: Healing Ourselves and the World Through Mindfulness* (New York: Hyperion, 2005).

16. J. M. Greeson, "Mindfulness Research Update: 2008," *Complementary Health Practice Review* (2009):10–18; A. Chiesa and A. Serretti, "Mindfulness-Based Stress Reduction for Stress Management in Healthy People: A Review and Meta-Analysis," *Journal of Alternative and Complementary Medicine* (2009): 593–600; P. Grossman, L. Niemann, S. Schmidt and H. Walach, "Mindfulness-Based Stress Reduction and Health Benefits. A Meta-Analysis," *Journal of Psychosomatic Research* (2004): 35–43.

17. J. Kabat-Zinn, A. O. Massion, J. Kristeller, L. G. Peterson, K. E. Fletcher, L. Pbert, W. R. Lenderking, and S. F. Santorelli, "Effectiveness of a Meditation-Based Stress Reduction Program in the Treatment of Anxiety Disorders," *American Journal of Psychiatry* (1992): 936–943; J. J. Miller, K. Fletcher, and J. Kabat-Zinn, "Three-Year Follow-up and Clinical Implications of a Mindfulness Meditation-Based Stress Reduction Intervention in the Treatment of Anxiety Disorders," *General Hospital Psychiatry* (1995): 192–200; S. Evans, S. Ferrando, M. Findler, C. Stowell, C. Smart, and D. Haglin, "Mindfulness-Based Cognitive Therapy for Generalized Anxiety Disorder," *Journal of Anxiety Disorder* (2008): 716–721.

18. D. Koszycki, M. Benger, J. Shlik, and J. Bradwejn, "Randomized Trial of a Meditation-Based Stress Reduction Program and Cognitive Behavior Therapy in Generalized Social Anxiety Disorder," *Behaviour Research and Therapy* (2007): 2518–2526.

19. J. M. Schwartz and B. Beyette, *Brain Lock: Free Yourself from Obsessive-Compulsive Behavior* (New York: First Regan Book/Harper Perennial Edition, 1997); J. Schwartz and S. Begley, *The Mind and the Brain: Neuroplasticity and the Power of Mental Force* (New York: Regan Books, 2002), 55.

20. L. Rapgay, A. Bystritsky, R. E. Dafter, and M. Spearman, "New Strategies for Combining Mindfulness with Integrative Cognitive Behavioral Therapy for the Treatment of Generalized Anxiety Disorder," *Journal of Rational-Emotive and Cognitive-Behavior Therapy* (2009); L. Rapgay and A. Bystrisky, "Classical Mindfulness: An Introduction to Its Theory and Practice for Clinical Application," *Longevity, Regeneration, and Optimal Health* (2009): 148–162.

21. J. J. Gross and O. P. John, "Individual Differences in Two Emotions Regulation Processes: Implications for Affect, Relationships, and Well-being," *Journal of Personality and Social Psychology* (2003): 348–362.

22. J. J. Gross and R. W. Levenson, "Hiding Feelings: The Acute Effects of Inhibiting Negative and Positive Emotion," *Journal of Abnormal Psychology* (1997): 95–103.

23. S. Bowen, K. Witkiewitz, T. M. Dillworth, and G. A. Marlatt, "The Role of Thought Suppression in the Relationship Between Mindfulness Meditation and Alcohol Use," *Addictive Behaviors* (2007): 2324–2328.

24. E. Garland, S. Gaylord, and J. Park, "The Role of Mindfulness in Positive Reappraisal," *Explore* (2009): 37–44.

25. J. D. Creswell, B. M. Way, N. I. Eisenberger, and M. D. Lieberman, "Neural Correlates of Dispositional Mindfulness During Affect Labeling," *Psychosomatic Medicine* (2007): 560–565.

26. G. O. Gabbard, J. S. Beck, and J. Holmes, *Oxford Textbook of Psychotherapy* (New York: Oxford University Press, 2007).

27. J. D. Teasdale, Z. Segal, and J. M. Williams, "How Does Cognitive Therapy Prevent Depressive Relapse and Why Should Attentional Control (Mindfulness) Training Help?" *Behavior Research and Therapy* (1995): 25–39.

28. J. Carmody, R. A. Baer, E. L. B. Lykins, and N. Olendzki, "An Empirical Study of the Mechanisms of Mindfulness in a Mindfulness-Based Stress Reduction Program," *Journal of Clinical Psychology* (2009): 1–14.

29. Rapgay, Bystritsky, et al., "New Strategies for Combining Mindfulness with Integrative Cognitive Behavioral Therapy."

30. J. Schwartz and S. Begley, *The Mind and the Brain: Neuroplasticity and the Power of Mental Force* (New York: Regan Books, 2002).

31. Teasdale, et al., "How Does Cognitive Therapy Prevent Depressive Relapse"; J. D. Teasdale, Z. V. Segal, J. M. Williams, V. A. Ridgeway, J. M. Soulsby, and M. A. Lau, "Prevention of Relapse/Recurrence in Major Depression by Mindfulness-Based Cognitive Therapy," *Journal of Consulting and Clinical Psychology* (2000): 615–623.

32. J. D. Teasdale, R. G. Moore, H. Hayhurst, M. Pope, S. Williams, and Z. V. Segal, "Metacognitive Awareness and Prevention of Relapse in Depression: Empirical Evidence," *Journal of Consulting and Clinical Psychology* (2002): 275–287.

33. M. A. Kenny and J. M. Williams, "Treatment-Resistant Depressed Patients Show a Good Response to Mindfulness-Based Cognitive Therapy," *Behavior Research and Therapy* (2007): 617–625.

34. N. N. Singh, G. E. Lancioni, S. D. Singh Joy, A. S. Winton, M. Sabaawi, R. G. Wahler, et al., "Adolescents with Conduct Disorder Can Be Mindful of Their Aggressive Behavior," *Journal of Emotional and Behavioral Disorders* (2007): 56–63.

35. W. L. Heppner, M. H. Kernis, C. E. Lakey, W. K. Campbell, B. M. Goldman, P. J. Davis, et al., "Mindfulness as a Means of Reducing Aggressive Behavior: Dispositional and Situational Evidence," *Aggressive Behavior* (2008): 486–496.

36. "Insight Prison Project," 2009, available at: http://insightprisonproject.org (accessed July 28, 2009).

37. D. B. Clark, A. M. Parker, and K. G. Lynch, "Psychopathology and Substance-Related Problems During Early Adolescence: A Survival Analysis," *Journal of Clinical Child Psychology* (1999): 333–341.

38. S. Bogels, B. Hoogstad, L. Van Dun, S. Schutter and K. Restifo, "Mindfulness Training for Adolescents with Externalizing Disorders and Their Parents," *Behavioral and Cognitive Psychotherapy* (2008): 193–209.

39. For advances in this area, see www.casel.org.

NOTES TO CHAPTER 7

1. J. H. Fowler and N. A. Christakis, "Dynamic Spread of Happiness in a Large Social Network: Longitudinal Analysis over Twenty Years in the Framingham Heart Study," *British Medical Journal* (2008): a2338.

2. A. Huxley, *The Doors of Perception and Heaven and Hell* (New York: Harper Perennial Classics, 2004), 26.

3. K. R. Jamison, *Exuberance: The Passion for Life* (New York: Alfred A. Knopf, 2004), 131–132.

4. J. Bolte Taylor, *My Stroke of Insight: A Brain Scientist's Personal Journey* (New York: Plume, first printing 2009), 68.

5. K. Nerburn, *The Wisdom of the Native Americans* (Novato, CA: New World Library, 1999), 1.

6. W. James, *The Varieties of Religious Experience: A Study in Human Nature* (New York: Modern Library, 2002), 76.

7. P. T. de Chardin, *The Phenomenon of Man* (New York: Harper & Row, 1959).

8. C. R. Cloninger, *Feeling Good: The Science of Well-being* (Oxford: Oxford University Press, 2004).

9. M. R. Leary, C. E. Adams, and E. B. Tate, "Hypo-egoic Self-Regulation: Exercising Self-Control by Diminishing the Influence of the Self," *Journal of Personality* (2006): 1803–1831.

10. M. Csikszentmihalyi, *Flow: The Psychology of Optimal Experience* (New York: HarperCollins, 1990).

11. M. E. P. Seligman, "Positive Psychology, Positive Prevention, and Positive Thinking," in *Handbook of Positive Psychology*, ed. C. R. Snyder and S. J. Lopez (Oxford: Oxford University Press, 2005), 3–9.

12. C. R. Snyder and S. J. Lopez, *Handbook of Positive Psychology* (Oxford: Oxford University Press, 2005); American Psychiatric Association, *Diagnostic and Statistical Manual of Mental Disorders (DSM-IV-TR)*, 4th ed. (Washington, DC: American Psychiatric Association, 2000).

13. R. F. Baumeister and K. D. Vohs, "The Pursuit of Meaningfulness in Life," in *Handbook of Positive Psychology*, ed. C. R. Snyder and S. J. Lopez (Oxford: Oxford University Press, 2005), 608–618.

14. Cloninger, *Feeling Good*, 4–5.

15. Ibid., 7–8.

16. S. Whittle, N. B. Allen, D. I. Lubman, and M. Yucel, "The Neurobiological Basis of Temperament: Towards a Better Understanding of Psychopathology," *Neuroscience and Biobehavioral Review* (2006): 511–525.

17. Cloninger, *Feeling Good*, 45.

18. Ibid., 128.

19. S. L. Smalley, S. K. Loo, T. S. Hale, A. Shrestha, J. McGough, L. Flook, et al., "Mindfulness and Attention Deficit Hyperactivity Disorder," *Journal of Clinical Psychology* (2009): 1087–1098.

20. C. R. Cloninger, *The Temperament and Character Inventory (TCI): A Guide to Its Development and Use* (St. Louis, MO: Washington University, Center for Psychobiology of Personality, 1994).

21. A. Berger, O. Kofman, U. Livneh, and A. Henik, "Multidisciplinary Perspectives on Attention and the Development of Self-Regulation," *Progress in Neurobiology* (2007): 256–286.

22. D. M. Svrakic, S. Draganic, K. Hill, C. Bayon, T. R. Przybeck, and C. R. Cloninger, "Temperament, Character, and Personality Disorders: Etiologic, Diagnostic, Treatment Issues," *Acta Psychiatrica Scandinavica* (2002): 189–195.

23. Cloninger, *The Temperament and Character Inventory*.

24. Ibid.

25. D. D. Coward, "Self-Transcendence and Emotional Well-being in Women with Advanced Breast Cancer," *Oncology Nursing Forum* (1991): 857–863; D. D. Coward and P. G. Reed, "Self-Transcendence: A Resource for Healing at the End of Life," *Issues in Mental Health Nursing* (1996): 275–288; J. H. Fanos, D. F. Gelinas, R. S. Foster, N. Postone, and R. G. Miller, "Hope in Palliative Care: From Narcissism to Self-Transcendence in Amyotrophic Lateral Sclerosis," *Journal of Palliative Medicine* (2008): 470–475; L. P. Joffrion and D. Douglas, "Grief Resolution: Facilitating Self-Transcendence in the Bereaved," *Journal of Psychosocial Nursing and Mental Health Services* (1994): 13–19; B. Nygren, L. Alex, E. Jonsen, Y. Gustafson, A. Norberg, and B. Lundman, "Resilience, Sense of Coherence, Purpose in Life, and Self-Transcendence in Relation to Perceived Physical and Mental Health Among the Oldest Old," *Aging and Mental Health* (2005): 354–362.

26. For more on this subject, see "The Art of Health, the Science of Happiness," Anthropedia Foundation, 2006, www.anthropedia.org.

27. T. S. Kuhn, *The Structure of Scientific Revolutions* (Chicago: University of Chicago Press, 1996).

28. K. Robinson, *Out of Our Minds: Learning to Be Creative* (Oxford: Capstone Publishing, 2001), 134.

29. J. Salk, *Anatomy of Reality: Merging of Intuition and Reason* (New York: Columbia University Press, 1983), 7.

30. A. Dijksterhuis, M. W. Bos, L. F. Nordgren, and R. B. van Baaren, "On Making the Right Choice: The Deliberation-Without-Attention Effect," *Science* (2006): 1005–1007.

31. M. Jung-Beeman, E. M. Bowden, J. Haberman, J. L. Frymiare, J. S. Arambel-Liu, R. Greenblatt, et al., "Neural Activity When People Solve Verbal Problems with Insight," *PLoS Biology* (2004): e97.

32. A. Einstein, "Wisdom Quotes," available at: www.wisdomquotes.com/ 003510.html (accessed February 23, 2010).

33. Thomas Paine, "The Age of Reason," in *Paine: Collected Writings* (New York: Library of America, 1984), 702.

34. K. W. Brown and R. M. Ryan, "The Benefits of Being Present: Mindfulness and Its Role in Psychological Well-being," *Journal of Personality and Social Psychology* (2003): 822–848.

35. E. Keogh, F. W. Bond, and P. E. Flaxman, "Improving Academic Performance and Mental Health Through a Stress Management Intervention: Outcomes and Mediators of Change," *Behavior Research and Therapy* (2006): 339–357; S. Rosenzweig, D. K. Reibel, J. M. Greeson, G. C. Brainard, and M. Hojat, "Mindfulness-Based Stress Reduction Lowers Psychological Distress in Medical Students," *Teaching and Learning in Medicine* (2003): 88–92; S. L. Shapiro, D. Oman, C. E. Thoresen, T. G. Plante, and T. Flinders, "Cultivating Mindfulness: Effects on Wellbeing," *Journal of Clinical Psychology* (2008): 840–862; S. L. Shapiro, G. E. Schwartz, and G. Bonner, "Effects of Mindfulness-Based Stress Reduction on Medical and Premedical Students," *Journal of Behavioral Medicine* (1998): 581–599.

36. A. Lutz, L. L. Greischar, N. B. Rawlings, M. Ricard, and R. J. Davidson, "Long-Term Meditators Self-Induce High-Amplitude Gamma Synchrony During Mental Practice," *Proceedings of the National Academy of Sciences* (2004): 16369–16373.

37. A. Lutz, J. Brefczynski-Lewis, T. Johnstone, and R. J. Davidson, "Regulation of the Neural Circuitry of Emotion by Compassion Meditation: Effects of Meditative Expertise," *PLoS ONE* (2008): e1897.

38. H. A. Slagter, A. Lutz, L. L. Greischar, S. Nieuwenhuis, and R. J. Davidson, "Theta Phase Synchrony and Conscious Target Perception: Impact of Intensive Mental Training," *Journal of Cognitive Neuroscience* (2009): 1536–1549.

39. S. H. Strogatz, *Sync: The Emerging Science of Spontaneous Order* (New York: Hyperion, 2003).

40. D. Siegel, *The Mindful Brain* (New York: Norton, 2007).

41. A. F. Leuchter, I. A. Cook, S. H. Uijtdehaage, J. Dunkin, R. B. Lufkin, C. Anderson-Hanley, et al., "Brain Structure and Function and the Outcomes of Treatment for Depression," *Journal of Clinical Psychology* (1997): 22–31.

42. R. L. Morehouse, V. Kusumakar, S. P. Kutcher, J. LeBlanc, and R. Armitage, "Temporal Coherence in Ultradian Sleep EEG Rhythms in a Never-Depressed, High-Risk Cohort of Female Adolescents," *Biological Psychiatry* (2002): 446–456.

43. M. R. Leary, E. B. Tate, C. E. Adams, A. B. Allen, and J. Hancock, "Self-Compassion and Reactions to Unpleasant Self-Relevant Events: The Implications of Treating Oneself Kindly," *Journal of Personality and Social Psychology* (2007): 887–904.

44. C. A. Hutcherson, E. M. Seppala, and J. J. Gross, "Loving-Kindness Meditation Increases Social Connectedness," *Emotion* (2008): 720–724.

45. Lutz, et al., "Regulation of the Neural Circuitry of Emotion."

46. L. E. Williams and J. A. Bargh, "Experiencing Physical Warmth Promotes Interpersonal Warmth," *Science* (2008): 606–607.

47. R. Soussignan, "Duchenne Smile, Emotional Experience, and Autonomic Reactivity: A Test of the Facial Feedback Hypothesis," *Emotion* (2002): 52–74.

48. T. Brach, *Radical Acceptance: Embracing Your Life with a Heart of the Buddha* (New York: Bantam, 2003), 266.

49. Oprah Winfrey, "Oprah Talks to Julianne Moore, Meryl Streep, and Nicole Kidman," *O Magazine* (2003): 113.

NOTES TO CHAPTER 8

1. See for yourself at http://viscog.beckman.illinois.edu/flashmovie/15.php.

2. William James, *The Principles of Psychology* (Chicago: Encyclopedia Britannica, 1955).

3. Ibid., 402.

4. M. I. Posner, B. E. Sheese, Y. Odludas, and Y. Tang, "Analyzing and Shaping Human Attentional Networks," *Neural Networks* (2006): 1422–1429.

5. J. Fan, Y. Wu, J. A. Fossella, and M. I. Posner, "Assessing the Heritability of Attentional Networks," *BMC Neuroscience* (2001): 2, 14.

6. M. I. Posner and M. K. Rothbart, "Attention, Self-Regulation and Consciousness," *Philosophical Transactions of the Royal Society of London Series B: Biological Science* (1998): 1915–1927.

7. Ibid.

8. G. A. Sunohara, W. Roberts, M. Malone, R. J. Schachar, R. Tannock, V. S. Basile, et al., "Linkage of the Dopamine D4 Receptor Gene and Attention-Deficit/Hxyperactivity Disorder," *Journal of the American Academy of Child and Adolescent Psychiatry* (2000): 1537–1542; A. N. Kluger, Z. Siegfried, and R. P. Ebstein, "A Meta-Analysis of the Association Between DRD4 Polymorphism and Novelty Seeking," *Molecular Psychiatry* (2002): 712–717; J. Fossella, T. Sommer, J. Fan, Y. Wu, J. M. Swanson, D. W. Pfaff, and M. I. Posner, "Assessing the Molecular Genetics of Attention Networks," *BMC Neuroscience* (2002): 1–11.

9. M. Skounti, A. Philalithis, and E. Galanakis, "Variations in Prevalence of Attention Deficit Hyperactivity Disorder Worldwide," *European Journal of Pediatrics* (2007): 117–123; J. M. Swanson, J. A. Sergeant, E. Taylor, E. J. Sonuga-Barke, P. S. Jensen, and D. P. Cantwell, "Attention-Deficit Hyperactivity Disorder and Hyperkinetic Disorder," *Lancet* (1998): 429–433.

10. S. L. Smalley, "Genetics and the Future of ADHD," *Advances in ADHD* (2008): 74–78.

11. S. L. Smalley, "Reframing ADHD in the Genomic Era," *Psychiatric Times* (June 2008): 74–78.

12. S. L. Smalley, S. K. Loo, T. S. Hale, A. Shrestha, J. McGough, L. Flook, et al., "Mindfulness and Attention Deficit Hyperactivity Disorder," *Journal of Clinical Psychology* (2009): 1087–1098.

13. L. Zylowska, D. L. Ackerman, M. H. Yang, J. L. Futrell, N. L. Horton, T. S. Hale, C. Pataki, and S. Smalley, "Mindfulness Meditation Training in Adults and Adolescents with ADHD: A Feasibility Study," *Journal of Attention Disorders* (2008): 737–746.

14. L. J. Harrison, R. Manocha, and K. Rubia, "Sahaja Yoga Meditation as a Family Treatment Programme for Children with Attention Deficit-Hyperactivity Disorder," *Clinical Child Psychology and Psychiatry* (2004): 479–497.

15. A. Lutz, H. A. Slagter, J. D. Dunne, and R. J. Davidson, "Attention Regulation and Monitoring in Meditation," *Trends in Cognitive Sciences* (2008): 163–169.

16. L. Rapgay, A. Bystritsky, R. E. Dafter, and M. Spearman, "New Strategies for Combining Mindfulness with Integrative Cognitive Behavioral Therapy for the Treatment of Generalized Anxiety Disorder," *Journal of Rational-Emotive and Cognitive-Behavior Therapy* (2009).

17. M. A. Tanner, F. Travis, C. Gaylord-King, D. A. Haaga, S. Grosswald, and R. H. Schneider, "The Effects of the Transcendental Meditation Program on Mindfulness," *Journal of Clinical Psychology* (2009): 574–589.

18. A. P. Jha, J. Krompinger, and M. J. Baime, "Mindfulness Training Modifies Subsystems of Attention," *Cognitive, Affective, and Behavioral Neuroscience* (2007): 109–119.

19. Y. Y. Tang, Y. Ma, J. Wang, Y. Fan, S. Feng, Q. Lu, et al., "Short-Term Meditation Training Improves Attention and Self-Regulation," *Proceedings of the National Academy of Sciences* (2007): 17152–17156.

20. D. Chan and M. Woollacott, "Effects of Level of Meditation Experience on Attentional Focus: Is the Efficiency of Executive or Orientation Networks Improved?" *Journal of Alternative and Complementary Medicine* (2007): 651–657; H. Wenk-Sormaz, "Meditation Can Reduce Habitual Responding," *Alternative Therapies in Health and Medicine* (2005): 42–58.

21. L. Pellerin and P. J. Magistretti, "How to Balance the Brain Energy Budget While Spending Glucose Differently," *Journal of Physiology* (2003): 325.

22. M. E. Raichle, A. M. MacLeod, A. Z. Snyder, W. J. Powers, D. A. Gusnard, and G. L. Shulman, "A Default Mode of Brain Function," *Proceedings of the National Academy of Sciences* (2001): 676–682.

23. H. A. Slagter, A. Lutz, L. L. Greischar, A. D. Francis, S. Nieuwenhuis, J. M. Davis, et al., "Mental Training Affects Distribution of Limited Brain Resources," *PLoS Biology* (2007): e138.

24. Ibid.

25. J. A. Brefczynski-Lewis, A. Lutz, H. S. Schaefer, D. B. Levinson, and R. J. Davidson, "Neural Correlates of Attentional Expertise in Long-Term Meditation Practitioners," *Proceedings of the National Academy of Sciences* (2007): 11483–11488.

26. Tang, Ma, et al., "Short-Term Meditation Training Improves Attention and Self-Regulation."

NOTES TO CHAPTER 9

1. J. Steinbeck, *Cannery Row* (New York: Penguin, 2002), 30–31.

2. M. S. Gazzaniga, *Human: The Science Behind What Makes Us Unique* (New York: Ecco, 2008).

3. E. Goldberg, *The Executive Brain: Frontal Lobes and the Civilized Mind* (Oxford: Oxford University Press, 2001).

4. J. McCrone, "States of Mind," *New Scientist*, March 20, 1999.

5. J. Jaynes, *The Origin of Consciousness in the Breakdown of the Bicameral Mind* (Boston: Houghton Mifflin, 1976).

6. A. Einstein, *The Expanded Quotable Einstein* (Princeton, NJ: Princeton University Press, 2000), 263.

7. The relationship between self-recognition and self-awareness is not completely clear, but they are thought to be associated; see M. Iacoboni, *Mirroring People: The New Science of How We Connect with Others* (New York: Farrar, Straus and Giroux, 2008).

8. G. Rizzolatti, L. Fadiga, V. Gallese, and L. Fogassi, "Premotor Cortex and the Recognition of Motor Actions," *Cognitive Brain Research* (1996): 131–141.

9. Iacoboni, *Mirroring People*.

10. Ibid., 143–152.

11. N. Gogtay, J. N. Giedd, L. Lusk, K. M. Hayashi, D. Greenstein, A. C. Vaituzis, et al., "Dynamic Mapping of Human Cortical Development During Childhood Through Early Adulthood," *Proceedings of the National Academy of Sciences* (2004): 8174–8179.

12. Iacoboni, *Mirroring People*, 133–134.

13. R. L. Buckner and D. C. Carroll, "Self-Projection and the Brain," *Trends in Cognitive Science* (2006): 49–57.

14. Ibid.; D. A. Gusnard, E. Akbudak, G. L. Shulman, and M. E. Raichle, "Medial Prefrontal Cortex and Self-Referential Mental Activity: Relation to a Default Mode of Brain Function," *Proceedings of the National Academy of Sciences* (2001): 4259–4264; H. C. Lou, B. Luber, M. Crupain, J. P. Keenan, M. Nowak, T. W. Kjaer, et al., "Parietal Cortex and Representation of the Mental Self," *Proceedings of the National Academy of Sciences* (2004): 6827–6832; B. Wicker, P. Ruby, J. P. Royet, and P. Fonlupt, "A Relation Between Rest and the Self in the Brain?" *Brain Research Review* (2003): 224–230.

15. Gusnard, et al., "Medial Prefrontal Cortex and Self-Referential Mental Activity."

16. D. P. Brown, "Mastery of the Mind East and West: Excellence in Being and Doing and Everyday Happiness," *Annals of the New York Academy of Science* (2009): 231–251.

17. D. Powell, "Crick Was Right About the 'Vision Filter' in the Brain," *New Scientist*, October 5, 2008.

18. B. Rosenblum and F. Kuttner, *Quantum Enigma: Physics Encounters Consciousness* (New York: Oxford University Press, 2008).

19. K. M. O'Craven and N. Kanwisher, "Mental Imagery of Faces and Places Activates Corresponding Stimulus-Specific Brain Regions," *Journal of Cognitive Neuroscience* (2000): 1013–1023.

20. T. M. Mitchell, S. V. Shinkareva, A. Carlson, K. M. Chang, V. L. Malave, R. A. Mason, and M. A. Just, "Predicting Human Brain Activity Associated with the Meanings of Nouns," *Science* (2008): 1191–1195.

21. H. D. Thoreau, *Walden, or, Life in the Woods* (Mineola, NY: Dover Publications, 1995).

22. E. Goldberg, *The Executive Brain: Frontal Lobes and the Civilized Mind* (Oxford: Oxford University Press, 2001).

23. Ibid., 78–79.

24. K. Foerde, B. J. Knowlton, and R. A. Poldrack, "Modulation of Competing Memory Systems by Distraction," *Proceedings of the National Academy of Sciences* (2006): 11778–11783.

25. J. Schwartz and S. Begley, *The Mind and the Brain: Neuroplasticity and the Power of Mental Force* (New York: Regan Books, 2002), 55.

26. S. Jain, S. L. Shapiro, S. Swanick, S. C. Roesch, P. J. Mills, I. Bell, et al., "A Randomized Controlled Trial of Mindfulness Meditation Versus Relaxation

Training: Effects on Distress, Positive States of Mind, Rumination, and Distraction," *Annals of Behavioral Medicine* (2007): 11–21.

27. B. K. Holzel, U. Ott, T. Gard, H. Hempel, M. Weygandt, K. Morgen, and D. Vaitl, "Investigation of Mindfulness Meditation Practitioners with Voxel-Based Morphometry," *Social Cognitive and Affective Neuroscience Advances* (2007): 55–61; S. W. Lazar, C. E. Kerr, R. H. Wasserman, J. R. Gray, D. N. Greve, M. T. Treadway, et al., "Meditation Experience Is Associated with Increased Cortical Thickness," *NeuroReport* (2005): 1893–1897.

28. Lazar, et al., "Meditation Experience Is Associated with Increased Cortical Thickness."

29. Schwartz and Begley, *The Mind and the Brain*, 88–90.

30. B. R. Cahn and J. Polich, "Meditation States and Traits: EEG, ERP, and Neuroimaging Studies," *Psychological Bulletin* (2006): 180–211.

31. R. J. Davidson, J. Kabat-Zinn, J. Schumacher, M. Rosenkranz, D. Muller, S. F. Santorelli, et al., "Alterations in Brain and Immune Function Produced by Mindfulness Meditation," *Psychosomatic Medicine* (2003): 564–570.

32. B. R. Dunn, J. A. Hartigan, and W. L. Mikulas, "Concentration and Mindfulness Meditations: Unique Forms of Consciousness?" *Applied Psychophysiology and Biofeedback* (1999): 147–165.

33. Cahn and Polich, "Meditation States and Traits."

NOTES TO CHAPTER 10

1. C. R. Cloninger, *Feeling Good: The Science of Well-being* (Oxford: Oxford University Press, 2004).

2. See, for instance, Anthropedia Foundation (2006), www.anthropedia.org; Human Metrics (1998), http://www.humanmetrics.com.

3. C. R. Cloninger, *The Temperament and Character Inventory (TCI): A Guide to Its Development and Use* (St. Louis, MO: Washington University, Center for Psychobiology of Personality, 1994).

4. Ibid.

5. Ibid.

6. Ibid.

NOTES TO CHAPTER 11

1. J. Salk, *Anatomy of Reality: Merging of Intuition and Reason* (New York: Columbia University Press, 1983), 113–114.

2. The relationship of quantum physics to consciousness may reflect aspects of meta-biology. Two reference books examining this relationship are by Henry P. Stapp, *Mindful Universe: Quantum Mechanics and the Participating Observer* (New York: Springer, 2007) and Bruce Rosenblum and Fred Kuttner, *Quantum Enigma: Physics Encounters Consciousness* (New York: Oxford University Press, 2008).

3. J. Salk, *The Survival of the Wisest* (New York: Harper & Row, 1973).

4. J. P. Carse, *Finite and Infinite Games: A Vision of Life as Play and Possibility* (New York: Free Press, 1986).

5. Clearly, there are millions of people working for change across the planet. Those who specifically enact change using the principles of mindfulness are beautifully described in Donald Rothberg's *An Engaged Spiritual Life* (Boston: Beacon Press, 2006).

6. J. K. Burgoon, C. R. Berger, and V. R. Waldron, "Mindfulness and Interpersonal Communication," *Journal of Social Issues* (2000): 105–127.

7. J. L. Krieger, "Shared Mindfulness in Cockpit Crisis Situations: An Exploratory Analysis," *Journal of Business Communication* (Urbana, IL) (2005).

8. Burgoon, et al., "Mindfulness and Interpersonal Communication."

9. P. G. Zimbardo, *The Lucifer Effect: Understanding How Good People Turn Evil* (New York: Random House, 2007), 72–73.

10. "Nonviolent communication," developed by Marshall Rosenberg, is an excellent model and training program for mindful communication and has been used worldwide to help individuals and communities. For more information, go to www.cnvc.org.

11. M. Gladwell, *Blink* (New York: Little, Brown, 2005).

12. Sharma, "Psychological Testing of Alice Project Students," ed. D. Winston (Varanasi, India: unpublished, 2002). For more information on the Alice Project, see www.aliceproject.org.

13. S. Kaiser Greenland, *Mindful Child* (New York: Simon & Schuster, 2010).

14. L. Flook, S. L. Smalley, M. J. Kitil, B. M. Galla, S. Kaiser-Greenland, J. Locke, et al., "Effects of Mindful Awareness Practices on Executive Functions in Elementary School Children," *Journal of Applied School Psychology* (2010): 70–95.

15. M. Napoli, P. R. Krech, and L. C. Holley, "Mindfulness Training for Elementary School Students: The Attention Academy," *Journal of Applied School Psychology* (2005): 99–125.

16. L. Lantieri and C. Malkmus, "The Inner Resilience Program," available at: http://projectrenewal-tidescenter.org/ (accessed July 28, 2009).

17. E. Keogh, F. W. Bond, and P. E. Flaxman, "Improving Academic Performance and Mental Health Through a Stress Management Intervention: Outcomes and Mediators of Change," *Behavior Research and Therapy* (2006): 339–357.

18. D. Oman, S. L. Shapiro, C. E. Thoresen, T. G. Plante, and T. Flinders, "Meditation Lowers Stress and Supports Forgiveness Among College Students: A Randomized Controlled Trial," *Journal of American College Health* (2008): 569–578.

19. S. L. Shapiro, K. W. Brown, and G. M. Biegel, "Teaching Self-Care to Caregivers: Effects of Mindfulness-Based Stress Reduction on the Mental Health of Therapists in Training," *Training and Education in Professional Psychology* (2007): 102–115; S. L. Shapiro, G. E. Schwartz, and G. Bonner, "Effects of Mindfulness-Based Stress Reduction on Medical and Premedical Students," *Journal of Behavioral Medicine* (1998): 581–599.

20. S. Cendrowski, "Green Mountain Coffee's Hot Stock Won't Cool Down," *Fortune*, June 4, 2009.

NOTES TO AFTERWORD

1. *The U.S. Meditation Market.* Marketdata; September 2017.

2. D. A. Scott, B. Valley, and B. A. Simecka, "Mental Health Concerns in the Digital Age," *International Journal of Mental Health and Addiction* (2017): 15(3), 604–613.

3. N. Stiglic and R. M. Viner, "Effects of Screentime on the Health and Well-Being of Children and Adolescents: A Systematic Review of Reviews," *BMJ Open* (2019): 9(1), e023191.

4. P. Blanck, S. Perleth, T. Heidenreich, et al., "Effects of Mindfulness Exercises as Stand-Alone Intervention on Symptoms of Anxiety and Depression: Systematic Review and Meta-analysis," *Behaviour Research and Therapy* (2018): 102, 25–35.

5. F. Bossi, F. Zaninotto, S. D'Arcangelo, N. Lattanzi, A. P. Malizia, and E. Ricciardi, "Mindfulness-Based Online Intervention Increases Well-Being and Decreases Stress after Covid-19 Lockdown," *Scientific Reports* (2022): 12(1), 6483.

6. S. G. Hofmann, A. T. Sawyer, A. A. Witt, and D. Oh, "The Effect of Mindfulness-Based Therapy on Anxiety and Depression: A Meta-analytic Review," *Journal of Consulting and Clinical Psychology* (2010): 78(2), 169–183.

7. B. Khoury, M. Sharma, S. E. Rush, and C. Fournier, "Mindfulness-Based Stress Reduction for Healthy Individuals: A Meta-analysis," *Journal of Psychosomatic Research* (2015): 78(6), 519–528.

8. H. Haller, P. Breilmann, M. Schröter, G. Dobos, and H. Cramer, "A Systematic Review and Meta-analysis of Acceptance- and Mindfulness-Based Interventions for DSM-5 Anxiety Disorders," *Scientific Reports* (2021): 11(1), 20385.

9. W. Kuyken, R. Hayes, B. Barrett, et al., "The Effectiveness and Cost-Effectiveness of Mindfulness-Based Cognitive Therapy Compared with Maintenance Antidepressant Treatment in the Prevention of Depressive Relapse/Recurrence: Results of a Randomised Controlled Trial (The PREVENT Study)," *Health Technology Assessment* (2015): 19(73), 1–124.

10. J. Li, Z. Cai, X. Li, et al., "Mindfulness-Based Therapy versus Cognitive Behavioral Therapy for People with Anxiety Symptoms: A Systematic Review and Meta-analysis of Random Controlled Trials," *Annals of Palliative Medicine* (2021): 10(7), 7596–7612.

11. B. Khoury, T. Lecomte, G. Fortin, et al., "Mindfulness-Based Therapy: A Comprehensive Meta-analysis," *Clinical Psychology Review* (2013): 33(6), 763–771.

12. W. B. Britton, G. Desbordes, R. Acabchuk, et al., "From Self-Esteem to Selflessness: An Evidence (Gap) Map of Self-Related Processes as Mechanisms of Mindfulness-Based Interventions," *Frontiers in Psychology* (2021): 12, 730972.

13. J. Gu, C. Strauss, R. Bond, and K. Cavanagh. "How Do Mindfulness-Based Cognitive Therapy and Mindfulness-Based Stress Reduction Improve Mental Health and Wellbeing? A Systematic Review and Meta-analysis of Mediation Studies," *Clinical Psychology Review* (2015): 37, 1–12.

14. T. Singer and V. Engert, "It Matters What You Practice: Differential Training Effects on Subjective Experience, Behavior, Brain and Body in the ReSource Project," *Current Opinion in Psychology* (2019): 28, 151–158.

15. L. N. Sun, J. W. Gu, L. J. Huang, et al., "Military-Related Posttraumatic Stress Disorder and Mindfulness Meditation: A Systematic Review and Meta-analysis," *Chinese Journal of Traumatololgy* (2021): 24(4), 221–230.

16. X. Liu, P. Yi, L. Ma, et al., "Mindfulness-Based Interventions for Social Anxiety Disorder: A Systematic Review and Meta-analysis," *Psychiatry Research* (2021): 300, 113935.

17. S. Y. Wong, B. H. Yip, W. W. Mak, et al., "Mindfulness-Based Cognitive Therapy v. Group Psychoeducation for People with Generalised Anxiety Disorder: Randomised Controlled Trial," *British Journal of Psychiatry* (2016): 209(1), 68–75.

18. M. de Abreu Costa, G. S. D'Alò de Oliveira, T. Tatton-Ramos, G. G. Manfro, and G. A. Salum, "Anxiety and Stress-Related Disorders and Mindfulness-Based Interventions: A Systematic Review and Multilevel

Meta-analysis and Meta-regression of Multiple Outcomes," *Mindfulness* (2019): 10(6), 996–1005.

19. J. J. Arch and C. R. Ayers, "Which Treatment Worked Better for Whom? Moderators of Group Cognitive Behavioral Therapy versus Adapted Mindfulness Based Stress Reduction for Anxiety Disorders," *Behaviour Research and Therapy* (2013): 51(8), 434–442.

20. R. Ferreira-Garcia, M. A. Costa, F. G. Gonçalves, et al., "Heart Rate Variability: A Biomarker of Selective Response to Mindfulness-Based Treatment versus Fluoxetine in Generalized Anxiety Disorder," *Journal of Affective Disorders* (2021): 295, 1087–1092.

21. A. Athanas, J. McCorrison, J. Campistron, et al., "Characterizing Emotional State Transitions during Prolonged Use of a Mindfulness and Meditation App: Observational Study," *JMIR Mental and Health* (2021): 8(3): e19832.

22. A. J. Athanas, J. M. McCorrison, S. Smalley, et al., "Association between Improvement in Baseline Mood and Long-Term Use of a Mindfulness and Meditation App: Observational Study," *JMIR Mental and Health* (2019): 6(5): e12617.

23. W. Hasenkamp, C. D. Wilson-Mendenhall, E. Duncan, and L. W. Barsalou, "Mind Wandering and Attention during Focused Meditation: A Fine-Grained Temporal Analysis of Fluctuating Cognitive States," *Neuroimage* (2012): 59(1), 750–760.

24. M. A. Killingsworth and D. T. Gilbert, "A Wandering Mind Is an Unhappy Mind," *Science* (2010): 330(6006), 932.

25. O. Singleton, M. Newlon, A. Fossas, B. Sharma, S. R. Cook-Greuter, and S. W. Lazar, "Brain Structure and Functional Connectivity Correlate with Psychosocial Development in Contemplative Practitioners and Controls," *Brain Sciences* (2021): 11(6).

26. N. A. Farb, Z. V. Segal, H. Mayberg, et al., "Attending to the Present: Mindfulness Meditation Reveals Distinct Neural Modes of Self-Reference," *Social Cognitive and Affective Neuroscience* (2007): 2(4), 313–322.

27. J. D. Creswell and E. K. Lindsay, "How Does Mindfulness Training Affect Health? A Mindfulness Stress Buffering Account," *Current Directions in Psychological Science* (2014): 23(6), 401–407.

28. S. W. Cole, M. E. Levine, J. M. Arevalo, J. Ma, D. R. Weir, and E. M. Crimmins, "Loneliness, Eudaimonia, and the Human Conserved Transcriptional Response to Adversity," *Psychoneuroendocrinology* (2015): 62, 11–17.

29. S. W. Cole, "Social Regulation of Human Gene Expression: Mechanisms and Implications for Public Health." *American Journal of Public Health* (2013): 103(Suppl 1), S84–S92.

30. B. L. Fredrickson, K. M. Grewen, S. B. Algoe, et al., "Psychological Well-Being and the Human Conserved Transcriptional Response to Adversity," *PLoS One* (2015): 10(3), e0121839.

31. D. S. Black and G. M. Slavich, "Mindfulness Meditation and the Immune System: A Systematic Review of Randomized Controlled Trials." *Annals of the New York Academy of Sciences* (2016): 1373(1), 13–24.

32. J. D. Creswell, A. A. Taren, E. K. Lindsay, et al., "Alterations in Resting-State Functional Connectivity Link Mindfulness Meditation with Reduced Interleukin-6: A Randomized Controlled Trial," *Biological Psychiatry* (2016): 80(1), 53–61.

33. P. Condon, G. Desbordes, W. B. Miller, and D. DeSteno, "Meditation Increases Compassionate Responses to Suffering," *Psychological Science* (2013): 24(10), 2125–2127.

34. D. Lim, P. Condon, and D. DeSteno, "Mindfulness and Compassion: An Examination of Mechanism and Scalability," *PLoS One* (2015): 10(2), e0118221.

35. S. K. Iwamoto, M. Alexander, M. Torres, M. R. Irwin, N. A. Christakis, and A. Nishi, "Mindfulness Meditation Activates Altruism," *Scientific Reports* (2020): 10(1), 6511.

36. J. N. Donald, B. K. Sahdra, B. Van Zanden, et al., "Does Your Mindfulness Benefit Others? A Systematic Review and Meta-analysis of the Link between Mindfulness and Prosocial Behaviour," *British Journal of Psychology* (2019): 110(1), 101–125.

37. N. J. Schork, "Personalized Medicine: Time for One-Person Trials," *Nature* (2015): 520(7549), 609–611.

38. L. I. Black, P. M. Barnes, T. C. Clarke, B. J. Stussman, and R. L. Nahin, "Use of Yoga, Meditation, and Chiropractors among U.S. Children Aged 4-17 Years." *NCHS Data Brief* (2018): (324), 1–8.

39. T. C. Clarke, P. M. Barnes, L. I. Black, B. J. Stussman, and R. L. Nahin, *Use of Yoga, Meditation, and Chiropractors among U.S. Adults Aged 18 and Over* (Hyattsville, MD: National Center for Health Statistics, 2018).

INDEX

For more information about the UCLA Mindful Awareness Research Center (MARC), MAPs classes, Training in Mindfulness Facilitation, and free meditations, among other resources, go to www.uclahealth .org/marc or the UCLA Mindful App.

ABOUT THE AUTHORS

Susan L. Smalley, PhD, is Professor Emerita of Psychiatry and Founder of the Mindful Awareness Research Center (MARC) at University of California, Los Angeles (UCLA). During her thirty-year career as a behavior geneticist, she received numerous National Institutes of Health (NIH) grants and published extensively on autism, attention-deficit/hyperactivity disorder, and mindfulness. She spent the last decade involved in human rights work supporting women and girls and investing in companies that focus on wellness. She works to bridge research with action through her involvement at MARC as well as the UCLA Bedari Kindness Institute that she helped create dedicated to kindness research and its translation to solve societal problems. She is a mother of three and lives in Los Angeles with her husband.

Diana Winston is the Director of Mindfulness Education at the Mindful Awareness Research Center (MARC). She is the author of *The Little Book of Being, Wide Awake: A Buddhist Guide for Teens*, and *Glimpses of Being*. She has taught mindfulness since 1998 in a variety of settings, including in health care, universities, businesses, nonprofits, and schools in the United States and internationally. Her work has been mentioned in the *New York Times, CNN.com, Los Angeles Times, Bloomberg, Women's Health*, among others. She created the evidence-based Mindful Awareness Practices (MAPs) Program and the University of California, Los Angeles (UCLA) Training in Mindfulness Facilitation. The *Los Angeles Times* calls her "one of the nation's best-known teachers of mindfulness." A former Buddhist nun, mother of a teenager, and Los Angeles resident, you can find her on the UCLA Mindful or Ten Percent Happier App, or at www.dianawinston.com.